Their Town

The Mafia, the Media and the Party Machine
Second Edition

Bill Freeman and Marsha Aileen Hewitt

James Lorimer & Company Ltd., Publishers
Toronto

Copyright © 1979, 2016 by James Lorimer & Company, Publishers.

All rights reserved. No part of this book may be reproduced or transmitted in any form or by any means, electronic or mechanical, including photocopying, or by any information storage or retrieval system, without permission in writing from the publisher.

James Lorimer & Company Ltd., Publishers acknowledges the support of the Ontario Arts Council. We acknowledge the support of the Canada Council for the Arts which last year invested $24.3 million in writing and publishing throughout Canada. We acknowledge the Government of Ontario through the Ontario Media Development Corporation's Ontario Book Initiative.

Cover design: Adam Hartling
Cover photo of John Papalia courtesy of the *Globe and Mail*

Library and Archives Canada Cataloguing in Publication
Freeman, Bill, 1938-, author
    Their town : the Mafia, the media and the party machine / Bill Freeman
and Marsha Aileen Hewitt. -- Second edition.

Revision of: Their town : the Mafia, the media and the party machine / edited
    by Bill Freeman and Marsha Hewitt. -- Toronto : J. Lorimer, 1979.
ISBN 978-1-4594-0946-0 (paperback)

    1. Political corruption--Ontario--Hamilton. 2. Business and politics--Ontario--Hamilton. 3. Organized crime--Ontario--Hamilton. 4. Hamilton (Ont.)--Politics and government. I. Hewitt, Marsha, 1948-, author II. Title.

JS1751.8.F74 2016   364.1'3230971352   C2016-900042-7

James Lorimer & Company Ltd., Publishers
117 Peter Street, Suite 304
Toronto, ON, Canada
M5V 2G9
www.lorimer.ca

Printed and bound in Canada

To Erik, Peggy, Jessica, Nathan and Justin

Contents

Foreword to the Second Edition — 4
Foreword to the First Edition — 7
Introduction: Hamilton politics and the ideology of business — 8

PART I: POLITICAL POWER

Welfare Hamilton style by Bill Freeman — 14
Business control in a working class town by Bill Freeman — 28
Hamilton Labour: The failure of an opposition group by Bill Freeman — 38

PART II: ORGANIZATIONS

John Munro and the Hamilton East Liberals: Anatomy of a modern political machine by Henry Jacek — 62
The Hamilton Mob and the politics of organized crime by Bill Freeman — 74
Independence or control: Ten years at *The Spectator* by Marsha Aileen Hewitt and Bill Freeman — 90
Selling out: The story of the Victoria Park Community Organization by Bill Freeman — 100

PART III: THE USES OF POWER: CASE STUDIES IN CITY POLITICS

The new city hall saga 1955–1972 by Marsha Aileen Hewitt — 112
Downtown redevelopment: The Civic Square project by Bill Freeman — 120
Arenas, libraries and parking garages: Downtown development in the seventies by Marsha Aileen Hewitt — 136
Hamilton Harbour: Politics, patronage and cover-up by Marsha Aileen Hewitt — 148

Index — 167

Foreword to the Second Edition

It is time for celebration when a book like *Their Town* is republished. It provides an alternative view of how cities operate and decisions are made. The continuing interest in the book illustrates that the public is keen to dig deeper than superficial news stories to understand how their city really works.

When *Their Town* was first published, over 35 years ago, it caused a considerable stir in Hamilton, and it continues to have its supporters and detractors. Some denounce it because it brought bad publicity to the city, and others welcome it as a realistic view of how the city operates. Most readers were simply fascinated by the book's contents.

A lot has happened since then, both in Hamilton, and to the two of us. We had moved to Montreal before the book was released to take up teaching positions. Today Bill is a free-lance writer living on Toronto Island, and Marsha is a professor of religion, teaching in Trinity College at the University of Toronto, and a psychoanalyst in private practice.

The genesis of every book is complicated and it is worth taking a moment to sketch out the origins of *Their Town*. In the late 1960s and early '70s Bill was living in Hamilton and had become involved in the Civic Square debate. Later he worked as an organizer for the Hamilton Welfare Rights Organization, possibly the most controversial group to hit the city since the Steelworkers Union began organizing in the steel mills. Later he ran for political office. But this involvement was tempered by his experience as a graduate student and teacher in McMaster's Sociology Department.

Marsha came to the project from a different perspective. She had grown up in Hamilton and studied English and Religion at McMaster University. For a time she was employed by the Victoria Park Community Organization, a group working with low income people in the north west part of the city. As a community organizer, Marsha worked with a group of residents who fought to preserve the last untouched piece of the bay at the far west end of Lake Ontario. The city was prepared to allow a private development that would have filled in that area of the bay for commercial use. This dedicated group of ordinary citizens who called themselves "Save Our Bay" successfully stopped the proposed landfill project. Today a beautiful park stands on the shores of the bay. The success of Save Our Bay demonstrated the power of ordinary people to protect their communities.

Bill had already published with James Lorimer and talked with Jim about doing a book on Hamilton. This seemed like a daunting task for one person, but when Marsha agreed to join the project as a co-researcher/author, it suddenly became a possibility.

Marsha brought another expertise to the project that was invaluable. The publisher wanted to bring the book out with illustrations. Marsha was not only a talented photographer, but with a detailed knowledge of the contents of the book, she knew what photos were needed to illustrate the text.

Bill and Marsha wanted photographs of Railway Street, once home of some of Hamilton's organized crime families. Already living in Montreal, Marsha visited Railway Street one summer day to take photos for the chapter on the mob. She had her infant daughter with her that day. A very large man, who looked like a character out of a Sopranos episode, was sitting on a lawn chair on the public sidewalk. As Marsha began to take photographs, the man approached her with an aggressive swagger. He told her she could not take photographs of the street, and ordered her to leave. The man's menacing tone was especially frightening given that Marsha's baby daughter was a few steps away. Marsha had no doubt the man would hurt her if she insisted on her right to photograph a public space. As she left the scene, she could not help but wonder, what kind of city is this?

All academic disciplines insist on rigorous, accurate research, and there is plenty of that in *Their Town*, but at that time there was vigorous debate among the faculty and students in sociology about the importance of elites. Who were members of elites, and how and why did they gain power? Bill's position was that you can only understand the importance of elites in a dynamic way by looking at how they shape issues. *Their Town* describes just that. The articles show how decisions were made, who benefited, who paid the price, and how did these decisions impact the City of Hamilton.

As the book developed we talked, sometimes for hours, about what should be included, what was important, and how it contributed to Hamilton and our understanding of the way decisions are made. Early in the project we agreed that each of us would work on the issues that interested us, and the book reflects that. The author's name is given for each article. This approach allowed for richer, diverse perspectives. This was also a deeply collaborative work and that meant hours of working together.

As a project like this develops often there are happy, unforeseen developments that crop up. Henry Jacek's article, "John Munro and the Hamilton East Liberals: Anatomy of a modern political machine", is a good example. Bill, who was working in the Sociology Department at the time, happened to mention the project to Jacek, a professor in the Political Science Department at McMaster. Jacek mentioned that he had an article that might fit. Not only did it fit, by describing how the Munro political machine worked, but it became the centrepiece in the section on organizations in the book.

The origins and development of the book are of interest, but what is more important are the articles themselves, the issues they addressed, and what they show about Hamilton. Of all the articles in *Their Town* the one that stirred the most controversy was Bill's exposé on organized crime, "The Hamilton Mob and the politics of organized crime."

Crime is always fascinating to readers, and some of the Hamilton crime figures had an almost legendary status. Marsha grew up hearing stories from her father about Rocco Perri, who gave him quarters each time the young man delivered a telegram to his home. In her father's words, he was "a gentleman." The careers of Rocco Perri, ("King of the Bootleggers,") and his "consort," Bessie, had been written about by others. Johnny Papalia had been identified as a kingpin of organized crime in Ontario and upper New York State several times. This article drew attention to the long history of organized crime in the city, explaining why Hamilton in particular had become a centre of organized crime in Ontario.

Johnny Papalia was murdered in broad daylight on May 31, 1997, in the parking lot of his vending machine company on Railway Street. Another organized crime group was moving in on his territory. That group, according to accounts, continues to operate in the city.

Marsha's article "Hamilton Harbour: Politics, patronage and cover-up," was equally explosive. It begins by making a startling observation: "The discovery of a fraudulent contract for dredging work in Hamilton Harbour, standard practice in Canada's dredging industry, it appears, provided a startling demonstration of the way in which some large enterprises regularly have done their business with the public."

Bill's article "Downtown redevelopment: The Civic Square project," follows this theme of corporate give-aways and back room deals. It exposes how then Mayor Vic Copps and Controller Jack MacDonald handled the negotiations. They used federal and provincial urban renewal funds to tear down the central core of the city's business district. Unfortunately, they had little to replace it with. In this case it was incompetence and favouritism toward one of Hamilton's leading families, the Pigotts. In the end the two most prominent politicians of the city agreed to a dreary looking shopping mall that contributed to the deterioration of downtown rather than encouraging its rejuvenation.

Is development any better today? No. Louder voices continue to dominate. We get wonderful housing for the affluent, but little for those with middle or low incomes. We continue to allow suburban sprawl to eat up valuable farmland, and at the same time create car dependent communities that contribute to the crisis of global warming. That is no surprise. Property developers have more political influence with municipalities and the province than any other industry, and our unaffordable, environmentally unsustainable communities are the result.

Hamilton has changed since *Their Town* was published. The steel industry, once the base of the city's economy, has shrunk and the Steelworkers Union has shrunk with it. Fortunately the city has not gone through the decline of "rust belt" industrial cities in the American northeast. The reason for this is not the strength of manufacturing and the private sector. It is the public sector. Today Hamilton Health Services is the city's largest employer, and McMaster University, along with the many enterprises that have been spawned by the university, makes a major contribution to the city's prosperity.

The long fight against the Red Hill Creek Expressway shows the strength of opposition groups in Hamilton. Community groups are flourishing across the city. CATCH News continues to publish detailed, evidence-based information, about the political decisions at city hall. Raise the Hammer is one of the best online alternative websites focusing on municipal issues in the province.

Only a mobilized public can change the political climate of a city. Citizen engagement is hard work. Asking questions, demanding that political decisions be transparent, insisting that policies benefit everyone, rather than business. The work of creating a democratic city is essential.

The lesson is that ordinary people have to build a strong, vibrant citizen's movement to take back Hamilton and make it their town.

— Bill Freeman and Marsha Hewitt, March 2016

Foreword to the First Edition

Our interest in Hamilton politics goes back many years, and stems mainly from our experiences as activists working with the Victoria Park Community Organization. We were involved in several issues there, but two major areas in Hamilton were the focus of our studies: Civic Square and Hamilton Harbour. It was, in fact, from these particular interests that the rest of the book grew. Bill's article on Civic Square was first published in *City Magazine* in 1975 and Marsha's article on Hamilton Harbour appeared there a year later. We found that the way in which both the downtown and the harbour development was carried out is typical of the inept planning and lack of overall vision that characterize city hall. Civic Square and Hamilton Harbour could have been exciting, people-oriented projects as well as commercially successful enterprises. Instead, the city politicians have allowed the private sector to take what it wanted, with no reference point beyond profit. The result has been failure with Civic Square and an inaccessible, dangerously polluted Bay that services only industry.

The long-overdue question we began to ask was: why and how are these things able to occur? Who is making the decisions and in whose interest? Most major development in Hamilton has long appeared to us to be against the best interests of the people who live and work there. Yet someone is clearly benefitting from their loss.

We decided that the best way to understand the political process at city hall was through a description and analysis of selected events. In this way the writing and format of this book parallels our own approach to Hamilton politics: rather than beginning with a fixed theory, we began with the issues themselves and discovered an underlying common element. The events described in these essays reveal the central dynamic of Hamilton political life. Our conclusions about the relationship between political power and business in Hamilton are self-evident.

Our ideas changed a great deal during the writing of this book, largely because the issues we were writing about are ever-changing, with new twists and developments frequently occurring. Most of the issues we discuss have yet to be resolved, so that in one sense this book cannot be complete. What we are offering here is by no means a definitive description of Hamilton politics because such a task would be near-impossible. We are presenting a glimpse of political power in a Canadian city as it is revealed in concrete issues. After all, it is in this way that the people of any city are most directly affected. Although what goes on in Hamilton happens to varying degrees in most North American cities, Hamilton is almost a classic example of the way in which special interest groups come to dominate society.

We wish to thank all those people who helped us with this book, especially Hank Jacek for his fine description of the Munro machine in Hamilton. For their ideas and suggestions, we thank Steve McBride, Gary Teeple, Bill Powell, Chairman of the Hamilton and Regional Conservation Authority; Alderman Bill McCulloch, Don Grey, Reg Wheeler, Ted McMeekin and Henry Merling; Herman Turkstra, Tom and Elena Moerman, Gary Proctor; journalists Bob Reguly, Ken Campbell, Jim Travers, Gerry McAuliffe, Warren Barton and Paul Warnick; Dick Leppert and the staff of the reference library of the Hamilton Public Library and its archivist, Brian Henley. Thanks also to our editor, Mark Czarnecki.

Jim Lorimer we thank for his encouragement during the various stages of the writing and especially for seeing the inherent value of what we were attempting to accomplish.

Finally, to those people who helped us but who for obvious reasons cannot be named, our gratitude for their trust and frankness in talking to us. These people gave us valuable insights and information which greatly aided our research and enhanced our book. We hope that they will recognize how much they helped us in the pages of this book.

— Montreal, January 1979

Introduction: Hamilton politics and the ideology of business

Business is fine in Hamilton. The grimy lunch-bucket town that regularly turns out the basic materials Canada needs to run her industries is still prosperous. The steel mills, employing approximately 35,000 people, are producing at record levels and the hundreds of secondary industries dependent on steel continue to flourish. Perhaps there is a deepening sense of economic crisis in the western world, but Hamilton appears to be untouched by it. For the moment most people seem content that the city and the industries operating within it are functioning as they should.

But beneath this veneer of prosperity and complacency there is a feeling shared by many that things are not quite as they could or should be. Many complain that the old neighbourhoods, such as Durand, Corktown and York Street, have been destroyed so that widened roads could be punched through, and high-rise towers could spring up. Still others complain that the mountain, one of the city's most beautiful natural assets, has been scarred with highways. There is a vague sense of unease whenever it is mentioned that the city's air is so befouled that the working-class East End has the highest cancer rate in Ontario.

For a substantial group of Hamiltonians, the unease changes to indignation whenever the Bay is mentioned. There are still a number of people, raised in the 1920s or earlier, who can remember when the Bay was the centre of the city's life. Not only was it the heart of heavy industry and trade, but in both winter and summer it was the major recreation spot for the entire area. People swam in its crystal-clear waters, fished, picnicked and sailed there in summer. Until the late 1920s there were regular steamboat connections across the Bay to Toronto, and excursions to the Thousand Islands. With autumn the ducks came in their thousands and hunters could easily bag twenty in a day. In winter there was ice fishing and skating. The water was so pure that until 1922 ice was cut off the Bay and sold for use in ice boxes across the city. All that is gone now. Fears of hepatitis and meningitis stopped swimming and picnicking a long time ago. Over one-third of the original surface of the Bay has been filled in for industry and the water that remains is so polluted that it is regularly termed a septic tank or an open sewer.

When people with some awareness are pushed to talk about political life in Hamilton, they will usually agree that they are dissatisfied with what is happening. City council, they admit, is unrepresentative of anything other than the business community, and most political activity is focussed on creating or attracting big impressive projects like Civic Square, hotels, arenas, convention centres, automobile races and industries. Relatively little attention is given to the problems of the neighbourhoods or the needs of less fortunate citizens; many people are aware that the former federal cabinet minister John Munro runs a political organization which depends on political patronage; they acknowledge that developers have virtually a free hand; and most know that organized crime is solidly entrenched in the city.

But despite the knowledge that the environment and communities have been despoiled, and the understanding that much of the city's political and social life is unsavory, to say the least, little has changed in Hamilton for decades, and today there are few cries for reform. The silence of some can be explained because they have benefitted tremendously from the political system in Hamilton. For others, no doubt, prosperity is enough. Most people, however, do not take such a cynical view of their world. The only reasonable explanation for their complacency is that they have become convinced that the political leadership of the city is the best they can hope for.

This book focuses on a puzzling set of problems. To express them in a succinct way: how are political groups able to gain and sustain power in spite of widespread dissatisfaction; and, how are they able to achieve their objectives and get them accepted as legitimate by the majority of citizens? No one will ever be able to answer these questions definitively, but we hope that this critical examination of issues and organizations begins the task. We begin with a general account of how the political system in Hamilton works, who gets elected, and how opposition is frustrated. Then we examine, one by one, some key political organizations: a political party machine, community groups, the city's only newspaper and even organized crime, to show the way they contribute to and reflect the power structure. Finally we look at some of the important issues that politicians have struggled with, and ask questions such as: who has benefited from development; who gains the most when the city takes on urban renewal; and, what is the real scandal behind the harbour. The central concept in all of these studies is power. Before going on to explain how we see power in Hamilton and the way this has shaped our view of politics there, it is worth noting briefly how other social scientists have understood this concept. There are two divergent points of view on power, held by competing schools of thought. For simplicity's sake we can term the two schools the Pluralists and Elitists.

PLURALIST THEORY[1]

Canadians are told in many different ways that ours is a pluralist society. Power, we are assured, is widely distributed among a great number of groups so that no individual, small faction or limited set of interests can rule society. This is the perspective of the pluralists. They hold that ours is a democratic society in which people can participate equally, or nearly equally, in the political decisions facing the community or the nation.

The most important element of the pluralist point of view is the belief that power does not rest with one group, or a small number of groups, but is fractured into hundreds of special-interest groups with widely different power bases. These groups compete openly in the political arena for power. An active agent in the decision-making process is the politician, who, faced with the competing claims of these different interests, must choose what course to take.

Pluralism has been attacked from a number of different points of view, but the most telling critique has identified pluralism as simply an affirmation of the dominant American ideology of liberalism. Pluralism assumes, rather than demonstrates, that political decisions result from the open debate of issues and denies that there are any coalitions of special groups who can impose their will.

When the theory of pluralism is applied to Hamilton political life it seems very naive. There are news outlets that could provide a forum for dissenting opinion, but they largely support the business community. City council gives some opportunity for the open debate of issues and politicians are pressured to act in a variety of ways, but if the major issues facing the council over the years are examined it is obvious that the business community has had by far the greatest influence on their outcome. What is more, the evidence shows that powerful elements in the community are adept at dealing with issues or groups that may create dissent. Although the Hamilton political system allows a limited amount of participation it is the business community that has the loudest voice, and there is very little effective opposition to its point of view.

THE THEORY OF ELITES

Among social scientists, the belief that small elites control political life has a much longer history than pluralism. In the nineteenth century this point of view was put forward mainly by right-wing social philosophers,[2] but in the mid-twentieth century the theory of elites was adapted by left-wing social scientists to launch a critique of the American political system.[3]

Those who hold the theory that elites run political life maintain that in spite of the facade of democratic politics, which gives the impression that political power is dispersed among a plurality of groups, a social and economic elite will be found in all communities and at the national level, running things behind the scenes. This results from the fact that in a society such as our own there are enormous differences in wealth, occupational position and social status. Inequality of political power, therefore, is a consequence of social and economic inequalities.

There are a number of problems with this conception. Elite theorists have been criticised because they ignore or downplay the disputes that arise in political life. Controversial issues often provoke serious differences of opinion among people within the economic elite. However, the real problem of the theory is that it presents a static view of political life. It assumes that a recognizable group of people is able to impose its will on the political process. Virtually all political life, therefore, is a conspiracy. This perspective denies the dynamic quality of politics. Alliances change constantly on many important issues, and occasionally decisions are made that go against the interests of people defined as the elite.

To some extent the theory of political elites is useful when looking at power in Hamilton. An analysis of political issues shows clearly that business groups have been able to obtain programs geared to their needs. It would be hard, however, to construct a list of Hamiltonians who are in the political elite, and to be able to justify, with a solid argument, why these persons are in the elite and others are excluded. To understand political power in the city it is necessary to have a much more dynamic model, which explains why the politicians and the public as a whole accept one approach to government and not others.

THE IDEOLOGY OF BUSINESS AND THE ROLE OF THE STATE

All the evidence from Hamilton's political and economic history points to the fact that the group which has held and continues to hold dominant power in the city is the business community. It has been able to do this, not as a small elite dictating its will to city council, but because the majority of politicians and a significant number of citizens believe that the proposals made by business are in the best interests of the city. The growth of business is thought to represent "progress" and that goal, in the twentieth century as much as in the nineteenth, remains the magical touchstone that is politically irresistible to all. To put it another way, the business community has held power over the years because the "ideology of business" has provided the dominant set of beliefs guiding the city's political life.

There is a persistent myth that the business community believes that government should be uninvolved in its affairs. If necessary the state should act as a referee in disputes, but competition and the free market should determine the success of a company or industry. This myth has virtually no resemblance to the facts. Throughout the history of this country, from the days of the fur trade, through railway development, to modern industry, the state has played a major role in subsidizing private firms with their policies, providing services and giving economic stability so that business can grow and make a high level of profit. The state, far from being uninvolved in the affairs of business, plays a major role by providing massive public subsidization of private interests.[4]

In the past century the federal government gave enormous subsidies to railways and developed a system of tariffs and bounties for manufacturers. More recently they have provided airlines, canals, harbour facilities, DREE grants and funds for research. The provincial governments have given roads, cheap hydroelectric power and education, to name only the chief programs.

The function of municipal governments in Canada has been to provide similar services to business on the local level. The chapter "Welfare: Hamilton Style" in this book points out that, as early as the 1850s, the city heavily subsidized railways directly from the public purse. At the same time an important water works was built to attract industry. The tax concessions and obvious given to industries prior to World War I were truly enormous in their scope. For example, bus companies were purchased when it was obvious that private enterprise could no longer run them at a profit. The urban redevelopment schemes designed and implemented in the late 1960s and early 1970s served a similar function. They were carried out primarily to revitalize the city core so that it would attract people downtown and improve the trade of the merchants.

Nowhere is the practice of subsidizing business more clear than in the policies affecting Hamilton Harbour. From the time the Desjardins Canal was cut in the 1830s, the harbour was always developed for commerce and industry. Shipping rates were kept low and ultimately, in the 1930s, eliminated. The Hamilton Harbour Commission maintains warehouses and makes sure that there are plenty of longshoremen to service the ships. It has even gone so far as to supply land to industry through the sale of water lots, so that companies can expand their operations.

It is clear that these programs did not come about by accident in Hamilton. They were guided by the belief that the major role of the state should be to meet the needs of the private sector. This belief, stated in many different ways, is promoted by the business community for its own economic ends, but it has remained the guiding principle in the formation of policy in the city for well over one hundred years.

One of the clearest statements of this ideology was made by Mayor Vic Copps in 1963, when he appeared before the Senate Standing Committee on Transport and Communications in Ottawa, dealing with the issue of who should retain power over Hamilton Harbour. At that hearing Copps said:

We think it is most essential and most necessary that we be left with this power to try and assist in developing the harbour in the interests of the city and in the interests of our industries that have such a big stake there . . . there has been great expansion [of the harbour since the seaway opened] and expansion in our industries . . . All this development is based on the co-operation they [the businesses] know they can get from the city and the harbour commissioners along the bay front.[5]

Clearly, in Copps' mind, the interests of the city and private industry are virtually identical, and the role of government should be to serve the needs of private interests.

In this attitude lies part of the answer to the question of how political groups are able to gain and sustain power in spite of widespread dissatisfaction. There is wide support among politicians and the public, in places like Hamilton, for the subsidization of business. There are certain consequences of this support, such as the pollution of the environment, the destruction of old neighbourhoods, and the domination of councils by business interests, but people either accept these problems as a cost of "progress" or find that their protests are ignored by the media and the political and business leaders.

It is not necessary, then, for business to enter into a conspiracy with the politicians in order to dominate political life, as elite theorists would suggest. The ideology of business is so pervasive that, as we will see, the majority of council members have always been willing to design programs for this special interest group. To the question: who has power in Hamilton? We must reply: the business community. It is able to sustain its power chiefly because belief in the business ideology is widely shared by groups beyond the business community itself.

POLITICAL POWER AND HAMILTON

The studies of Hamilton political life found in this volume have both shaped and been shaped by this view of political power. Unlike others who hold that elites run political life, we have made no attempt here to try to identify exactly who makes up the political elite in the city.[6] Rather, we reject this as too static a view of the political process. Our approach is to look at the issues themselves to see how power works. We believe that politics can only be seen and understood in any fundamental sense as power is used and that this by necessity leads to a detailed study of political life as well as organizations and issues.

The studies in this book show that politics is an extremely complex social process, and that decisions are made as a result of a wide variety of factors. The business group in Canada — or in Hamilton at least — is not so well integrated a class that it can simply impose its will on the political process. Often there are serious disputes among politicians, businessmen and political activists, and the outcome can be unpredictable. Nevertheless, the widespread agreement on the "rules of the game," which dictate that programs designed for business should be supported because they are in the best interests of everyone, means that business, more often than not, is able to win the issues.

One result of political disputes is that, frequently, they make it possible for the public to discern the important political interests in the city, and to identify the recipients of the benefits in different public programs. It is because of this that studies such as those on aspects of development in part three of this book are possible. Urban renewal programs, for example, can reveal a tremendous amount of detail about the use of power that is not available in any other way. However, we do not pretend that these studies reveal all there is to know about political life in the city or even uncover everything that went on in the resolution of these issues. A great deal of political life goes on behind closed doors. Nevertheless these cases illustrate the way power is used in our cities, and the richness of detail gives a glimpse into political life operating in the real world.

As a final note of introduction we should comment on our own orientation in preparing these studies. This book arises out of both an academic interest in political life and a commitment as political activists. The understanding of urban politics in Canada is still elementary; indeed, outside the major cities of Montreal, Toronto, Winnipeg and Vancouver it is virtually non-existent. This book in a small way begins to fill this gap and gives new insights into the operation of political power and organizations.

At the same time, these studies were written in an effort to stimulate political discussion and change. Much about Hamilton political life disturbs us greatly. We would like to see fundamental change that challenges the "ideology of business" and replaces it with a new set of political values stressing the involvement of citizens in discussions and debate, an emphasis on preserving and strengthening neighbourhoods, and a movement to clean up the devastation left by environmental pollution.

For us, two symbolic events will mark the beginning of a new and revitalized Hamilton. The first will be the emergence of a vigorous opposition group in the city, effectively criticising the "ideology of business" that has guided our public life for so long, and opening an extensive public debate on city programs and policies. The second symbolic event will be the reclamation of Hamilton Bay by the people. When the water becomes clean enough for swimming and people can picnic on what remains of the beaches, that will be a beginning. Maybe the ducks will come back in their thousands, and the long dead fish will be resurrected from the muck. When these things have happened it will be a time to celebrate. This book is a contribution to that end.

1. The clearest statement of the Pluralist Theory is in Robert Dahl, *Who Governs?* (New Haven: Yale University Press, 1961); and Nelson Polsby, *Community Power and Political Theory*, (New Haven: Yale University Press, 1963).

2. The best-known works of the Elitist School in the nineteenth century are: Vilfredo Pareto, *The Mind and Society*, Vol. III (New York: Harcourt, Brace and World, 1935); Gaetano Mosca, *The Ruling Class*, (New York: McGraw-Hill, 1965); and Robert Michels, *Political Parties*, (New York: Dover, 1959).

3. The best-known works of the modern Elite Theorists are: Robert and Helen Lynd, *Middletown and Middletown in Transition*, (New York: Harcourt and Brace, 1920 and 1937); C. Wright Mills, *The Power Elite*, New York: Oxford University Press, 1951); and Floyd Hunter, *Community Power Structure*, (New York: Anchor Books, 1963).

4. The best description of this political economy approach is still: Rick Deaton, "The State's Fiscal Crisis," *Our Generation*, Vol. 8, No. 4.

5. The Senate of Canada, "Proceedings of the Standing Committee on Transport and Communications," 30 October 1963, p. 36.

6. Canadian elite studies have proliferated in recent years and have become the major way of viewing power by sociologists and political scientists. The best known are John Porter, *The Vertical Mosaic*, (Toronto: University of Toronto Press, 1965); and Wallace Clament, *The Canadian Corporate Elite: An Analysis of Economic Power* (Toronto: McClelland and Stewart, 1975).

Part I
Political power

Much of the writing about politics, no matter what the political orientation of the writer, focuses on the power brokers who make things happen. This may provide interesting gossip on political and business leaders, but it is not very fruitful in explaining political life because it denies the way politics is practised in this country. All policies or programs represent the promotion of a set of interests that favours one section of the population over another. Legislation is not designed for individuals; it is for interest groups, and particularly certain economic interest groups. The important set of questions around the issue of power, then, are: what interest group is able to gain the major favours of the political system and, how is it able to maintain power in the face of competition from others? These questions provide the theme for the three chapters in this part.

The first chapter looks at the broad pattern of city government policies over the last 150 years in Hamilton, and compares the use made of municipal funds and resources to assist business to the help provided to the city's poor. The second chapter examines how local government is structured and explains how business interests have managed to capture and hold political power in what is basically a working-class town. The final chapter is a history of the attempts by labour, at times almost successful, to wrest power from the dominant business interests, and an analysis of the reasons for labour's failure to win political control of Hamilton's city hall.

Welfare Hamilton style

Bill Freeman

In 1935, Mr. Ross McMaster, then the president of Hamilton's largest firm, the Steel Company of Canada, said: "The main fault to be found with most [government] plans is that their effect tends to stultify individual initiative. Governmental action educates the public to believe that they have no responsibility for their own welfare. This is directly opposed to the principles which helped build up this country."[1]

This statement by Hamilton's leading corporate citizen at the time is a clear expression of the dominant ideology of our society. It says, essentially, that ours is a country where success depends on individual initiative. Those with money and power gained it through their own or their forefathers' efforts, while the poor are responsible for their own plight because they lack the initiative and capacity for hard work necessary for success. Hence welfare in any form is to be opposed, because it allows people to be lazy rather than encouraging them to enter into the enobling struggle for wealth.

This is a convenient ideology for those who are well off. It both congratulates them for having achieved so much through their own efforts and shifts the blame for poverty away from our economic system which allows for social inequality, to the poor themselves. The only problem with this belief is that it has little basis in fact.

The reality is that from the earliest development of the city the poor in Hamilton have been forced to live under welfare systems that treat them as unwanted parasites who are a drain on the municipality's finances. As a consequence many have suffered hardship and deprivation, often resulting in the disintegration of their families and of their image of themselves as worthwhile members of society. On the other hand, the rich in the city have benefitted from a sophisticated type of corporate welfarism, designed by their friends in government to lessen the risks of development, fatten profits and increase enormously the wealth of the few.

The policy of Hamilton's city government has not been guided by the belief that all subsidies are wrong. Quite the contrary. Policies have been shaped by the belief that government should provide support to private enterprise whenever and wherever they are able. The "ideology of business," as we have called it, is particularly evident when the political life of Hamilton is viewed historically. City council has frequently given concessions, in the form of investments, direct grants or tax holidays to companies, when industries faced high risks or when there was competition among municipalities for the investment dollar.

There have been three distinct periods of the city's history when different types of industries received the benefits of municipal give-aways. The first was during the era of railway buildings, from 1850 to 1860; the second was during the period of industrial expansion, from 1890 to 1918; and the third was the recent period of the real estate development boom, from 1962 to 1976. Contrasting this type of corporate welfarism with the support given the poor in these historical periods gives an accurate picture of how the welfare system has actually worked in the city.

THE BUILDING OF THE RAILWAYS 1850-1860

For the early Hamilton businessman the chief attraction of the city was its location. Situated at the extreme west end of Lake Ontario on a magnificent natural harbour, with ready access to the hinterland to the southwest and north, the city seemed destined to become one of the major trading centres of the province. In 1837 the Desjardins Canal was opened through to Dundas, making that town, for a time, the centre of commerce. It was soon obvious, however, that this narrow, shallow waterway could not accomodate heavier ships. By the late 1840s Hamilton had firmly taken the lead in economic growth.

With the beginning of the railway era the Hamilton business community saw the opportunity to make Hamilton the centre of trade for the region around the city and greatly expand commerce. As early as 1834 a group of local businessmen received a charter from the Legislature of Upper Canada incorporating a railway between London and Hamilton. Because of the heavy financial risks the project never materialized.[2] It was clear that the major problem in undertaking a project of this size lay in raising sufficient capital, and it was not long before a group of railway businessmen emerged with a plan to tap the public purse in order to gain the needed funds.

Sir Allan MacNab, a man still revered in Hamilton as the city's greatest nineteenth-century businessman and statesman, was the chief architect of this policy. MacNab was a man of enormous prestige, political power and personal wealth in the middle of the last century. He came from a family of Scottish Highland chieftains, had been a child hero in the War of 1812 and played an important part in quelling the Mackenzie Rebellion of 1837. He sat in the Canadian legislature for many years as a supporter (indeed he himself was a member) of the Family Compact, the Tory ruling group in Upper Canada. In 1854 he was speaker of the house and for a brief time was prime minister. MacNab had been knighted for his role in putting down the 1837 Rebellion and in 1856 he was given a baronetcy.

In spite of these honours MacNab was primarily a businessman who looked on politics as a way of gaining personal wealth. For some time he was the chairman of the Legislative Assembly Standing Committee on Railways,[3] and he used this position to promote his own financial interests and block competition."Railways are my politics,"[4] he once stated frankly, and there can be no doubt that he intended this in a literal sense.

In 1834 MacNab had been one of the chief promoters of the London and Gore Railway Company, which had been unable to raise enough money to begin their project. By 1845 the railroad's

Sir Allan MacNab (Hamilton Public Library).

name had been changed to the Great Western Railway, MacNab had been made the company president, and their proposed project had become much more ambitious. Instead of the modest objective of building a rail line for the eighty miles between London and Hamilton, the promoters proposed to build a railway from Niagara Falls, through Hamilton, Brantford, Woodstock, London, Chatham and Windsor. They claimed that the line would not only be a means of bringing the products of Southwestern Ontario to the port of Hamilton, but would also become the most frequently travelled rail link between New York City and Boston in the east and Chicago in the west, because it was considerably shorter than the route through the United States.

MacNab and his associates saw that the only way of raising enough money to make their railway a reality was to create the right political climate, in which government subsidies would become available. From 1845 on they made a concerted effort to achieve their objectives. In that year Hamilton's Board of Trade (the forerunner of the Chamber of Commerce) was organized, and the most important project they promoted was the railway. But even with speeches at public dinners and wordy legislation giving moral support, the railroaders were unable to raise much money. In

An old lithograph of Dundurn Castle (Hamilton Public Library).

1845 Hamilton town council voted the paltry sum of £25 to the railroad, although the chief engineer had estimated that it would cost about £4332 for every mile of construction.[5]

Sir Allan MacNab and his fellow promoters of the Great Western were not about to accept this setback. In the following five years the campaign urging public support for the railway was unremitting. Newspapers, pamphlets and letters to the editor spread the word of the great benefits the railway would bring. One remarkable treatise written at the time, called The Philosophy of Railroads, claimed that "Local proprietors of real estate . . . could have no better security for their investment than that contingent upon the increase of population, wealth and traffic."[6] This, the author argued, would only come with the railways. Railways, in other words, would increase property values, and this was a potent argument in an era when the only municipal voters were property owners. What the author conveniently omitted to mention, however, was that the railway was a private scheme with the intent of making profits for the owners alone.

By 1849 the railroad promoters were beginning to have some success. In that year an act was passed in the Canadian parliament, at the prompting of railway owners such as MacNab, to provide capital to railway companies on certain conditions. It proposed that the government would "lend to companies incorporated for the construction of railways not less than seventy-five miles in length, a sum sufficient to complete the road, when one-half of the work had been performed to the satisfaction of the Public Works Department."[7] (Only later was it learned that Sir Francis Hincks, the promoter of this bill, had received $250,000 worth of stock and other favours from the Grand Trunk Railway for services rendered to the company.)[8]

Despite promotion by the companies there was still public resistance to this subsidy program. In 1849 there was pressure on Hamilton town council to buy railroad stock, but the motion merely to discuss the idea was passed by only one vote. But when the Great Western promoters announced that they were considering running the railroad along the mountain brow and avoiding the city altogether, town council threw caution to the winds and launched a policy of direct subsidization of the railroad that almost bankrupted the city.[9]

Initially it was found that it was illegal for municipalities to invest in railway stocks, but after MacNab, Hincks and other railway promoters who controlled the Canadian parliament changed this legislation, Hamilton council passed a by-law authorizing the purchase of £100,000 of Great Western stock. This was a staggering amount of money in those days. It was only after some citizens

The Great Western Railway yard about 1875 (Public Archives Canada).

pointed out that the total assessed value of the city's real estate was only £94,000 that the value of the shares purchased was reduced to £50,000. Even with this reduction the city population was burdened with additional taxes. In order to raise sufficient money for the purchase, a special tax had to be levied of one shilling per person.[10]

The promotion of the Great Western Railway to municipalities was handled by Sir Allan MacNab's right-hand man, J. T. Gilkson, who at the time was both a Hamilton alderman and the secretary of the railroad. Gilkson's success was impressive. A total of 2,464 acres of valuable land was given free of charge to the railroad by virtually every town along the route, and thousands of pounds of municipal taxes were given as grants or invested in Great Western stock. In addition, between 1852 and 1855, the Canadian government loaned the company £770,000 for the completion of the railroad.

The Great Western was not the only railway that was subsidized by Hamilton town council in the 1850s. In 1853 the council approved a motion to invest £10,000 in shares of the Galt-Guelph Railroad and in 1856 this was increased to £50,000. In 1855 Sir Allan MacNab was promoting the Hamilton-Port Dover Railway and the city bought £50,000 of its stock.[11] Tax money was also invested in the Preston-Berlin Railroad.

The railway promoters in the middle of the last century were viewed as the great capitalists of the age, but their business dealings were not always ethical even by the lax standards of that time. Sir Allan MacNab's activities were often tinged with scandal. In 1857 stockholders of the Great Western met in Hamilton to protest the action of the company directors in granting £5000 to MacNab for services he had rendered the railroad. Despite calls for a royal commission nothing was done.[12] MacNab had made himself a fortune in railways and by the mid-1850s he lived in splendour in Dundurn Castle, his magnificent estate on Burlington Heights overlooking the Bay. He was honoured to the end, but the fact is that the Laird of Dundurn had made his fortune by using his public posts to further his own private interests.

The municipal policy of subsidizing private interests was disastrous for Hamilton. By 1860, $938,880 in debentures had been issued to pay for railroad stocks, general debentures amounted to $556,812, and there was an additional set of debentures for $774,412 for construction of the water works. In that year the city paid out $334,136 just to service the debt—77.5% of the total expenditure.[13]

In spite of the promises of the railway promoters, economic conditions worsened in the city. In 1858, at the height of a boom, there were 25,000 people living in Hamilton, but with the onset of

An old drawing of the Desjardins Canal Railway Disaster of March 12, 1857 in which sixty people were killed (Hamilton Public Library).

a depression and the burden of heavy taxes the population decreased to 19,000 in 1862. At one point in that year it was estimated that one-third of all the dwelling places in the city were standing vacant and some areas were virtually deserted.

This sparked a serious financial crisis in the city. In 1862 some of the creditors became impatient with the city's slow payment of their debts and got a judgement against the municipality. The sheriff sold the furniture in the city hall to meet the court order, but because the judgements were coming in faster than they could be satisfied he was instructed to place a special assessment on property to pay off the debt. It was estimated that a tax of this type would have amounted to ten shillings and six pence payable for every pound's worth of real estate owned — 55% of its value. This would have been impossible to collect. The city was rescued only when Thomas Beasley, the city clerk, locked up the assessment tolls in a warehouse, hid the key, and on his doctor's advice took a much-needed rest in some unknown spot. His "cure" lasted until it was past the court term for a special assessment.[14] In that year the city was able to overcome its financial crisis by negotiating new debentures, but for many years it was crippled with enormous debt for the period of railway subsidization. In 1864 almost 86% of tax revenues had to be applied to service the debt and by 1873 the amount was still 50%.

The political and economic power of the railway barons can be seen in the enormous financial concessions they obtained from municipalities such as Hamilton and from the Government of Canada, but it was also shown in the way they operated their lines and the scant regard they showed for the safety of their workers and passengers. Although millions of dollars were advanced to the Great Western, the railway was so poorly constructed that numerous wrecks caused considerable loss of life on the line: "At Lobo (near London) on June 2, 1854, six passengers were killed and fourteen injured; at Thorold, on July 16, 1854, seven passengers were killed and fourteen injured; a terrible wreck at Baptist Creek, on October 27, 1854 caused the death of fifty-seven persons and the injury or mutilation of forty-six."[15] A commission of the legislature was formed to investigate these accidents in 1854 and found evidence of poor and faulty construction. Because of the political power of the railway interests no official was ever punished or even charged.[16]

There was a public outcry but conditions on the Great Western continued in a general state of disrepair. Finally, on March 12, 1857, a train crossing the Desjardins Canal on its entrance into Hamilton plunged through the bridge into the waters below, killing sixty people. A later enquiry showed that, although the bridge was originally to have been built of oak timbers, the company had constructed it of pine, and it had been kept in bad repair. Government regulations at the time required trains to stop before crossing the bridge, but the rule had been disregarded by the company. However, despite evidence of neglect, company officials were exonerated of blame for the tragedy and paid only small compensation to the families of the victims.

While the city of Hamilton was involved in what can only be described as massive subsidization of the wealthy railroad interests in the 1850s, its support for the poor in the municipality was shockingly inadequate. In 1852 a hospital and a "House of Industry" (the new name used for the poor house) were built. Those unable to support themselves crowded into the House of Industry and subsisted largely on the charity of churches and private individuals.

When the depression came in 1861, caused in part by the railway subsidies which left the municipality close to bankruptcy, the city fathers attempted to save money by restricting help to the poor. On April 1, 1861 the council instructed the high bailiff "to discontinue the issue of bread tickets on behalf of the relief committee until further notice."[17] Again in 1861 a resolution was passed in council which said:

Resolved that the Hospital Committee be required to enquire into and report upon the present state of the House of Refuge with a view to removing therefrom such women as may be capable of earning their own support, and also to adopt some plan for apprenticing to farmers all boys over ten years of age now in the institution.[18]

It is difficult to imagine the results of such a policy. Women with dependents, children over ten, and men unable to support themselves were left in destitution in the midst of a depression which virtually eliminated the opportunity for even the able-bodied to get employment. The result must have been wide-spread misery. Meanwhile the Great Western, built in large part at the public's expense, reaped profits for the railway barons.

THE AGE OF INDUSTRIAL DEVELOPMENT 1890-1918

The history of Canada's industrial growth is another story of huge subsidization and protection of private interests by all levels of government. The basis for this development was laid out in John A. Macdonald's National Policy of 1879, but Hamilton added to this to provide a level of subsidization for local industry that reached almost all manufacturers in the city.

By the time the National Policy was legislated, Hamilton was already a growing industrial centre, and it is not surprising that political leaders in the city were among the major promoters of protective tariffs for the Canadian market. Isaac Buchanan, a leading city merchant and member of parliament, published a book advocating protective tariffs for Canada as early as 1848, and for the next thirty years he was the policy's chief proponent. The *Spectator,* the Hamilton newspaper, followed his lead by becoming the country's most ardent protectionist newspaper.[19] When John A. Macdonald was finally convinced of the policy he was reported to have said in Hamilton, in a blunt manner he would never have dared to use in other ridings: "Let each manufacturer tell us what he wants and we will try to give him what he needs."[20]

An extensive system of tariffs existed by 1890, when Hamilton city council began a policy of direct cash payments and municipal tax reductions to encourage companies to locate in the city. By that time it was clear to the city's business community that Hamilton's position as a financial and trading centre was fading, and that its future growth would depend on industrial expansion. Because of that concern, "The finance committee in that year (1890) recommended that all manufacturers locating in the city should be exempted from paying taxes for ten years on all of their buildings, machinery, tools, income and personal property."[21]

Although the motion did not pass, it marked the first trickle of what was to become a vast outpouring of subsidies to industrial firms in the city. In 1893 the first grants were given to the steel industry. A group of New York capitalists were given a free site of seventy-five acres of land and a bonus of $100,000, if a $400,000 blast furnace and a $400,000 open hearth mill were built and running by 1894.[22] The land given to the company, valued at $35,000 at the time,[23] was known as Huckleberry Point, a beauty spot famous among local residents for its oak and walnut woods, and a popular landing site for boaters and outdoorsmen. Today there is nothing left of the beauty of Huckleberry Point among the huge installations of the Steel Company of Canada. The by-laws of the city in the 1890s are filled with special tax exemptions and bonuses paid to new companies that located in the city, but it was only after the turn of the century that the subsidies handed out by Hamilton became enormous. In 1897 Westinghouse located in the city and in 1903 an inducement given to the company stated that, "The taxes . . . on all property existing or thereafter established were fixed at $1,500 per annum for 1905 to 1909, $3,000 from 1910 to 1914, and $4,500 from 1915 to 1919."[24]

In that same year Hamilton city council ran into its first real problem in granting bonuses to industry as an inducement to locate in the city. In 1902 Alexander Dunn, a hotel owner, alderman and member of the city finance committee, heard that the Deering Agricultural Implement Company

An early drawing of the International Harvester Works on Hamilton's bayfront (Hamilton Public Library).

(later to become a part of International Harvester) was searching for a location for its Canadian branch plant. Dunn negotiated directly with the company and agreed that the city would pay the Deering Company $50,000 if it chose to locate in Hamilton. It was expected that the by-law would be ratified by the population in a referendum with little problem, but to the surprise of the city councillors it was defeated by a sizeable majority. All of the labour unions in the city had campaigned against the by-law because Deering kept an open shop in its main plant in Illinois.

A *Spectator* article, written in 1920, shows how city council responded and incidentally illustrates some of the biases of Hamilton's leading newspaper of the day.

It was a sad night in Hamilton for those who had looked forward with hopes of an industrial city. The matter was dropped for the time being but in 1903 it was again revived. With the new council, a new financial committee was appointed . . . the Deering Company was invited to again visit Hamilton and a more inviting proposition was made. It was proposed to annex to the city limits a large block of farm land that the Deering Company had selected for its plant, which the finance committee and the city council would have assessed at the then township valuation and on which the rate of taxation of 1903 would prevail for the next twenty years. The suggestion of the committee was at once ratified by the council, and for the past seventeen years the company has been enjoying the ownership of 200 acres of land within the city limits at the rate of assessment and taxation of township farm lands. It was a good thing for the company that the labour unions defeated the $50,000 bonus.[25]

This by-law was an important development in Hamilton's system of industrial subsidies. The changes eliminated the need to take the risky political step of putting the issues of bonuses and tax reductions to a referendum of all voters, and also provided a structure of municipal subsidies which could continue for years without having it debated each time a new grant was to be given.

The slice of land the city annexed in order to accommodate the needs of Deering was a part of Barton Township running east from Sherman Avenue to near Gage, between Barton Street and the Bay. Within a short time this became the centre of industrial development in the city. Today it may well be the most heavily industrialized piece of land in all of Canada. After the by-law was passed all companies locating in the area or new additions to the assessed value of a property were to be taxed at the old Barton Township rate for fifteen years. The tax rate of Barton in 1903 was 6.875 mills. In Hamilton in the same year it was 20 mills and fifteen years later it was 27 mills.[26] Not only were the assessment rates low but the assessed values of a property were also lower than the actual value of the property.[27]

It is difficult to calculate the full extent of the city's subsidy program at this time because of the complicated tax concessions that were given

The interior of one of the steelmaking mills at the Steel Company of Canada, about 1920 (Public Archives Canada).

to companies. David Russell, however, made an extensive review of the subsidies given to the city's largest firm, the Steel Company of Canada, and found a history of giveaways over the years that were so generous that it is questionable whether the company even paid for the city services it received in the early part of the century.

In 1893, when Stelco's parent, the Hamilton Blast Furnace Company, located in the city, it was given seventy-five acres of land and a bonus of $100,000. By 1906 the company was preparing to make extensions to its plant. The firm was already being taxed at the Barton Township rate of 6.875 mills but to give further inducement for it to make improvements, "rather than move elsewhere," the city agreed to assess the total plant in 1907 at a mere $287,000, and from 1908 to 1919 inclusive at only $300,000. In 1910 the company became part of Stelco and additional property was acquired. A new assessment was made by the city and the value of the property was set at not more than $400,000 effective until March 13, 1918.

This municipal assessment of the value of the company property had little relation to its true value. In 1902 it was estimated that the capitalization of the Hamilton Steel and Iron Company, then the name of the firm, was $3,035,200 and when it became part of the Steel Company of Canada in 1910 its value had increased 150%. By 1918, with rapid inflation and a war-induced boom that placed a high demand on steel, the value of the property had increased substantially, and yet that year the company had to pay municipal taxes of only 6.875 mills on $400,000, 28 a total annual tax bill of just $2,750.

By the early 1920s subsidy programs designed to attract companies to municipalities were in disfavour and they were stopped altogether by the provincial government. It is difficult to see the benefits that the program brought to the city. The subsidies did attract new industries but the taxes they paid were so low that in many cases they were a drain on the resources of the municipalities rather than a benefit. As David Russell wrote: "Whether the inequalities of such a system placed a burden upon the tax payer of the city exceeding the benefits received is more than a debatable question."[29]

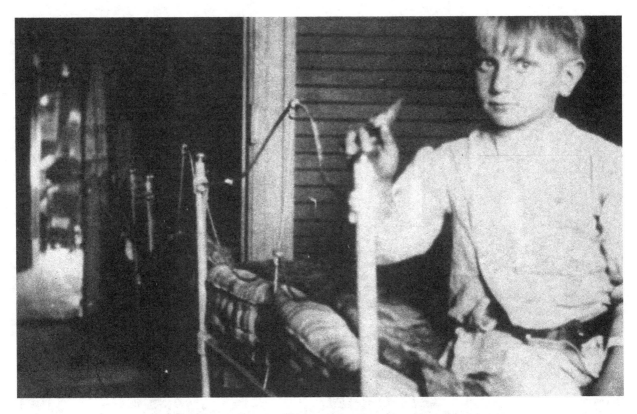

Poverty in the Northeast section of Hamilton, prior to World War I
(McMaster University, Labour Studies Collection).

The subsidies were of benefit to one group alone, and that was the owners of the companies. There can be little doubt that this program took money from the ordinary tax payer to swell the profits of companies that were already large, prosperous and financially stable.

Although the needs of the industrialists were more than adequately taken care of in this period, this was certainly not true of the less fortunate citizens. In the pre-industrial era the problems of poverty could normally be handled within families, but as Hamilton became industrialized after 1890 destitution became more, rather than less, common. Most people in the city were wage earners and when illness or an accident struck the wage earner the family immediately would be in desperate straits. There were large numbers of immigrants with no family in the country to help them if they fell on hard times. When one of the periodic depressions swelled the unemployment rolls, large numbers of people were faced with destitution.

In spite of the need, a comprehensive welfare program for the poor never emerged in the period of rapid industrial development from 1890 to 1918. The city assumed limited responsibilities for the sick, the elderly, the young and women with dependent children, but this was only after the family's financial resources were completely exhausted, and where local residency could be clearly established.[30] Some volunteer welfare organizations such as the Children's Aid Society were founded, but they were not set up to help the poor as much as to see that minimum standards of care were maintained for children or the aged. Throughout the period the burden of welfare work was still borne by volunteer agencies — particularly the churches.

It was not until the economic crisis of the 1930s that a welfare system of the kind that exists today was established in Hamilton, but it was hardly generous. The amount given in 1936 was approximately $100 a year per person. In February of that year the average monthly payment was $8.73. This was made up of: food, $4.66; fuel, $1.60; shoes and shoe repair, $0.26; miscellaneous, including rent, light and medical expenses, $2.21.

The system emphasized the control of those on relief, to see that the money was not misspent and that the recipients caused no trouble to the city. When a person applied for relief an investigator was sent out to the house to check that the family did not own unnecessary items such as a car or spend the money on liquor. Although there were thirty-one investigators employed by the city, in the early days of welfare the recipient had to go to the office to apply in person. In time the administrators recognized that this caused problems. One observer noted, "A large crowd gathered around the relief office, many of which arrived there hours before the office opened. This

Twenty-three Bulgarian men shared thirteen beds in this house
(McMaster University, Labour Studies Collection).

brought unnecessary humiliation to those on relief and made disturbances by the ubiquitous 'red' a continual source of trouble to the department."[31] As a result the welfare department came to rely on the home investigation.

In Hamilton the contrast between the welfare system devised for the rich during this period and that for the poor could not be sharper. While hundreds of thousands of dollars were granted almost for the asking to the large corporations, the poor were questioned and closely watched to see that they were deserving and grateful. It took the Great Depression to bring about a system of welfare for the poor in which there was a degree of universal coverage for people in dire distress. Even then, however, they were policed to such an extent that it is obvious that those in control of the municipality viewed the recipients of relief as irresponsible with money and potential political troublemakers.

THE REAL ESTATE BOOM 1962–1976

In the early 1960s the municipal leaders of Hamilton devised a new form of subsidy to yet another industry. After the Second World War many North American cities had seen demolition and reconstruction of their downtown cores, but Hamilton had changed little in fifty years. The business community was concerned. Was the city facing deterioration and ultimate decay? How would it be possible to attract new investment to rejuvenate the area? In the light of Hamilton's history it is not surprising that political leaders found the answer in the municipal subsidization of private investment.

Soon after Vic Copps became mayor in 1962 it was clear that his administration would aggressively promote downtown redevelopment. Already a large part of the central area of the city to the south and west of the new City Hall had been zoned for high rise and through the 1960s many beautiful old houses, built before the turn of the century, were demolished and replaced with large apartment buildings. But redevelopment of the downtown area was occurring too slowly for the business community that dominated the city's political life.

The politicians wanted downtown redevelopment but the developers were more cautious. Some developers claimed that because of the industrial character of Hamilton's economy the city did not have much need for office and commercial development. If they were to be enticed into investing their money in the downtown area, inducements would have to be offered. Copps and the people around him with ambitions to make

Hamilton one of the great cities of Canada were only too eager to comply.

The first project involving municipal subsidization of developers that was promoted by Copps was Terminal Towers. A large piece of property in the downtown area, bounded by Main, Catherine and King Streets, had been a vacant parking lot for a number of years. In 1959 it had been announced by Mayor Jackson that there would be a development on the site but it failed to materialize. After Copps became mayor in 1962 he was able to persuade the developer to build on the site but not without a substantial inducement. In the negotiations the city agreed that if the project was to go ahead they would take a twenty-year lease on 2,699 square feet of the project and pay an annual rent of $113,436, that is, $42 per square foot. This was a price considerably higher than the going rental rates in the city at the time. In the building the city located its new Magistrate's Court (now called the Provincial Judge's Court) and paid an additional $220,000 to build the interior of the courtroom.

For the developers this was an ideal arrangement. They would have a twenty-year lease with a prime tenant who would spend $2.5 million over the term of the agreement for the use of only a fraction of the building. This was enough for them to announce that construction of the $12 million complex would begin.

It was clear that the deal that Copps and the Board of Control negotiated with the Terminal Towers owners was a subsidy designed to spark development in the downtown area. Brian Morison, a city controller at the time, stated the case very clearly: "We don't want to see downtown Hamilton left the way it is now. We want a bustling metropolis typical of the core of other major Ontario centres. I'm voting for this proposal because I want the downtown heart of Hamilton to live. I've been on council for twelve years and I've seen our downtown core dying."[32] By a vote of nineteen to one the motion to rent the court space in the project passed council.

The Terminal Towers project shows the beginning of a new type of subsidy for the development industry in Hamilton, but by far the most important extension of this program was the Civic Square Urban Renewal project in the heart of the city. Urban renewal was, for the Hamilton politicians, the ideal solution to the problem of the deteriorating city core. Land could be assembled by using their powers of expropriation and costs would be shared 50% by the federal government, 30% by the province and 20% by the municipality. This would solve the sometimes difficult problems that developers faced in assembling land, and it would allow a sizeable package of property to be developed as one unit. It was widely believed in the 1960s that this was the answer: providing a massive influx of public and private money would rejuvenate the downtown core of the city and spark redevelopment in the entire surrounding area.

Not surprisingly, Vic Copps and numbers of other political and business leaders enthusiastically advocated urban renewal for Hamilton. In 1965 city council unanimously voted in favour of a by-law designating forty-four acres of land in the heart of the city as an urban renewal project. This was the largest and most comprehensive project anywhere in Canada.

Again, the essential intent of the program was to provide incentives to attract investment into the downtown core. Initially, 10.4 acres of the project was to be devoted to commercial development but this later rose to 18 acres. The rest of the property was to be used for a theater-auditorium, an art gallery, board of education headquarters and other public facilities. This was to be only the beginning. *The Spectator* commented at the time that the downtown area would soon be ringed with apartment buildings "built to accommodate the people who will flock to this exciting new concept of living," and Controller Brian Morison was quoted as saying: "This will attract the private investment so badly needed in our central business core."[33]

Twelve years after these statements, and the investment of millions of dollars of public money, one can state categorically that the Civic Square project has been a failure. To summarize what happened: the public buildings of the square were nearing completion by the late 1970s; however only a fraction of the commercial development seems likely ever to be finished. The public buildings are crowded into the narrow space between King and Main Streets while acres of land available for development as commercial property lie vacant. The second phase of the development scheme was reduced in size; there seems to be no possibility of attracting the once-promised hotel, and the prestige residential development in the square is unlikely to go ahead. Downtown urban renewal in Hamilton has been a failure of such magnitude that it has speeded rather than stopped the deterioration of the central core.

There was one other important attempt by the city council to spur development in Hamilton by giving subsidies: the Century 21 project. As early as 1959, developer Alf Frisina purchased property on the corner of Main and Catherine Streets, across from the site of what was to become Terminal Towers. Frisina had come to Canada from Italy in 1950 with virtually no assets and for several years had worked as a contractor.[34]

Eventually, he accumulated enough capital to purchase the land and start the planning of a twenty-storey office building (which would have been the city's tallest building at the time), but he could not arrange financing. Over the years he added to his property and his dreams grew bigger. In 1969 it seemed as if the financing was all arranged and a

A welfare protest march on Barton Street in the 1930s (McMaster University, Labour Studies Collection).

large billboard was put up, announcing that the project would be completed in August 1971. Again the deal fell through when Frisina could not find enough tenants to go ahead.

Members of city council favoured this project, believing that it would help stimulate development of the downtown, and a group of council members began negotiating with Frisina. Finally in January 1972 council agreed to rent 15,000 square feet of office space at $8.33 a square foot, or $125,000 a year, an amount well above rental rates at the time. On the basis of this incentive Frisina was able to get the rest of the mortgage money for the project. However, as Century 21 began construction it was announced that it had again grown in size. Now the building was to be a forty-five storey, $10 million project with ten floors of office space and thirty-five floors of apartments which were to rent from $200 to $1000 a month. On the ground floor and basement there were to be stores and a recreation centre, and on the forty-fifth floor a restaurant-nightclub.

By 1974, in the midst of construction, problems were multiplying for the Frisina project. The city' decision to rent space in the building was over turned by the Ontario Municipal Board. Vic Copps tried to come to the developer's aid. In April 1974 he met with then Ontario Attorney General Robert Welch to discuss a proposal to expand the provincial court into the Century 21 tower. In his usual frank manner Copps said at the time that he "wanted to give the developer a hand to find tenants for his building,"[35] but his efforts failed.

A month later, in May 1974, both Frisina and the developers of Civic Square, Yale, were engaged in an attempt to attract the new regional government offices. Finally, with the help of his political friends, Frisina was able to win the contract at $6.31 a square foot, a considerable drop from the $8.33 a square foot once offered by the city.

Despite all of these subsidies the Frisina project went bankrupt in the summer of 1977. By that time the financial affairs of Century 21 were in a

A model of Terminal Towers.

hopeless state. There were still 100 apartment units that had never been rented, most of the retail space was still unoccupied, much of the office section of the building had never been completed, and a tenant was never found for the restaurant-nightclub.

Two other projects that the development-oriented city council attempted to lure to Hamilton by municipal subsidies in the last few years are notable for the fact that they never got off the ground — literally — in spite of promised city subsidies. For a time there was talk of the city making a heavy contribution towards an arena and ice rink in the East End to house a World Hockey League team. When this fell through, members of city council entered into negotiations to build an arena on the vacant land in Civic Square. This plan was turned down by the voters in a 1976 referendum when it appeared that, once again, it was just another way to subsidize private developers. With the end of the development boom in the 1970s this appeared to be the city's last chance to redevelop the downtown by subsidizing private developers.

The type of redevelopment Copps and the people around him designed failed for two reasons. First, since the turn of the century Hamilton has been an industrial rather than a commercial or financial centre; there has never been the need for large office complexes in the central business district that could sustain the scale of development the business community and politicians wanted. Second, what the politicians were trying to do, in essence, was to support downtown businessmen and ensure the success of the developers. When this aim came into conflict with the legitimate desire of the citizens for a rejuvenated downtown, the interests of business were given priority.

Rather than recreating a new central core, redevelopment in Hamilton became a subsidy scheme for business that failed. The taxpayers paid the costs of the original subsidy and now they have to pay the costs of living with a downtown divested of much of its life.

Of course direct subsidies for downtown developers are only the most blatant form of support by city governments for the real estate interests of the city. As James Lorimer points out in his book *A Citizen's Guide to City Politics*, "When you look closely at the functions of city government it becomes quite apparent that almost everything city hall does is related to real estate."[36] With the pro-development council that Hamilton has always had, land has been zoned to serve the interests of the developers. For example, the servicing of land in several parts of the city, but particularly in parts of the East Mountain, have proved to be a massive subsidy to those owning the land. In many cases the owners of property are ordinary citizens, but in Hamilton, as in every other Canadian city, large businesses have been taking over the real-estate industry. The people provide the subsidies through their taxes while the corporations reap the profits.

While a massive subsidy program was developed for business interests of the city in the land development era of the 1960s and 70s, what of the welfare system for Hamilton's poor in the same period? By the end of World War II, a system had evolved in which the poor could receive income support, but it was and has remained grossly inadequate. In order to be eligible a family has to be completely destitute, with no savings and no means of support. Those physically and mentally capable of taking work are forced to take any job offered them or they can be cut off assistance immediately.

In the year 1971, when the Hamilton Welfare Rights Organization operated, the organizers were swamped with complaints of almost every imaginable kind. Many recipients received payments from the welfare department that were less than they were entitled to; others had been declared ineligible for welfare when they were obviously entitled to support under the legislation; there were complaints by recipients that they were berated by the workers; the bureaucracy was difficult to understand, especially for those applying for the first time; and there were many examples of people waiting all day in the welfare office to be served.

As the year progressed, and the Welfare Rights organizers and members became more experienced, appeals multiplied until they occupied almost all the efforts of the group. Because of the political pressure a number of reforms were instituted, making it easier to appeal, and reducing the waiting time at the welfare office. (The policy seems to be similar to that of the 1930s. Recipients were moved out of the welfare office so that they would not come into contact with the "ubiquitous" Welfare Rights organizers.) These reforms made the welfare system in Hamilton more efficient and removed some of the injustices, but did not improve the living standards of the recipients by one dollar.

In 1971 the maximum payment for a single person was $150 a month and for a family of four in the neighbourhood of $375. Out of this people had to provide for all of their needs. Many families had to use money allotted for food to cover their rent. Often people would not have enough money to get through the month and would be forced to turn to churches or friends. Some told stories of being forced to steal; women went into prostitution and the loan sharks "got their hooks into" a number of others.

Comparing the welfare system for the rich to the program for the poor leaves no doubt about who receives the lion's share of the benefits. The poor are forced to live in squalor, blaming themselves for their poverty, while the major subsidy programs are directed at those who already have power, wealth and prestige. It is the "ideology of business," dictating that private enterprise should be supported whenever possible and subsidized when business thinks it necessary, which has been the guiding principle of Hamilton politics for well over a hundred years.

It should also be remembered that municipal subsidies for business are only a small part of the support program for business in this industry. Most manufacturing industries are protected by a high tariff from outside competition and there is a complex system of programs, from subsidized loans to DREE Grants, to aid almost every industry in the country. The tax system gives allowances for depreciation of equipment and many special concessions to increase the profits of business.

If government plans "tend to stultify individual initiative" and welfare is "directly opposed to the principles which helped build up this country," as Ross McMaster suggested, then it is surprising that business has prospered in Hamilton, for it has been the major recipient of the welfare programs designed by the politicians.

1. The Hamilton Public Library, Newspaper Clipping Files, "Stelco," 1935.

2. C.M. Johnston, *The Head of the Lake* (Hamilton: Wentworth County Council, 1958) p. 182.

3. Gustavus Myers, *A History of Canadian Wealth* (Toronto: James, Lewis and Samuel Publishers, 1972) p. 155.

4. Myers, p. 169.

5. Johnston, p. 188.

6. Johnston, p. 188.

7. Myers, p. 189.

8. Myers, pp. 170-171.

9. David Russell, "A Financial History of Hamilton" (BA Thesis, McMaster University, 1936).

10. Paul C. Warnick, "The History of Rail Transportation in the Hamilton Area 1845-1865" (MA Thesis, McMaster University, 1954) p. 54.

11. Warnick, p. 73.

12. Warnick, p. 48.

13. Russell, p. 27.

14. Russell, p. 28.

15. Myers, p. 190.

16. Myers, p. 191.

17. Hamilton City Council Minutes 1861, p. 331.

18. Minutes 1861, p. 369.

19. William Kilbourn, *The Elements Combined: A History of the Steel Company of Canada* (Toronto: Clark Irwin, 1960) p. 39.

20. Kilbourn, p. 41.

21. Russell, p. 48.

22. Kilbourn, p. 48.

23. Johnston, p. 241.

24. Russell, p. 46.

25. The Hamilton Public Library, Newspaper Clipping Files, "International Harvester," 1920.

26. Russell, p. 46.

27. Russell, p. 47.

28. Russell, p. 47.

29. Russell, p. 48.

30. Andrew Armitage, *Social Welfare in Canada: Ideals and Reality* (Toronto: McClelland and Stewart, 1975).

31. Russell, p. 101.

32. *The Globe and Mail*, 12 December 1963.

33. *The Hamilton Spectator*, 10 April 1965.

34. *The Hamilton Spectator*, 2 February 1974.

35. *The Hamilton Spectator*, 6 April 1974.

36. James Lorimer, *A Citizen's Guide to City Politics* (Toronto: James Lewis and Samuel, 1972) p. 4.

Business control in a working class town

Bill Freeman

One of the most striking things about Hamilton political life is that it is virtually unintelligible to any but those who follow political events in detail. On voting day the citizen is faced with a choice of one vote for mayor, four votes for controller, two votes for alderman, and two votes for Board of Education candidates. To make things more difficult there is almost no way for the voter to tell one candidate from another. There are normally no political parties or caucuses with sets of policies; in fact there is not even any agreement among the candidates to help one another get elected. Why would anyone design such a confusing system and why has it been retained for seventy years?

THE ROOTS OF HAMILTON POLITICS

The structure of government in Hamilton, like other large Ontario municipalities, is a peculiar hybrid. In the early years of the city's history, city government was modelled on the British system. There was a council of aldermen elected from local wards; they would be delegated certain responsibilities and bring their recommendations back to council for final approval. In 1909 the present system was introduced by the Ontario government: a mayor, four members of the Board of Control elected by all voters across the city and a council of aldermen elected in different local wards. In 1912 the system was altered slightly so that there became a mayor, a four-person Board of Control and sixteen aldermen, elected two to a ward. This remains the structure of Hamilton city government.[1]

The origins of this local government structure are not British, but American. During the latter part of the nineteenth century and the early twentieth century, most large American cities were governed by political machines, drawing their power from political patronage. The causes of this are thought to be rooted in the large number of immigrants with little knowledge of the electoral system who flooded into American cities, the absence of social welfare programs or a professional civil service, and the existence of unregulated business corporations willing to pay for favours from municipal politicians.[2]

In response to the corruption of these political machines a number of middle-class reformers, drawn from the Progressive movement, emerged in the last century and for many years had broad influence in both the United States and Canada. Among the "reforms" they advocated was the introduction of non-partisan politics to municipal government (that is, the elimination of political parties); they were also in favour of "at large" elections, in which politicians are elected by all the voters rather than from local constituencies, and many supported the city manager plan. All of these changes were designed to attack what they perceived as the source of municipal corruption: the ward-heeling party boss who bought votes by political patronage.

Another important element of the ideas of these "reformers" was the belief that city government had nothing to do with politics. They believed that the problems of cities could be managed simply according to the business principles of efficiency and economy. They failed to realize that politics is the promotion of a set of policies that favour one section of the population over another. As one writer put it, they felt "that political parties introduce irrelevant issues into local administration and that they were inherently corrupt."[3]

Ironically, despite the fact that not a city in Canada at this time had machine politics, and in fact few had political parties, the ideas of these American urban reformers had a very great influence on this country. In part this was because of our proximity to the United States, American immigration to the Canadian west at the time these ideas were current, and because the Progressive movement was a very powerful influence on our political life until the late 1920s. However, these ideas were particularly influential because the notion of non-partisanship and the belief that "politics" was inappropriate for city government fit very well with our political values.

Canadians generally view their country as a classless society without a political ideology. As Richard Whittaker has pointed out, the watchword of our political life is "pragmatism." Politics are supposedly guided not by ideology "but by a practical application of what will work in a given situation."[4] A set of political beliefs or ideals based on something other than pragmatics, somehow smacks of a class-based society and is rejected as inappropriate. The voters, therefore, do not expect that there will be ideological differences between the parties, and in fact there are few differences between the Liberals and the Conservatives, the two major parties. With a set of political values such as this it is not surprising that Canadians would approve the elimination of political parties at the municipal level, and accept the assertion that it is through parties that corruption arises.

Perhaps the most important consequence of these ideas is that non-partisan politics has remained the pattern of Hamilton political life to this day. Each candidate in the city runs his own campaign, recruits his own organization, prints his own literature, and refuses to adopt any label or political party identity. As an example of the set of beliefs that sustains this system, Donald Clark, the opponent to the Labour politician Sam Lawrence in 1943, built his campaign around the charge that Lawrence would bring party politics to city hall. Clark said he was urged to stand for election by representative citizens and taxpayers who:

Two of Hamilton's postwar mayors: Victor Copps (on the left) and Lloyd D. Jackson (on the right) (Hamilton Public Library).

knew the inevitable consequences of party government in civic administration, an administration which would be clogged by party patronage, an administration whose costs would be increased by partyism, an administration in which the party or individual party candidates, if elected, would not be primarily responsible to the electors, but would have a first responsibility to the party executive, and not to the public who pay the costs. This they strongly opposed and so do I.[5]

The vehemence with which Clark stated these views perhaps grew out of the fear he and others had of a labour takeover of the city. There can be little doubt, however, that the charge of "partyism" struck a responsive chord in Hamilton voters. Although Lawrence was elected, the rest of the labour slate was defeated and a system of party politics has never become institutionalized in Hamilton municipal political life.

The lack of party identification for individual politicians has important consequences for the city's politics. Perhaps the most significant is that there is little political debate among politicians in the city. Virtually all of the candidates tend to agree that there are no issues other than things like personal honesty or administrative ability. They all promise good government, better roads and good street

Victory for Vic Copps in one of his early elections (Hamilton Public Library).

lights. Most will defend the police department, criticize the public transit system and blame either the higher levels of government or the school board for increased taxes. There is a predictability in the way candidates deal with issues.

An equally important consequence of the Progressives' influence on Hamilton political life was the creation of the Board of Control system. Hamilton's twenty-one-member city council is divided into two separate bodies. The Board of Control, made up of the mayor and four controllers, all elected by city-wide vote, is collectively responsible for administration. They are to prepare the budget, and hire, fire and administer all of the departments. In turn, their decisions must be ratified by the entire council.

This political system has led to serious problems of leadership, and a personal competition that often degenerates into the petty and banal. Leadership is expected to be given by the mayor, but he is in a very weak position to get his programs implemented. The four controllers have all been elected by a city-wide vote and because there is no party system they owe no loyalty to the mayor. In fact if a serious campaign is to be mounted against the mayor in a subsequent election it is likely to come from one of the four controllers. Consequently, controllers often gear everything they say and do to the goal of gaining public attention. Usually there is no better way of doing this than showing themselves to be opposed to the mayor. There is an equally important tension between the Board of Control and other members of council. The aldermen are elected by their own wards and the lack of a party system means they are quite independent of any of the other councillors. Many of them want media attention to help their chances in the next election and often get this attention by criticizing the recommendations of the Board of Control.

Hamilton's political system, therefore, is competitive but it is a bickering competitiveness — a game of political one-upmanship — rather than the political competitiveness that would arise from policy debates and disputes. There is little or no co-operation among the members, even among those who consistently are in the opposition. It is simply a free for all, with everyone involved in the struggle for recognition.

Political figures react to this political climate in various ways. Vic Copps, the mayor for many years, tended to ignore the political issues and stress the social aspects of his job. He was skilled in greeting visiting dignitaries, and he attended innumerable dinners, weddings and funerals, but he never provided much more than a casual leadership of council. Jim Campbell, a long time controller, provided little input into policy making and made a career of taking pot shots at others. While he was on Board of Control, Jack MacDonald provided the real leadership of council. He did it by dint of hard work, knowing intimately how government worked and consistently representing the business point of view.

As a consequence of the structure of city government and the lack of a party system, there has been a shift away from issues and policies to a focus on the personalities of the councillors themselves. Some attention is given to neighbourhood issues such as roads, streetlights and so on, but there is little concentration on city-wide programs such

The Hamilton Club (Bill Freeman).

as transportation, development, zoning policies or pollution control. The lack of political debate makes it seem that the city has no policies on these issues, and that the only important concerns are strictly local problems.

As well as encouraging a shift away from an interest in policy, this system leads to a lack of accountability. The British system of municipal government follows the parliamentary structure. The mayor is the leader of the largest party in council, and he governs with its support. Most American cities today follow the presidential model. The mayor is elected by all voters but the office has tremendous power that he alone can wield. In both of these systems there is a concentration of power in the hands of the leader and the acceptance of political responsibility for the leader's policies. As a result the electorate can hold politicians accountable for their actions and if they do not like them can vote them out of office in the next election.

In a system such as Hamilton's, political responsibility is fragmented, so that it is impossible to hold any single individual or group responsible for the policies of the city. Not only are there twenty-one independent members of council, each with a say in policy making, but there are also semi-political bodies such as planning and library boards as well as the Board of Education. In this system the electorate can neither assign blame or praise to anyone on council. Because there is no party system, there is no way to elect the new group that could shift the policies of the city in some new direction. It is a static system, resistant to change and subject to the worst form of the politics of personality.

WHO GETS ELECTED?

It is vital to perceive the effects of this system upon who gets elected and how they get elected, in order to understand Hamilton political life. The confusing electoral system, the absence of parties and the issueless campaigns produce very little interest and anticipation in the city's politics. Voter turnout in Hamilton is usually less than 35% and sometimes as low as 20%. This reflects one of the lowest participation rates in the country.

The poor and working class, particularly, have little interest in municipal politics. Political scientists and sociologists have shown that, as a general

United Steelworkers Centre (Bill Freeman).

rule, the lower the socioeconomic status of the individual or group, the lower their participation in political life, and the lower their rates of voting.[6] There are working-class aldermen in Hamilton but by and large the city's political life is dominated by the middle and upper classes, even in the strongly working-class wards in the central part of the city, the East End and on the Mountain. Middle-class residents are the ones who get out to vote, and it is their candidates who are elected to council.

Campaigns for alderman are normally rather casual affairs. There are a few meetings at which the candidates are present but they are usually badly attended. Most incumbents will have printed no more than their personal card, but new candidates will often spend more money to become better known. Generally the candidates elected are the ones with the deepest roots in the community. There is a strong tendency for people to vote for their friends, and candidates poll strongest in areas where they were raised and where their spouses were raised.

Another important factor in the election of candidates, particularly for mayor and Board of Control, is the support they receive from different organized groups. Vic Copps' backing is an interesting example that sheds light on the way candidates are elected. The story has often been told that in 1958 or 1959 the late Ken Sobel, the millionaire owner of CHML radio station, CHCH-TV, and a number of other businesses, became involved in an argument at city hall. He went back to his radio station, happened to see Vic Copps, one of his sports announcers and salesmen, in the hallway, and in a moment of inspiration said: "Vic, we're going to make you mayor!"

Ken Sobel clearly was the force behind Vic Copps in his early elections. Once he had decided on his candidate, Sobel got others involved in the task of lining up support. They were given organizational help and donations by various business groups, and the strong backing of the Liberal Party. Capitalizing on the fact that Copps was a Catholic, they received support from the Knights of Columbus and over time built links with other ethnic clubs and associations. Using this support in 1960 Copps won a position on Board of Control and in 1962 became mayor.

All candidates must have support from groups such as business associations, political parties and men's clubs if they are to be successful in Hamilton city politics. It is from these groups that politicians get the money and recruit the volunteers to run their campaigns, and this backing helps to give them the social contracts they need to reach large numbers of influential people. Of the associations in the city the Chamber of Commerce is the most important. It informally supports candidates and monitors issues between elections, making sure council always knows the point of view of business. Other important business groups are the Rotary Club, the Downtown Businessmen's Association

Knights of Columbus Hall (Bill Freeman).

and the Hamilton Apartment Association. The Hamilton and District Labour Council has played a similar role for the NDP candidates, but this help has been in the form of relatively small amounts of money rather than a commitment of political supporters.

Political parties are perhaps even more important for city politicians. Although council members all deny that party politics has anything to do with what goes on at council, virtually every one of them is an active supporter of one of the major political parties. This is no accident. The parties provide money to their members for election campaigns and are an important source of political activists who are of real benefit in a campaign. City politicians deny that parties have any influence at council because they want to get votes from all segments of the population, but links as strong and as clear as this indicate that the parties could have great influence on their members in council if they chose.

A variety of men's clubs have played a role in getting people elected. The Knights of Columbus are best known for helping Vic Copps, but they also gave considerable support to Bill Foley, an NDP member, when he ran for Board of Control and have helped other aldermanic candidates. Some claim that the Masons support selected politicians, but little is known about their political activities. At the ward level, groups such as the Kiwanis and Lions' Clubs are the base of support for some candidates.

Community groups made up of local citizens have had little influence in electing candidates in Hamilton. Reg Wheeler's candidacy in the East End is an exception to this rule, but other politicians tend to use community groups by showing up at meetings to answer questions and shake hands. Unlike the political parties, business groups or men's clubs, they rarely provide the basic source of support for candidates, as they have done in some other cities.

Although special-interest groups are important in providing support for people running for council, this does not mean that power is distributed among hundreds of different groups. Quite the contrary. A striking feature of Hamilton political life is that the significant groups controlling the political process are associations of businessmen. The major way that they have been able to control politics is by providing their candidates with the necessary financial and organizational support to get elected. A look at the occupations of council members shows clearly that individuals with links to business dominate city council. Tables I and II give some indication of this by a simple grouping of the occupations of candidates and winners in two elections in the Copps era.

These figures clearly show that council during the Copps era was dominated by people with

TABLE I: THE 1962 ELECTION: OCCUPATIONS OF CANDIDATES AND WINNERS

MAYOR AND BOARD OF CONTROL

Occupations of Candidates	Number Ran	Number Elected
Lawyers	2	1
Other Professionals	1	-
Owners of Businesses	5	1
Managers	-	-
Sales	4	2
Skilled/Unskilled Workers	1	-
Others	2	1
Total	15	5

1962 ALDERMANIC ELECTIONS

Occupations of Candidates	Number Ran	Number Elected
Lawyers	5	4
Other Professionals	-	-
Owners of Businesses	5	4
Managers	6	3
Sales	1	1
Skilled/Unskilled Workers	9	2
Others	4	2
Total	30	16

TABLE II: THE 1972 ELECTION: OCCUPATIONS OF CANDIDATES AND WINNERS

MAYOR AND BOARD OF CONTROL

Occupations of Candidates	Number Ran	Number Elected
Lawyers	-	-
Other Professionals	1	1
Owners of Businesses	4	2
Managers	1	-
Sales	2	2
Skilled/Unskilled Workers	1	-
Others	1	-
Total	10	5

1972 ALDERMANIC ELECTIONS

Occupations of Candidates	Number Ran	Number Elected
Lawyers	-	-
Other Professionals	3	2
Owners of Businesses	6	5
Managers	8	5
Sales	5	-
Skilled/Unskilled Workers	10	4
Others	-	-
Total	32	16

close connections to the business community. The 1962 council had five owners of businesses, three managers and three sales people, for a total of eleven councillors out of twenty-one who were directly linked to business. Added to this, several of the five lawyers on the 1962 council had close ties with business, particularly real estate, interests. Ten years later, in 1972, council had no lawyers but it did have seven owners of businesses, five managers, and two salesmen, for a total of fourteen out of twenty-one members closely linked to business. This is representative of council not only in the Copps years but for the entire history of Hamilton municipal government.

These figures do not express the additional fact that the people who run for Mayor or Board of Control tend to be wealthier and better established than the other council members. It is very expensive to run a city-wide campaign and few people have the necessary personal wealth or political backing to afford the costs. As a result, the city's most senior elected political body — the Board of Control — tends to be dominated even more clearly by those who support business.

Another intriguing factor in Hamilton politics concerns the people who do not run for council. None of the executives of the big firms in the city were candidates during the Copps years. Virtually all of the managers were drawn from the foreman and supervisor levels. Of the professionals it was almost entirely the lawyers and a handful of high school teachers who stood for election. There was a pharmacist on council but in his actions he seemed more of a small businessman than a professional. In all of the Copps elections there was never a candidate from the medical profession, the civil service, and few drawn from the university community. Skilled and unskilled workers ran for council, some year after year, but although the city is populated by large numbers of blue-collar workers few have ever been successful. There can be little doubt that the business community has been the dominant force in municipal politics in Hamilton.

One final factor is the power of the incumbents to get re-elected. It is striking that, in the seven elections during the Copps era, from 1962 to 1973, only two incumbent Board of Control members were ever defeated, and even more striking, only two incumbent aldermen were defeated. Once a person has a seat on council it is virtually impossible to remove him. If it were not for retirements and the fact that some aldermen choose to run for Board of Control, creating vacancies, council would be almost unchanging from election to election.

THE FAILURE OF OPPOSITION

The major reason for the static nature of Hamilton's city council is that opposition to the business community and their representatives at city hall has been badly organized over the years and at most times almost non-existent. The reason for this stems in part from the tradition of non-partisan politics, the cumbersome structure of the Board of Control system, and the consequent lack of interest in municipal politics. It also stems, however, from inadequacies in the opposition groups themselves.

The group that has provided the most consistent opposition over the years has been labour. Just after World War I the labour group was so successful that it came close to holding the majority of seats on council, and between 1943 and 1949 its candidate Sam Lawrence was mayor. In various elections, labour, along with political allies, the Independent Labour Party, the CCF and the NDP, have run elections using the party label. Despite this constant effort labour's success has been very limited and today, although candidates use the label of "labour," their programs and their actions once on council show that they are virtually indistinguishable from any other members of council. (This issue is further explored in the next chapter.)

Another source of opposition that emerged in the 1960s and early 1970s was community groups organized to try to stop certain developments. The group called Save Our Square (SOS) that fought the First Wentworth plan for Civic Square in 1968 did not save the square, but it had an effect on the city's political life. Another group that emerged to stop a Lax family development in the west end of the harbour had more success, but by far the most successful was the Durand group. This organization of residents of the old middle-class and wealthy neighbourhood south and west of city hall was able to get zoning changes to stop high-rise development and obtain a small park in their community.

Opposition to development that disturbs existing communities is still an important, if latent, issue in Hamilton. Today there are more people both on and off council who would oppose projects of this kind than ever before, but they have never come together in a municipal political movement. Their opposition to the business community has been limited to particular projects, and these groups have never advocated new policies that would lead the city in new directions. In fact many of the people involved in these protests still strongly believe in the business ideology, that the role of government should be to support and subsidize development.

For instance, considerable opposition was generated around the First Wentworth plan for Civic Square in the late 1960s, but the way it was

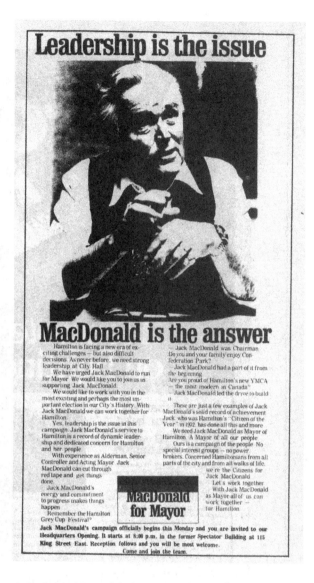

A Jack MacDonald election brochure. MacDonald, known for years as the leader of the business interests on council, was able to gain the support of business and the Conservative Party in running a very slick advertising campaign in his 1976 victory over Vince Agro.

expressed was significant. During the controversy no one ever criticized the fact that government was providing a massive subsidy scheme so that private business could reap big profits. Those who led the fight against First Wentworth always made it clear that they were not critical of urban renewal as such but only of the plans put forward by this company. (See the chapter "Downtown Redevelopment: The Civic Square Project" in Part III of this book.)

Though a few opposition groups have existed, none has ever been in a position to challenge seriously the business interests who run the city. In most instances groups have emerged to protest certain issues and after these were dealt with they

Vince Agro's brochure in the 1976 campaign stresses that he is fighting for the little people at city hall. From the results of the election it is evident that they did not believe him.

simply faded away. Only labour has had a sufficient power base to provide opposition for any length of time. Yet, over the years they have been ineffective, badly organized and often without an alternative set of policies.

HOW BUSINESS RULES

The influence of business over the years has been so pervasive in Hamilton and its ideology, which dictates that the major role of government is to subsidize the interests of private concerns, is so accepted that business groups in the city do not need to be well organized or co-ordinated. Often to dominate city government individuals who represent business compete with each other for political office and frequently disputes among them break out into the open. There are two competing major political parties that support business candidates in Hamilton elections, and a host of different business groups promoting their own particular issues. Business groups can allow themselves the luxury of dissent in their ranks because they control the process so thoroughly that at no time are they threatened.[7]

Debate is so rarely focussed on policy that the impression given to the public is that there is no alternative to the present way of doing things, and in fact few people are aware that there are policies of any kind guiding city government. The assumption by most is that the only principle of importance is one of "efficiency" or "good government."

The confusion of the political system, in other words, plays an important role in Hamilton political life. It is a perfect solution for the business group that runs the city. The politicians can implement policies at city hall designed for special interests and at the same time continue to claim that they are the "government of all the people." In view of the fact that business is such a small group in an overwhelmingly working-class city, this is a remarkable achievement.

1. Marjorie Freeman Campbell, *A Mountain and a City* (Toronto: McClelland and Stewart, 1966) p. 223.

2. Jack K. Masson and James D. Anderson, *Emerging Party Politics in Urban Canada* (Toronto: McClelland and Stewart, 1972) p. 3.

3. J.D. Anderson, "Nonpartisan Urban Politics in Canadian Cities," in Jack K. Masson and James D. Anderson (ed.) *Emerging Party Politics in Urban Canada* (Toronto: McClelland and Stewart, 1972) p. 13.

4. Richard Whittaker, "Introduction" in William Irvine, *The Farmers in Politics* (Toronto: McClelland and Stewart, 1976) p. v.

5. Quoted in: John M. McMenemy, "Lion in a Den of Daniels: A Study of Sam Lawrence, Labour in Politics," (MA Thesis: McMaster University, 1965) p. 83.

6. Seymour Martin Lipset, *Political Man: The Social Basis of Politics,* (Garden City, New York: Doubleday, 1960) p. 92-97.

7. There is evidence suggesting that when business control is seriously threatened, business can co-ordinate its activities very quickly. This was the case in Hamilton in the early 1920s, when the Independent Labour Party was strong, and the political systems in Vancouver and Montreal show considerable discipline on the part of business. In Hamilton, where the opposition has been traditionally weak, the business group can afford competition among its members.

Hamilton Labour: The failure of an opposition group

Bill Freeman

On Friday, November 5, 1976 John Ball and Ben DesRoches, two leaders of the Hamilton and District Labour Council, got into a furious argument following a meeting at the Textile Workers' Hall. The argument turned into a shouting match, then the men began shoving each other and a moment later they were rolling on the floor, punching and kicking, until finally other members of the council were able to pull the two combatants apart. The fight between DesRoches and Ball concluded an evening of particularly bitter debate, concerning labour's involvement in municipal politics, that had wracked the council, but its cause was much more complex than the events of that night.

One of the most persistent images of Hamilton is that of a "lunch bucket" town. The working class supposedly dominates the city and imposes its style of life on all activities. Politically, however, this is not the case. Despite the high proportion of workers engaged in manufacturing and the approximate 40% of the work force that is unionized, business and not labour has dominated the political life of the city from its founding to the present day, and there are no indications that labour, or any political party allied with labour, will ever be able to mount a challenge to business control. But the real failure of Hamilton labour is not in its lack of electoral success. It is that, except for brief periods, the leaders of the movement have been unable to develop an effective alternative to the "ideology of business." Like other politicians labour leaders and labour politicians have become defenders and promoters of business interests at the expense of the majority of the population who are working class.

Part of the cause of the November 1976 fist fight was the fact that Ball and DesRoches have different political views on how the business group of Hamilton should be challenged by the trade union movement. The two men represent conflicting political factions within the labour movement whose history stretches back to the earliest decade of this century. These divisions have pitted unionist against unionist and have been a major factor in keeping labour from mounting an effective and unified opposition to the business interests that control the city. Therefore, even though neither DesRoches or Ball would have recognized it at the time, their fight had historic overtones which symbolized the years of frustration and lost political battles. By charting the course of the political wing of Hamilton labour from the early decades of this century to the present day one can clearly see the failure of the movement, and the reasons for the impotence of its leaders.

THE INDEPENDENT LABOUR PARTY

Unionism began in Hamilton as early as 1827, but it was not until the 1870s that the movement became a political force in the city. In 1872 several thousand of the city's workers staged a massive demonstration in support of the 9-hour-a-day movement and there was a round of strikes across the city and the province in support of the demands.[1] By 1881 the Knights of Labour, an idealistic and politically motivated group originating in the United States, had begun their Canadian organizational drive by establishing groups in Hamilton. Within a short time the Knights had twenty-five assemblies in the city.[2] Soon they were nominating their members to run for political office, but none met with success. By 1901 the Knights of Labour were in decline; the American Federation of Labor expelled them and adopted the conservative policy of Sam Gompers: the non-involvement of labour in direct political action.

But Canada was not to follow the American model. In Hamilton, as in much of the rest of the country, the influence of British immigrant workers was strong and they brought with them the direct political action approach of the British Labour Party.[3] In 1906 Allan Studholme, an iron moulder by trade and long-time unionist, ran and was elected as a labour representative to the provincial seat of Hamilton East. He held this seat until his death in 1919. An even more important event came in 1907 when the Independent Labour Party was founded to "consolidate the labour vote in Ontario."[4] The ILP drew its strength from urban centres across the province, but the Hamilton delegation was one of its most important elements. The first president and most active leader was Walter Rollo, a broom maker and unionist from the city. However, the time was not auspicious for the young labour party, and by the outbreak of World War I in 1914, the Hamilton branch was the only functioning group in Ontario.

Hamilton was known as a conservative labour city in the pre-World War I era. Labour News, a local pro-labour paper, commented in 1912 that although the city was "one of the best organized [it] is one of the most conservative labour cities in America. Strikes are rarely resorted to [and] labour leaders are cautious. Hamilton has the reputation of a 'no-strike' city."[5] The main reason for this was that, compared to other parts of the country at the time, Hamilton workers were well paid with good job security. Despite this conservatism about economic demands, the city's working class was highly organized, with the most politicized workers in Canada.[6]

By 1916, in the midst of wartime conditions, there were new political demands by Ontario labour, and in April of that year the Independent Labour Party met in London to reconstitute itself. The Hamilton group again played a leadership role and Walter Rollo was re-elected to his position of Ontario president. By mid-June of 1917 there were thirteen local branches of the ILP and seven more in the process of formation.[7] In the federal election of that year the party ran several candidates in Ontario and Walter Rollo, standing for election in Hamilton East, was named their national leader.

Nine Hour Movement demonstration in Hamilton 1872 (Hamilton Public Library).

Although the ILP did not elect any of its candidates it received a substantial vote, which encouraged the party to consider other political activities.[8]

In the election of 1917 there were indications of a serious split in the Independent Labour Party which was a preview of things to come. Fred Flatman, the ILP candidate for Wentworth, was considered a radical by others in the party. There were serious objections to his candidacy and Walter Rollo had to use his prestige to hold the party together. Flatman continued as the candidate but not without causing divisions within the party.[9]

By 1919 social conditions had changed so much that the Independent Labour Party found itself in a position of political ascendency. The inflation that followed World War I rapidly undermined the living standards of the working class and led to labour agitation on a scale never seen before or since in Canada. The Winnipeg General Strike in the spring of that year ended with government intervention, but not before a militant display of labour's power. In the United States the great steel strike paralyzed industry for months and the trade

This picture of a smashed streetcar is the only photographic record of the November 1906 strike of Hamilton Street Railway Employees. During this strike there were several serious disturbances. On one occasion mounted cavalry with sabers drawn charged a crowd that had gathered in support of the strikers. Several people were injured and the crowd in turn vented its anger on this street car. (McMaster University, Labour Studies Collection).

union movement across North America grew enormously in size and power. Even the Hamilton steel industry, which had a paternalistic anti-union personnel policy, saw 1300 workers organized into three lodges of the Amalgamated Association of Iron, Steel and Tin Workers.[10]

This social climate had a strong impact on Hamilton's political life. The militant or radical wing of labour grew in size and importance. The one identifiable leader of this group was Fred Flatman, the 1917 ILP candidate for Wentworth. Flatman had previously worked at the Dominion Steel Foundry and was a representative of the Amalgamated Society of Engineers, an English union operating in Canada. He led a strike at the steel mills in 1916,[11] and by 1919 he had founded the radical labour newspaper, *The New Democracy*. In issue after issue in 1919 and 1920, Flatman praised the work of the One Big Union, the radical syndicalist union group that played an important role in the disturbances around Winnipeg, and his paper featured favourable articles about the Bolshevik Party and its victories in Russia. "Capitalism is breaking down by its natural inefficiency,"[12] *The New Democracy* declared, and Flatman and people like him, no doubt, anxiously awaited the consequences.

Radicalism was by no means limited to a small group. *The Spectator* often warned that militants were fomenting trouble in the "foreign element" of the city. A story on January 8, 1920 claimed that one person had told the newspaper:

that meetings are held regularly in the north-east part of the city by foreigners who speak in foreign tongues and that one set, which meet in a hall owned by a church organization, was so revolutionary in character that the permission to use the hall was withheld some weeks ago, although some of the men were contributes to church funds. The police seem to ignore the "red" danger.[13]

On the one hand social conditions contributed to radical activity in Hamilton, but they also contributed to a broader labour political movement. The Independent Labour Party, representative of all political shades in unions, grew rapidly in strength and support. By 1919 the three ILP branches in the city were large and effective organizations, and in the provincial election of that year they ran candidates for the three local ridings. George Halcrow, a young ILP city controller, was to contest the working-class riding of Hamilton East; Walter Rollo, the president of the party, was the candidate in Hamilton West; and Will Crockett, a labour-farm candidate, was to run in the riding of Wentworth.

The outcome of the election was a surprise to the whole province: the Conservative government was overwhelmingly defeated. Eleven of the thirty-two ILP candidates were elected, and in Hamilton all three labour candidates were sent to Queen's Park with comfortable majorities. Even more surprising, the United Farmers of Ontario (UFO) gained forty-five seats in the election to become the largest party in the house. In the face of almost total opposition by the press and business groups, the victories of the farmer-labour candidates were remarkable.

A few weeks after the provincial election the ILP began preparing for the municipal election to be held on New Year's Day. On December 11, 1919 over 400 members met at the Moulder's Hall at King and Walnut Streets to nominate their slate of candidates. As *The New Democracy* reported it, all those present agreed that workers should control city hall and were dedicated to bringing it about. Controller H. J. Halford, a city barber, prominent union man, and founding member of the ILP, was nominated to contest the position of mayor. At first Halford refused the position but when members of the assembly persisted he asked the convention if it was unanimous:

Like a mighty roll of thunder came the answering chorus "yes" from all sides of the hall. "Well then boys, go to it," was his parting shot. It was the signal for an outburst of applause that shook the building. Men flocked around the controller.[14]

Two other candidates were named by the ILP to contest Board of Control and altogether thirteen aldermanic candidates were nominated. The slate was made up of a plumber, two painters, a secretary, a carpenter, a blacksmith and a moulder, a truly working-class group. Including candidates for the Board of Education and Hydro Board there were twenty-two ILP candidates in that election, by far the biggest undertaking of the local labour party up until that time.[15]

On election day labour made striking gains. Although Halford, the mayoralty candidate, was defeated, the ILP elected two members to Board of Control and six aldermen. The Liberal faction on council also elected eight members and the Conservative and soldier candidates made up the balance. The business group in the city was worried about the power of labour, and there were discussions of a merger between the Liberals and Conservatives.

The tide of labour support in Hamilton was very strong in the early 1920s. Each of the three branches of the ILP in the city met every two weeks to discuss political issues and plan social occasions. Their membership was large and actively involved in a number of projects. Not only did the labour party promote candidates but it also sponsored a baseball team and every summer organized a mammoth labour picnic at Wabasso Park or the Dundas Driving Park, attracting thousands of people. At those events there would be rides and races for the children, bake sales and

Walter Rollo (Ontario Archives).

political speeches. One ILP carnival even featured the unusual attraction of a 648-pound fat lady.

By 1920 the ILP in Hamilton had produced a number of important political leaders. Walter Rollo, the provincial member for Hamilton West and president of the party, was the best known and most respected. George Halcrow, the Labour member for Hamilton East, was unpredictable and at times critical of the party. He was, however, an effective speaker in the days when politicians reached the public mainly by speaking from soap boxes in the market square or on neighbourhood street corners, and had to contend with organized hecklers. Ex-controller Halford, who ran for mayor in 1920, was a well-known union leader who went to international labour conventions in both the United States and Europe. One of the most interesting of the ILP leaders was Mary MacNab, a granddaughter of Sir Allan MacNab, the railway baron and Hamilton Tory politician. She was a graduate of the University of Toronto and, despite the disapproval of her family, a lifelong socialist and labour supporter.[16] In those days when women politicians were still rare Mary MacNab was a long-standing member of the Ontario ILP executive, and frequently the feature speaker at Labour political meetings.

The Independent Labour Party was hardly a radical group, but it consistently supported what it felt were the political demands of labour at the time. The party members believed in working through the established electoral system and saw themselves as allied to other "producer" groups or parties in a struggle to win political power. Mary MacNab, for example, wrote in *The New Democracy* that farmers and labour — the two "producing classes" — should come together to "build a party of producers in opposition to those who do not work."[17] The ILP was a class-based party which saw itself as opposed to the business interests that had controlled the city, province and country for so many years.

The policies of the party, although not clearly worked out, reflected the members' concerns with job protection, working conditions and wages. The ILP advocated legislation for the eight-hour day and six-day week, government inspection of industry, a minimum wage, the abolition of the contract system for government projects, voluntary arbitration of labour disputes, the prohibition of prison labour in competition with free labour and the exclusion of all oriental immigration.[18] The ILP also advocated a number of other programs such as free compulsory education, tax reform, abolition of the Senate, no property qualification for the franchise, direct legislation through referendum and the public ownership of utilities.[19]

One thing that is particularly striking about the ILP is the exclusiveness of its class membership and political appeal. With the exception of Mary MacNab, the party's leaders had all been manual workers. They had risen to prominence first in their respective unions and then in the ILP. Their political activity was an extension of their trade union beliefs. These workers were attempting to gain their economic objectives, which could not be achieved through collective bargaining, by using the political process. Thus the party was a true opposition to the business interests, because it was dedicated not only to gaining power but also to redirecting the policies of the city so that the working class could reap the benefits of legislation. It is not surprising, therefore, that there were rumours that the Liberals and Conservatives on Hamilton city council would come together in a coalition. If the ILP were able to gain control of council its policies would seriously challenge the domination of business and could lead to a radical change to programs that favoured the working class.

The activities of the provincial wing of the ILP were significant for the development of the party in the city. Shortly after the 1919 election, when the Independent Labour Party had elected eleven members to the Ontario legislature, the party met to decide on a course of action. At first Walter Rollo argued that the circumstances were not ripe for a coalition of the party with the United Farmers of Ontario. He felt that they should simply hold the balance of power and stand alone.[20] Malcolm McBride, still the mayor of Brantford and elected to the Ontario house for the ILP, suggested that labour should enter into a coalition with the Liberals. However, the majority of the caucus decided that they wanted to take political power, and when E. C. Drury, the UFO premier, approached the labour contingent they agreed to enter into a coalition. In return for their support Drury made Walter Rollo, president of the ILP and the member for Hamilton West, the Minister of Labour in the new government.

From the beginning there were serious differences between labour and the farmers that led to continual problems. One of the most important was over the issue of tariffs. The farmers, wanting cheap farm machinery and markets for their produce, advocated the elimination of tariffs. Labour, and this was especially true of the Hamilton members, took a protectionist position because they saw any reduction of the tariff as an ultimate reduction of jobs in manufacturing.

Prohibition was an even more contentious issue. Generally in Ontario, as elsewhere in North America, the rural population and the urban middle class supported prohibition while the working class was strongly opposed to it. Because of the commitment of E. G. Drury and his Attorney-General W. E. Raney to the temperance movement, the farmer-labour government made a sustained effort to stamp out any violations of the law. The caucus members of the Independent Labour Party were split on this issue but some were very outspoken in their opposition. At almost every opportunity George Halcrow, from Hamilton East, condemned the Ontario Temperance Act, calling it the worst piece of legislation ever put on the statute books. "It has made barrooms of the homes,"[21] he once said.

The coalition government faced other serious problems. Labour members constantly criticized Drury for doing nothing about industrial issues, and when it was clear that the premier would bow to the pressure of farmers and not legislate the eight-hour day, he was denounced publicly.[22] For his part Drury spoke out several times against "class" legislation. Government, he said, must not be "prostituted by class legislation but . . . the welfare of all classes must be kept in mind."[23] This approach was an attempt by the United Farmers to broaden their political appeal, but it was also a direct attack on labour, which was almost exclusively an urban working-class party advocating legislation to improve conditions of this group.

As early as January 1920, only three months after their election, members of the labour group began to voice serious objections to the coalition. Mayor Malcolm McBride of Brantford was dissatisfied that he had not been given a cabinet post. He spoke out several times against the coalition, threatened to resign from the party, and finally crossed the floor of the house to sit as an Independent. In April 1921 he was expelled from the ILP. George Halcrow often voiced his dissatisfaction with the policies of the government, and it took the considerable influence of Walter Rollo, Mary MacNab and other ILP leaders to keep him in the party. In an obvious attempt to placate him Halcrow was made the house leader of the labour caucus in December 1920,[24] but if the ILP leaders hoped this would silence his criticism they must have been disappointed. The internal wranglings within the party were seriously damaging the image of the ILP and had repercussions on Hamilton city politics. In the 1921 municipal elections labour again put up a strong slate, led by George Halcrow who ran for mayor. On election day the ILP returned two members to Board of Control and five to council.[25] This was a drop of only one member from the previous election but Halcrow's substantial defeat gave some indication of the future.

The internal wranglings of the party that became apparent to the public were limited to the parliamentary wing of the ILP, but there was another far more serious split in the ranks of labour that was to have much broader implications. In the early years of the party the ILP was made up of a wide coalition of people who supported the general objectives of labour. Some were radicals like Fred Flatman who advocated the style of industrial union organizing shown in the One Big Union, and supported the new Bolshevik government in Russia; most were social democrats who followed the model of the British Labour Party, but others were Gompers-styled unionists who believed labour should stay out of active politics. In the early days of the ILP these groups were all part of the party, but the economic and political conditions of the post-World War I period were to create splits that could not be healed.

The years 1920 to 1923 were a time of economic depression in Canada, and Hamilton was hard hit because it was an industrial centre. By July 1920 there was a serious housing crisis in the city. Many people, mostly families of returned soldiers, were living in tents on the outskirts of the city in primitive conditions. By December of that year thousands of unemployed workers in the city were living close to starvation. Even the conservative *Spectator* featured stories about how men were sleeping in doorways on cold autumn nights, with no means of support, and dependent on charity just to be fed. A group called the Discharged Soldiers and Sailors Federation, meeting with city officials in December, described how every night between fifteen and twenty men competed for lodgings in the prison cells of the Hamilton police station.[26]

Through the fall of 1920 there were meetings of the unemployed to focus attention on their plight and demand government help. In those days before unemployment insurance and welfare, the chief responsibility for looking after the poor fell to the municipal government. Hamilton, with its strong labour caucus in council, did provide some assistance. The ILP held meetings with the members of the Chamber of Commerce,[27] a sewer project in the East End of the city was begun and a hostel for single men was opened at Scott barracks. These modest measures did little to ameliorate the suffering of the poor.

By January 1921 conditions in the city sparked a series of protests, to which the municipal government responded with repressive measures. On January 7 there was a meeting of the unemployed in the market square. Several hundred people showed up and the crowd became unruly. *The Spectator* reported there was a "determined effort made by several agitators to stir up trouble." To a cheering crowd Edgar Haslem shouted: "Have you left your courage in France? Let's go out and get what we want!" "Where's the ammunition?" someone replied and there were more shouts of encouragement.[28] The crowd set off on a march to city hall, adding people along the way until it had swelled to three times its original size. Someone pounded on the door demanding to see the mayor. "He's not here," they were told by the caretaker. So they marched over a mile to his house on Queen Street. When Mayor Coppley placated the demonstrators with promises of help, the unemployed marched back downtown and dispersed.[29]

This and other agitations coming soon after the serious working class disturbances of 1919, alarmed some groups in the city. Mayor Coppley and the police moved quickly to prevent any further trouble. On February 5, four leaders of the unemployed were arrested for sedition. The formal charge read in part:

That you did within three months last, in Hamilton, act as an officer of an unlawful organization and society whose professed purpose is to bring about governmental, industrial and economic change within the Dominion of Canada by use of force, violence and physical injury to persons and property and which' teaches, advocates, advises and defends the use of violence, terrorism and physical injury....[30]

The four men were arrested at a meeting of the unemployed. Bail was set at $2000, an impossibly high figure for any working man to raise at the time.

For two months the men waited in jail for their trial. The evidence piling up against them seemed considerable. The police had the minute book of their organization, which was filled with various "radical" statements, and Bolshevik pamphlets were found in the home of Edgar Haslem, one of the accused. During the trial evidence was given that the four men had urged radical action at the January 7 rally in the market. Mayor Coppley was called to testify how the four accused had made angry, threatening remarks during meetings with him and called him a "profiteer." Despite all of this evidence the jury refused to accept the argument

Mayor George C. Coppley (Hamilton Public Library).

that the unemployed organization was an illegal society and the men were found not guilty. On hearing the verdict the people in the courtroom broke into loud applause.[31]

Those who held political power, such as Mayor Coppley, reacted to these disturbances of the unemployed by using constituted legal authority to suppress them. Even the unions and the Independent Labour Party, however, gave the leaders of the unemployed little support. After the January demonstration the ILP was quick to point out that they were in no way connected with the disturbances.[32] When the four men were arrested the Hamilton Trades and Labour Council took up a collection for their families but made it clear that the council was giving no support to their defence because they had openly denounced the labour movement.[33]

By this stage, the leaders of the ILP and the unions in the city were concerned about radicalism in labour's ranks and determined to stamp it out. As a good example of the changes that had come between 1919 and 1921, the city's labour newspaper, *The New Democracy*, had been sold by 1920 and its radical editor Fred Flatman replaced. The new editor featured articles that kept up a sustained attack on radicalism of any kind whether it was the One Big Union, Bolshevism, or even J. S. Woodsworth, the leader of the labour group in the House of Commons. Often they ran stories claiming that labour and management were partners rather than competitors. One editorial proclaimed: "While we have hands to work and brains to reason, we, the workers in Canada, shall gain our ends and reach our destiny through paths of peace," and on another occasion they approvingly quoted Gompers as saying: "Bolshevism is against human evolution."[34]

By late 1920 and early 1921 at least two different wings of labour had emerged. The majority had retreated to a very conservative position. As the decade wore on the successful attacks on them by business and the shrinking membership of unions made this group even more conservative. However there was still a small group of radical socialists, operating within the trade union movement and in the labour political groups, which was constantly agitating for more militant action. Obviously an organization like the ILP could not contain such divergent political factions and so it was not surprising that in late May and early June of 1921 a small group met in a barn outside Guelph to create the Communist Party of Canada.[35] This split was to have serious repercussions in labour political movements that have continued to this day.

By late 1921 the Independent Labour Party was in a serious state of disarray. The party nominated a slate of candidates for the municipal elections, fully expecting to repeat its past performances, but on election day, January 1, they were overwhelmingly defeated. In the previous election they had won seven of the twenty-one seats, but in this election their numbers were reduced to three. One of those three, however, was Sam Lawrence, who became alderman for the working class Ward 8 in the East End of the city. In time Lawrence would play a very important role in Hamilton labour and political circles.

The 1921 split in the labour movement widened as time went on. The 1922 May Day march, led by the radical left wing, ended in what *The Spectator* called a "general riot." At 2:30 p.m., at the corner of King and James Streets the "International Wing of the Unemployed" confronted the police. This is how the paper described the event:

The police drew batons and charged the mob. Many heads were cracked and a number of arrests were made. Several women sympathizers, who carried the red flag at the head of the procession, were taken into custody. (The marchers) had ignored Chief Whatley's order that the red flag was not to be carried (When they approached King and James) the traffic officer grabbed the red flag and was immediately attacked by the reds. The reserve squad (of police) was then called into action with drawn batons and it took but a few minutes to disperse the crowd. After the leaders and women were taken into custody the (group) reassembled on the market square where torrid speeches were made.[36]

In the 1920s demonstrations like this one led by the Communists probably had little support from the majority of the working class and certainly did not have the support of the union leaders or the Independent Labour Party. However, by 1922–23 the ILP was facing much more serious problems than this break with the Communists. In the 1923 municipal election two of the ILP leaders were denied endorsement in party nomination meetings,[37] and on election day only two of the labour slate were elected.

Provincially the party had become a "shadow organization."[38] Only twenty-eight delegates attended the 1922 provincial convention in Hamilton and in 1923 only sixteen of the party faithful came to the Brantford convention.[39] In the spring of that year an effort was made to line up labour candidates for the expected provincial election, but even some of the sitting labour MLAs refused to run for the party. George Halcrow from Hamilton East was one of these. Rather than blaming the weakness of the party for his disillusionment, however, he returned to his old theme of dissatisfaction with the coalition government:

If I must swear constant fealty to Drury [the premier] during the next four years then I cannot accept the nomination . . . The time has now come when I must say that my ideals of what a Labour Party should be and those of the party are vastly different.[40]

Halcrow's refusal to run for the party was symptomatic of internal problems that had left the ILP little more than a number of bickering, disunited factions. In the provincial election the farmer-labour government was swept from power and replaced by the Conservatives, led by G. Howard Ferguson. All three Hamilton labour candidates were resoundingly defeated and the Independent Labour Party for all practical purposes ceased to exist.

The outstanding success and equally spectacular collapse of the ILP is not only a reflection of the party's initial vigour and subsequent failure to deal with internal problems but also a reflection of the social conditions of the time. The economic hardships faced by large numbers of working people in Hamilton during and after World War I led individuals to seek radical solutions. The ILP, whose leadership and active membership was drawn almost exclusively from the ranks of organized labour, appeared to be a viable alternative to the city's business-dominated political life. Because of this a large number of people, a much broader group than those in the trade union movement, voted for and supported the party.

The failure of the ILP is in part attributable to poor leadership and continual internal bickering. A more plausible explanation of the collapse, however, takes into account the wider social conditions that weakened party support. The most important factor was the lessening of economic hardship as inflation was reduced, unemployment levels dropped and the housing crisis gradually eased. Throughout the 1920s, furthermore, capitalists mounted a major attack on unions by advocating the open shop. From 1919 to 1929 the number of unionized workers in the country was drastically reduced so that the party lost the base of its strength. However, it was also obvious to the public by 1922 that the ILP was not going to provide them with policies or government that would challenge or change social and economic conditions. By 1922 the party, finding itself with no wide base of support, died a natural death.

In 1919 and 1920 it had appeared that the ILP presented a real challenge to the business interests who ran the city. The party had a program which was limited, in that it dealt mainly with trade union issues, but it was in favour of using the power of government to help workers and the unemployed. When the ILP elected as many as eight members to the twenty-one-seat council, Hamilton business groups became frightened of labour. They saw that it was possible for them to lose control and that ultimately, the extensive government subsidization of their interests could be called into question. However, as early as 1921 it was becoming obvious that this threat from labour was more imaginary than real. The farm-labour government had done little to curb business and it was unlikely that a few elected councillors in Hamilton could do any more. By 1922 the voters had rejected the ILP, and the crisis for business had passed.

SAM LAWRENCE AND THE CCF

In the 1922 municipal election, when the size of the Independent Labour Party caucus suddenly shrank from seven to three numbers, one new labour candidate rode against the tide and was elected alderman for Ward 8. This new labour city council member was Sam Lawrence. He was to become one of the most durable politicians on the Hamilton political scene and more than this, a central figure in labour struggles in the city for the next thirty years, and a major figure in the trade union movement and the CCF.

Lawrence was born in 1879 in Somerset, England, the fourth child in a family of five boys and five girls. He left school at the age of ten to work twelve hours a day at his father's trade of stone masonry. By the age of ten he had started his apprenticeship, at seventeen had joined a union called the "Operative Stone Masons" and by eighteen was a union steward. After army service during the Boer War Lawrence returned to London, England and again took up his stone mason's trade

Sam Lawrence demonstrating for a labour cause in the 1930s (McMaster University, Labour Studies Collection).

and union activity. For two terms he was on the executive board of the stone mason's union and in 1906 stood for election in Battersea Borough Council. In 1912 he followed three of his brothers and one sister across the Atlantic to Hamilton.[41]

As a long-time trade unionist Lawrence was a follower of the British Labour Party approach to politics: direct participation of workers in the electoral process. When he arrived in the city the Independent Labour Party was five years old and had elected unionist Allan Studholme to the provincial parliament for Hamilton East. It was natural for Lawrence to become a vocal party member and participate in the ILPs surge to power in 1919. In 1921 he ran for alderman for the first time, and in 1922 was able to land a seat on council.

Lawrence's victory in Ward 8, despite an electoral swing away from labour, was partly the result of his running in what was then, and still is, the most solidly working-class area of the city, but it was also a reflection of his political style. Lawrence, always known as "Sam," was a friendly, approachable man with whom ordinary people could identify. Lawrence was not particularly sophisticated or well read but was a practical man whose political commitment was expressed in his daily activity.[42] John McMenemy, who wrote a thesis on Lawrence's career, recorded this tribute to the labour politician:

A communist organizer who participated in many public events, particularly during the depression, pays him the highest compliment by describing him as a "modest unaffected man whose mind was instinctively clear of nationalism, racism and possessed of class internationalism." Lawrence's class position was strong; he was a socialist almost by instinct.[43]

After the collapse of the Independent Labour Party in 1923 the political wing of the trade union movement was hopelessly divided. On the left was the Communist Party of Canada. Despite the fact that the party was outlawed through much of the 1920s its members were involved in unions, and, in Hamilton, were particularly successful in organizing the unemployed. Although always small in numbers the Communists had wide influence because of their unstinting work and their disciplined, co-ordinated activities.

The bulk of the unionists and trade union leaders in the middle and late 1920s had returned to the support of the Liberal and Conservative parties. Craft unions were still the dominant form of labour organization. The American Federation of Labor leaders rejected direct labour political participation and advocated a policy of supporting labour's friends on an individual basis. John Flett, the Canadian leader of the AFL and a close associate of Samuel Gompers, lived in Hamilton most of his life and had at best been only a lukewarm supporter of the ILP even in its heyday of 1919. By 1923 the policy of labour's non-involvement in politics re-emerged.

By 1927 the only functioning remnant of the ILP in Ontario was the Hamilton East branch led by Sam Lawrence.[44] Many of the people across the province who were still committed to the moderate socialist approach of the ILP had become involved in the Canadian Labour Party. This group had been created in 1918 by the Trades and Labour Congress and in the mid-1920s included 10,000 members who were affiliated through their unions. During the 1920s the party admitted the Worker's (Communist) Party and the remnants of the ILP cooperated but were not affiliated.[45] By 1927 the Canadian Labour Party was hopelessly divided and finally split along Communist/noncommunist lines.

Through this period Sam Lawrence continued to be re-elected as alderman in his East Hamilton ward, but the labour representation on council shrank. By 1924 there were only two labour members and in October of that year a group calling itself the "Labour Representative Political Association" ran a slate of five trade unionists. They included Fred Flatman, who had remained an Independent Labour Party supporter, Humphrey Mitchell, who had been an ILP member and was to play an important role in Hamilton labour politics, and Sam Lawrence.[46] The entire labour slate with the exception of Lawrence was defeated. However, despite the poor record of labour in the middle and latter part of the 1920s Lawrence's personal popularity and following increased. In 1928 he ran and was elected to the Board of Control.

In those years Lawrence's politics included three important elements. The most fundamental of these was his resolute defense of the working man and the unions that struggled to represent him. A Hamilton newspaper editorial once commented: "As a devout socialist . . . Lawrence brought his conscious participation in the class struggle into a field of public office where it did not belong."[47] An exchange at a council meeting on October 1929 gives an indication of the kind of stance the labour politician took. Mayor Burton, a representative of the business community, came out in favour of forcibly suppressing meetings the Communists were holding in the market square. "We should stamp out this Communist menace as we would a diphtheria epidemic," he said. "It is affecting the prosperity of Hamilton. It is more prosperous today than it has been for years." In the debate Lawrence replied by saying that the Communists deserved the rights of free speech just like anyone else. He pointed out that even the AFL, which had often been attacked by the left-wing group, supported their right to associate and put forward their views. Then he concluded: "I don't call it prosperity when men are getting 25 cents an hour."[48]

Lawrence gave unquestioning support to labour but he also advocated what could now be called a "pre-development" policy. In his nomination speech of 1928, when he ran for Board of Control for the first time, he was reported by *The Spectator* as saying:

A vigorous policy of publicity should be maintained stressing the advantageous position of our city to those in search of a location on which to establish an industry, its advantages as a convention city and a city that should be included in the itinerary of all motorists visiting this part of Canada.[49]

A third very important element of Lawrence's program which he returned to regularly, was his promise to keep taxes down for the homeowner.[50] With the exception of his solid defense of labour Lawrence might have been difficult to distinguish

A supporter of the 1946 Stelco Steel Strike (McMaster University, Labour Studies Collection).

from any other business politician in Hamilton. He generally supported the concept that the role of government should be to promote the interests of business. His only major difference from the business politicians was that he believed that labour should be allowed to develop without interference from government. His policies were pro-labour and pro-business at the same time and Lawrence was able to use this obvious contradiction to his advantage. He was a populist, with something for everyone: low taxes for homeowners, promotion of the interests of business, and support of the trade union movement. Rather than presenting a challenge to the business interests that ran the city, Lawrence, and labour politicians like him, supported their objective of using the power of government to subsidize private investment.

The deepening of the Depression in the

1930s gradually changed the political climate of Canada. At first it appeared that there would be a resurgence of trade union political power. In 1931 Humphrey Mitchell was elected to the federal parliament in a by-election for Hamilton East. Mitchell had a similar background to that of Sam Lawrence. He was an Englishman and a hydro engineer by trade who settled in Hamilton after World War I. Soon he became involved in both the trade union movement and the Independent Labour Party. In 1928 he was elected on the labour slate to Sam Lawrence's aldermanic seat in Ward 8, when Lawrence successfully ran for Board of Control. After his election to the federal house it was expected that Mitchell would join the small labour group in parliament led by J. S. Woodsworth but he refused and sat as an Independent.[51]

The most important event for Hamilton labour in the early 1930s was the creation of the Co-operative Commonwealth Federation (the CCF). The new social democratic party, which emerged after the 1933 Regina convention, was to be an amalgamation of farm, labour and middle-class reform groups. In Ontario there seemed to be a base of support for the new party. Labour in Hamilton began to find a new purpose after its long years in the political wilderness. In March Humphrey Mitchell appeared with J. S. Woodsworth in Hamilton and they were "loudly supported by the largest audience given a political speaker since the 1930 campaign as they denounced the dictatorship by financial interests of the federal government."[52]

Municipally Sam Lawrence played a vital role in leading what remained of the Independent Labour Party into the new federation. In past years he had either been topping the polls in his elections for Board of Control, or had run second, and in December 1933 he led a CCF slate of candidates into the field. *The Spectator* fumed:

Have you ever stopped to consider what would happen if the distribution of relief got into the hands of an irresponsible clique or political party — the favouring of political friends and ward heelers that would go on — the fattening of the few and the neglect of the many — the opportunities for graft and the building up of party machinery that would be afforded?[53]

This editorial slandering the CCF, which went on to call the party members demagogues and elitists who betrayed the real interests of the working class, was published two days before the election. *The Spectator* need not have gone to such excesses. The entire slate went down to defeat with the exception of Sam Lawrence. He again topped the polls of Board of Control.

As the Ontario CCF moved into its second year it had already developed an enthusiastic and dedicated cadre of workers, but they were badly organized and deeply divided. Many of the party faithful believed that the public would flock to them in rejection of the Conservatives who held power in both Ottawa and Queens Park. Instead it was the Liberals who were to gain the political advantage in the economic crisis. In the July 1934 provincial election, Mitchell Hepburn, the St. Thomas onion farmer and populistic Liberal leader, toured the province blaming the Tories for all the woes facing the country. In the Liberal sweep to power the CCF were able to gain only one seat. This was Hamilton East and the candidate was Sam Lawrence.

The 1935 federal election was an even more disappointing showing for the CCF, who were unable to win a seat in the entire province. Humphrey Mitchell had been attracted to the new party not long after it was formed, but he returned to his independent status. Despite his political maneuvering he was defeated.

Although the CCF faced a string of disappointments in its early years, the 1930s created conditions that put the social democratic party on a firm footing in English-speaking Canada. One of the important elements favouring its establishment was a sudden reversal of policy by the Communists. In the early 1930s the Party was in an extremely radical phase and it continually vilified any labour political initiatives other than its own. In 1935 it suddenly shifted policy in the interests of promoting a common front against the fascist threat in Europe. This began a phase of real cooperation between the two most important branches of labour. In Hamilton, for example, May Day rallies saw both wings of the labour movement co-operating in the demonstrations. In 1936 Sam Lawrence praised the "different attitude adopted by the Communists who no longer set themselves apart from the working class movement but who were willing to do some reforming ... from within."[54]

This co-operation between the two political wings of labour was also of major significance in the growth of the new industrial unions. It was in 1935 that John L. Lewis formed the CIO and started the drive for industrial unions in North America. In 1936 the Steelworkers Organizing Committee (SWOC) was founded. The Communist-led Workers' Unity League, (1930–1934), had already been organizing Steelworkers in Hamilton, and they joined with SWOC in their long and difficult organizing drives in the mills across the country. In the same month that the Steelworkers was founded in the United States the Hamilton steelworkers met to form local branches. At that meeting both Sam Lawrence of the CCF and J. B. Salsberg of the Communist Party and the now-disbanded Workers' Unity League pledged their support to the new union.[55]

Up until 1935 very little union organizing had gone on in the enormous steel mills in the East End of the city. At Stelco three locals of the Amalgamated Association of Iron, Steel and Tin Workers had been formed in 1919, but by 1932 they had all lost their charters. In 1934 an Independent Steelworkers Association was organized in Stelco's sheet mill department, and in 1936 this group became the core of the members who organized the union. (At one time Dofasco was more organized than the workers at Stelco but a determined management fired the entire union executive in 1938. There has been little union activity in the plant since.) These efforts by the Steelworkers were ultimately to bring about radical change in the political life of labour groups by providing a strong political base of support.

The co-operation between the CCF and Communists caused some problems for Lawrence. On more than one occasion he was called a Communist by right wing trade unionists in an effort to smear his reputation,[56] but this did not appear to affect his political career. In 1937 he was defeated in his re-election bid for the provincial parliament, but a few months later he was given the largest number of votes in the Board of Control election, and he repeated his performance several times in elections that followed.

Despite Lawrence's support of the Communists in the late 1930s and early 1940s they met with a number of problems. In 1940 Harry Hunter, one of the original Workers' Unity League organizers in the city and a SWOC official, was elected alderman of Ward 7. A group of council members demanded his resignation because he was a Communist and Lawrence along with only three other councillors rallied to his support.[57] An even more serious attack to the left wing came from within the trade union movement. In 1940 Charles Millard was appointed Canadian director of the CIO. Soon afterwards he fired Hunter and other Communist Party members from their positions in the Steelworkers and replaced them with staff people who were supporters of the CCF. The control of the Steelworkers by the CCF (later NDP) faction was of major importance for the development of the party in Hamilton and Canada.

For ten years following its founding in 1933 the CCF struggled with little success, but unexpectedly in 1942 the party surprised even itself by winning a number of federal by-elections. In 1943 there was a sudden surge of support for the party, and the provincial election of that year saw the CCF jump from no seats at all to 34. This was only four seats short of the Conservatives, the largest party in the house. In Hamilton the CCF won every seat, and across the Niagara Peninsula the party captured every seat but one. In late 1943, at the height of the CCF's new popularity, Sam Lawrence, the veteran labour politician, decided to run for the top municipal position in the city. He accepted the nomination as the leader of the CCF-Labour slate to run for the position of mayor.

For the first time since the surge of support for the Independent Labour Party in the early 1920s labour was a serious political threat to the business interests that controlled the city. Not only was labour presenting a large slate of candidates but its program advocated a set of priorities favouring the working class. These included: "public ownership of distribution and services wherever feasible in the public interest, a federal and provincial financed municipal housing scheme, more equitable property assessment, lower fuel costs, and better street lighting."[58]

Hamilton's business group in 1943 was worried, and businessmen mounted a vigorous and well-financed campaign led by the Conservative candidate for mayor, merchant Donald Clark. *The Spectator* featured daily front-page editorials that denounced Lawrence and the CCF. One said:

There are men in Canada who in their reach for power are betraying dangerous social tendencies which threaten both good order and good government in this country. Some of their utterances sound ominously familiar — not unlike the wild men of Europe who bellowed from balconies and microphones, inflaming their dupes to mob violence and worse ...

These malcontents are known as the CCF Party. Locally, they are out to plant their totalitarian boot on the neck of Hamilton's civic administration ...

The singleness of aim, it is plain enough, is to wreck Canadian Democracy and Canadian enterprise by forcing an alien and totalitarian ideology upon this country and clamping it down with a ruthless dictatorship.

This is the party that seeks to dominate Hamilton's city council and turn its civic administration into a small-scale laboratory for totalitarian experiments.[59]

The results of the contest show that the massive campaign launched against the CCF was successful. Sam Lawrence was elected mayor but with a very narrow majority of 1,689 votes out of a total of 46,606 cast. Only two other members of the CCF slate were elected and both of these were in the strong labour Ward 8. Labour may have been able to elect a mayor but he would be powerless to implement any of the CCF policies that were so feared by business.

Sam Lawrence was to remain mayor from 1943 to his retirement in 1949. Of all the issues that he dealt with in those years by far the most contentious and important was the 1946 Stelco Steel strike. This strike was of fundamental importance to labour's political development in Hamilton.

The organization of Stelco had gone very slowly from the time of the first meeting of the Steelworkers Organizing Committee in 1936. The company had responded to the organizing drive by creating a "works committee" or "company union" as the Steelworkers called it. It was not until 1943 that the unionists had taken over this organization and finally in 1945, under new legislation forcing the company to bargain in good faith, the union was able to get its first contract.

When this contract was due to terminate in July 1946, it was obvious that both sides were preparing

Nora Frances Henderson confronting the strikers (McMaster University, Labour Studies Collection).

for a major conflict. The Steelworkers demanded a raise in wages of nineteen and a half cents an hour, a forty-four hour week, two weeks paid vacation after five years service, and union security with automatic check-off of dues.[60] For its part the company led by their president Hugh Hilton, made it clear that it intended to oppose the union and if possible break it. As a counter-offer it proposed five and a half cents an hour wage increase, and rejected all of the union security demands.[61] Soon it became known that the company was preparing an air strip inside its property, and extra help was hired in early July, many of whom were high school students. It became clear that Stelco planned to maintain production, keep its customers supplied with steel and force the workers back to work under company terms. When the strike broke out on July 14 everyone knew that it would be a protracted affair, and one of vital importance for unionists in Hamilton and across the country.

Curiously, one of the most important participants in the strike was the old ILP supporter and one-time labour federal member of parliament from Hamilton East, Humphrey Mitchell. When in Ottawa in the early 1930s Mitchell had been friendly with all political groups and later admitted that he would have been made Minister of Labour had he been re-elected in the 1935 election, whether the Liberals or Conservatives formed the government.[62] During the war he was named by Mackenzie King to a number of posts and finally became Minister of Labour in 1941, after he won a federal seat in Welland as a Liberal. When the 1946 strike broke out he was still the Minister of Labour, and in the eyes of many Hamilton labour supporters he was the real enemy backing Stelco's bid to break the union. In the year of his death, 1959, Sam Lawrence still remembered Humphrey Mitchell as "the only man he thoroughly disliked."[63]

From the beginning of the strike there were calls for the police to open the Steelworkers' picket lines so that the 2000 to 2500 employees inside the plant could come and go as they chose. On this point the Steelworkers refused any compromise. To them, the men inside the plant were scabs trying to take their jobs, and working with management to break their strike and the union. They did not intend to lift the picket line until a settlement was

The War Veterans' march in support of the strikers, August 26, 1946 (McMaster University, Labour Studies Collection).

reached. Soon there were violent incidents on the picket line and it was claimed that the police were needed to maintain law and order.

The strike in the giant steel mill rapidly polarized political opinion in the city and the municipal politicians were in the centre of it. Mayor Sam Lawrence, true to his labour beliefs, took part in a march in support of the strikers. At its conclusion thousands gathered in Woodland Park to hear his speech, which left no doubt where his loyalties lay. Declaring he was a "labour man first and chief magistrate second," he concluded by saying that "as a union man he was 100% behind the workers in their struggle."[64]

In opposition to the mayor Controller Nora Frances Henderson argued forcefully that the picket lines should be opened by the police. In statements she made to the press she deplored the city's "state of lawlessness,"[65] and insisted that the provincial police be called in to open the lines and deal with the emergency. On August 2 she marched alone to the picket line and demanded to be let into the plant. The picture of her tiny figure surrounded by a huge crowd of burly steel worker picketers was spread across the front pages of Canadian newspapers, making her a symbol to those who believed the union should be forced to obey the law. In fact, the strikers courteously let her through the lines rather than provoke the inevitable backlash.[66]

When she reappeared from the plant Nora Frances Henderson argued the issue of law-and-order to its fullest. "This form of picketing is illegal," she said to the press. "There is intimidation and threats of violence ... What burns me up is that 2700 men inside the plant are denied free access to the municipality."[67] Later she said, "I will not bow to mob rule," and called for a Board of Control meeting to deal with "the state of lawlessness in Hamilton at the present time."[68]

On August 9 a council meeting was held to deal with the issue. Thousands of strikers and their supporters converged on city hall, only to find that all the seats of the chamber were taken by the office personnel of the city's strike-bound plants, but a huge crowd stayed to hear the outcome. Whenever Mayor Lawrence or the union supporters on council spoke they were booed and heckled by the office workers, and whenever Controller Henderson or her supporters took the floor the strikers treated them the same way. The high point of the evening came when Police Chief Joseph Crocker claimed that there were no major problems on the picket line and noted that to date only thirty-three arrests had been made. After four hours of debate council voted nine to seven that provincial police were not needed.[69]

As the strike lengthened into August and September the conflict grew to include dropping leaflets by air, an aerial dogfight between company and union airplanes, and a virtual embargo on all boats trying to leave or approach the company docks by the union powerboat, the *Whisper*. The political battles between Nora Frances Henderson and Sam Lawrence continued. Finally on August 21 there was a clash on the picket line between police and strikers. The chief stated at the police commission meeting of August 23 that the law could not be enforced without extensive reinforcements.[70] At the meeting Lawrence cast a dissenting vote but the request for additional police was made. Soon the RCMP and the OPP had agreed to send in 250 men each to maintain law and order.

It was a tense period in Hamilton. Charles Millard, the Steelworkers' Canadian director, restated the union position that they would not open the picket line until an acceptable settlement was made and they would not back down in the face of government threats. On August 26 there was a march of 10,000 people demonstrating their support of the union. Telegrams were received and deputations arrived at the Steelworkers office, all declaring support should the police try to break the picket lines. There was talk of a general strike. The picketers believed that the police would arrive at any moment. Huge crowds of people waited expectantly at the plant gates for what some believed would be the final showdown between the company and the government on the one side, and the union and their political supporters on the other. But in the end the police did nothing. The solidarity of the Hamilton workers and the trade union movement appears to have convinced the different levels of government to wait, letting an agreement between the company and union emerge rather than opening the picket lines by force.

It took until October 1 for a final settlement to be arranged. The agreement gave the union an immediate increase of thirteen and a half cents an hour and an additional 5 cents before the end of the year. The issue of union recognition was settled on the basis of voluntary dues check-off after a majority of workers voted in favour of the union. The Steelworkers had been firmly established by the strike and a major battle for the acceptance of industrial unions in Canada had been won.

Lawrence's role in the strike demonstrates the sure touch of a master politician. As McMenemy points out, his "problem was to remain consistent to his socialist and labour principles while upholding the public trust. By every standard Lawrence's words and actions can be judged successful."[71] There can be little doubt that if a person less sympathetic to the cause of labour had been the mayor of Hamilton that summer the results of the 1946 strike and even of labour's future in Canada could have been much different.

It was widely predicted by the press that Lawrence would be defeated in his bid for re-election after the strike, but in December of 1946, just six weeks after the strike was settled, he was returned with a comfortable majority. In 1949 the popular labour mayor retired and was replaced by Lloyd D. Jackson, owner of Jackson's Bakeries and a prominent representative of the business community. Lawrence came back to win re-election to Board of Control in the 1950s but the era of his prominence in Hamilton politics was over.

Lawrence's career is instructive, because it stands in such contrast to the trends of the period. He was clearly a labour man and even supported various Communist activities, which could hardly have been popular with many people even in the late 1930s and 1940s. He was successful not only because of his personal qualities but because, while the policies he supported were broadly acceptable to the working-class base of his support they were not impossible for business to accept. Despite the barrage of slanderous editorials written about him, Lawrence was hardly a radical. What he stood for that was different from the attitudes of those in the normally-dominant business groups was the right of the trade union movement to operate openly and be accepted as an established element in Canadian industrial life.

There was only one time in Lawrence's long career that he was ever a threat to the business group who dominated the city. This was in 1943, when it appeared to be possible that the CCF slate of candidates could win a majority at city hall. They had a political program that favoured the working class and was aimed at curtailing the power of business. But although Lawrence was elected mayor the business group was able to mount a successful campaign against other members of the CCF and maintain political power.

The 1946 steel strike appears to have ended in a clear victory of labour over business and there can be no doubt that it is a milestone in the development of the trade union movement in this country. Yet it is important to remember that business and their political supporters were divided on the issue of unionization in 1946. Hilton, the president of the Steel Company at the time, represented a conservative business point of view while others could see that the establishment of unions did not represent a serious threat to their power.

By 1946 union security was an idea whose time had come and the support Lawrence received in

The union plane bombarding the plant with leaflets (McMaster University, Labour Studies Collection).

his elections after the Stelco strike shows that the majority of Hamiltonians felt that it was a perfectly acceptable and reasonable demand. The business group had not lost power in the strike; it was simply forced to alter its tactics in order to maintain control. The subsequent history of the trade union movement has shown that union demands can easily be accomodated in our economic and political system.

LABOUR IN POSTWAR HAMILTON

During the 1940s the trade union movement of the city finally achieved one of its major goals, organizing the majority of the industrial work force. Not only did the Steelworkers win recognition at the giant Stelco plant but unions were organized at Westinghouse, Firestone, International Harvester and scores of smaller firms in the city. The labour movement progressed in those years and its performance was impressive. But despite these significant breakthroughs, politically it continued to be weak, ineffective and badly divided. Today labour is as far away from gaining political power in the city as it has ever been in the past.

The Steelworkers are one of the most political unions in the country. Beginning in 1940, when Charles Millard was placed in charge of the union by the American leaders of the CIO, the union's policy has been one of open and consistent support of the CCF and its successor the NDP. To this day all steel staff are expected to attempt to identify the party with the union as much as possible and to use their position within the trade union movement to encourage members to support the party.

In the 1940s the major opposition to Millard's policy of labour alliance with the CCF came from unions led by members of the Communist Party. The most important of this group was the United Electrical Workers, or the "UE" as they are called. Irving Abella, writing about the Electrical Workers in the immediate postwar era, notes: "Of all the congress (CCL) unions the UE was the most continuously and accurately identified with the Communist Party."[72] Since its founding in the 1930s the UE has been led by C. S. Jackson and a remarkably talented group of organizers who built a union which has had strong support from the rank and file and a reputation for militancy and effectiveness. In Hamilton the UE organized the three large Westinghouse plants and a handful of smaller locals to make up a membership of about 5000. In terms of size it became the second largest union after the Steelworkers in the city. Because of the diametrically opposed political views of the Steelworkers and the Electrical Workers, a contest between them became inevitable.

The conflict between the Communists and the unionists supporting the CCF went on at many different levels in the city. For a time there was competition within the Steelworkers itself for political control of the union. When Millard fired

Harry Hunter and others from their Steelworker organizer's positions, the left wing mounted a challenge against the CCF leadership of the union, but this ultimately failed.[73] More significant for Hamilton was a series of struggles for political control within a number of locals. In Hamilton's Steelworker local 1005, the unit struggling to represent the workers at Stelco, the left-wing group under the leadership of Tom McClure, the president, was the dominant force for many years. In 1944 Millard moved Larry Sefton into the city as the chief steel organizer, with the specific job of eliminating the Communists from positions of influence. Within a short time he had put together a CCF group in the local and in the 1945 elections McClure was defeated for president by Reg Gardiner, a well-known CCF supporter.

In the 1940s the most intense competition between these two branches of the trade union movement was at the Hamilton Labour Council. At every meeting the acrimonious debates went on for hours. They were not debates in the sense that people could be persuaded by the arguments to support one side or another; the political climate was much too polarized for that. After 1944 the conflict became even more intense. On the side of the Steelworkers and the CCF, Larry Sefton "knocked up the vote," as he liked to put it, while on the left men like Bill Walsh of the UE led the debate and kept their supporters in line. On most issues the CCF group had the votes to dominate the council, but the competition was fierce, and as time went on the two groups became increasingly intractable and hostile to one another.

This competition had a negative influence on the political effectiveness of labour in the city. Often CCF candidates for municipal office found that their major opponents were from the Labour Progressive Party (the name adopted by the Communists in 1943). As they competed for the labour vote they would frequently split their support and give a representative of business the opportunity to win. Hard feelings about this electoral issue peaked in the 1945 federal and provincial elections.

In 1943 the CCF had come within four seats of becoming the largest party in the Ontario legislature, and it was widely predicted that the CCF would form the next government of Canada. As it turned out, this did not happen. In the June 1945 Ontario election, CCF strength in the house shrank from 34 to 8 seats and the Conservatives won a comfortable majority. In the federal election, held a week later, the party won only 28 seats, none of which were in Ontario. Casting about for an explanation for their defeat, many CCF supporters turned on the Communists. In a book on the Ontario CCF published as recently as 1973, Gerald Caplan, a prominent NDP organizer, puts forward this explanation:

The Communists, realizing Hepburn [the Liberal leader] had little chance of victory, were attempting to help return Drew [The Conservative Premier] to office by defeating as many CCF candidates as possible. Despite all their public protestations of hatred for "reactionary Toryism," this conclusion is inescapable. The L. P. P. contested thirty-seven seats in the Ontario election. No less than twenty-seven of these were ridings held by the CCFers since 1943 . . . The intention, of course, was simply to split the CCF vote wherever possible.[74]

Like many CCF supporters of the day, Caplan's interpretation blames the Communists for the party's defeat. It is implied that the Labour Progressive Party had no right to run in the election because it might harm the CCF chances. The Caplan interpretation also ignores the fact that the Communists ran in ridings held by the CCF because they perceived their strength to be in the working-class ridings, a large number of which were already held by the CCF. The most interesting thing about Caplan's views is that they reflect the bitterness between the two left-wing political parties, which came to a climax around the 1945 elections and lingers to this day.

After 1945 the strength and prestige of the Communist Party waned rapidly in Canada and Hamilton. The beginning of the Cold War in 1946 with the Gouzenko affair and the resulting arrest, trial and conviction of the Labour Progressive member of parliament, Fred Rose, led to a rapid loss of support. With the Korean War, the McCarthy hearings in the United States, and revelations about Russia under Stalin, the party's influence noticeably weakened. In Hamilton after the Stelco strike of 1946 the CCF unions were now clearly in the position of strength. Harry Hunter, an early trade union organizer in Hamilton who had been alderman as a Labour Progressive candidate on two occasions, was unable to get re-elected, and Helen Anderson, an LPP member who had once sat on Board of Control, was defeated. As Communist Party support shrank their institutions became more vulnerable; in 1949 the United Electrical Workers was expelled from the Canadian Congress of Labour. As a consequence the UE was forced to drop out of the Hamilton Labour Council, leaving the CCF wing of labour in virtually total control.

In the Cold War period there were few organizations in which attacks on Communists were more vehement than in the trade union movement. The CCF unions saw this as their chance to destroy the Communists once and for all and the passion with which they went about their task suggests that they were motivated by revenge as well as some notion that they were cleansing themselves of the Communist menace. But if the leaders of the trade union movement thought that the expulsion of the Communists would improve the political standing of labour and the CCF they were disappointed. The Cold War and the postwar economic boom

Larry Sefton, one of the important leaders of the Steelworkers strike. The poster on the wall,"We Don't Take the Spec." refers to a strike that was going on at *The Spectator* at the same time as the 1946 Stelco strike. Unlike the steel strike, however, *The Spectator* strike was lost when the company maintained production (McMaster University, Labour Studies Collection).

created a political climate unfavourable to all left-wing parties and after 1945 the CCF in Ontario went into a period of sharp decline.

These developments were paralleled in Hamilton. Through the 1940s Sam Lawrence led the CCF slate in a number of municipal elections but few were ever elected with him. When the labour mayor temporarily retired in 1949 the slate was completely defeated and when Lawrence ran again for Board of Control in 1950 he was the only CCF candidate to win. Even he suffered from the change of political climate in the 1950s. On two occasions in the next five elections Lawrence ran fourth, the lowest position on Board of Control.

One practice that emerged in the 1950s was that the CCF did not run a slate of candidates. Rather, the Labour Council directly endorsed candidates and gave them a small donation for their campaigns. The Council insisted that these people hold a membership in the CCF and support a four or five point program but in practice, most gave little more than give lip service to the support of unions in the city. Now the CCF/labour candidates were little different from candidates of the old line parties. They did not represent a challenge to business; they did not have a set of policies that presented an alternative to the development oriented business representatives; they were simply a number of individual politicians promoting whatever policy suited them. Most CCF candidates, in any case, could not get elected.

During the 1950s the success of labour-endorsed candidates was minimal. David Lawrence, a nephew of Sam, was elected alderman in 1951 for one of the East End wards, and was re-elected year after year. In the 1956 election, the year that Sam Lawrence finally retired from his Board of Control position, labour made its most serious challenge in several years by putting up nine candidates. Jim Stowe, who had been president of the AFL Trades and Labour Council since 1952 and now was president of the united Hamilton Labour Council, ran for Board of Control. However, the slate was badly defeated, and the only labour candidate elected was David Lawrence. Stowe stood eighth in a field of nine candidates.[75]

At the end of the 1950s the fortunes of labour began to revive and through the 1960s they continued to improve. In 1959 Reg Gisborn was elected to the provincial legislature from Hamilton

East for the CCF. In 1960 both Bill Foley, a staff man with the Textile Workers and Bill Scandlon, a Steelworkers representative, joined David Lawrence as labour member of council. By the mid-1960s Bill Powell and Jim Stowe were elected alderman. Finally in 1966 and again in 1968 Bill Foley was voted onto the Board of Control. He became the first labour representative on the Board since Sam Lawrence.

By 1968 it appeared as if the NDP (which had held its founding convention in 1961) and labour were in a state of revival similar to that in the early 1920s. The party held three of the six provincial seats in the area, and in 1968 they won five seats on council, more than at any time since 1922. The only setback was the loss of Dr. Bill Howe's federal seat of Hamilton Mountain in that year, but that was attributed to "Trudeaumania" rather than a rejection of the NDP. The morale and membership of the party was high and the time seemed ripe again to make a major challenge of the business interests who continued to control the city's political life.

Through much of the 1950s and 1960s there had been considerable dissatisfaction within the NDP about the performance of the labour-endorsed politicians at city hall. The major criticism was that the group was no different from any of the other members on council. They did not provide a critique of the policies of city hall, nor did they caucus or act together to promote certain programs. On issues such as development, the major issue facing the council of the day, they usually supported the developers. The opposition to the controversial Civic Square project, for example, was led by Reg Wheeler, a Liberal, Bill McCulloch, a Conservative, and Bill Powell, a New Democrat. The other NDP council members were strong supporters of the business groups promoting the scheme. (See "Downtown redevelopment: The Civic Square project" in Part III.)

There had long been discussions within the Hamilton NDP about the failure of the labour councillors but it was felt that party members could not legitimately challenge them because technically they were sponsored by the Labour Council rather than the NDP. If the council chose to ignore their councillors between elections then the party was powerless to do any more.

The 1968 NDP provincial convention in Kitchener changed all of this. A group of Toronto New Democrats involved in municipal politics put forward a set of resolutions at this convention in support of party politics at a municipal level. Essentially they proposed setting up a party structure much like that in federal or provincial politics, in which candidates would run across the city, committed to a common program worked out by the party as a whole. Once elected, the NDP group on council would regularly caucus, take common positions on policy, and provide an administration of the city based on the principles set down in the party program. The changes proposed by the Toronto NDP municipal group were designed to be not only a way of reforming city politics but also a way of reforming the party and controlling those NDP members of council who had labour endorsement.

The Hamilton NDP group was outside any of the discussions that led to these proposals but they were deeply influenced by them. Here was a practical way of bringing about reforms, both within the party and at council, that could easily be implemented. In the 1969 NDP Hamilton-area council the proposal to run candidates for city council under the party label became the chief issue of debate. The party was badly split on the issue. On one side was a group of young party activists who argued strongly that this was the only practical means of reforming city politics, in order to make the electoral process more meaningful to the voter and radically alter the type of politics at city hall. This group was joined by the leaders of the Steelworkers, who were by far the most influential group within the Hamilton NDP. Men like Stew Cooke, Bob McKenzie and Reg Gisborn were more pragmatic but in essence they claimed that the NDP was now not strong enough to mount a challenge to the business groups who dominated city hall. They argued that although the NDP would not be able to gain power immediately, party politics at city hall would be a beginning in the transformation for political life in Hamilton.

The resolution to run party politics at a municipal level was opposed primarily by the sitting NDP council members. Aldermen Bill Powell, Dave Lawrence and Jim Stowe all spoke against the issue at the convention and said, basically, that the NDP was not strong enough to run on party politics. They pointed out that in their campaigns they got support from people of all parties, and a clear party identification would lose them votes and possibly the election. Despite these arguments the debate went against them and the resolution saying the NDP would run a slate of candidates in the next election was strongly endorsed.

In the year leading up to the 1970 municipal election the Hamilton NDP became seriously divided over the issue. The provincial riding association of Hamilton Centre was strongly identified with alderman Bill Powell. The riding association as a whole opted out of the commitment to run in the election and did not support NDP municipal candidates or provide money for the campaign. Two other labour aldermen, Jim Stowe and David Lawrence, said they would run as Independents rather than on the party slate, and only alderman Bill Scandlon agreed to run under the party label.

The plans went ahead despite these divisions. In the early summer a party program was drafted at a convention in an attempt to redirect the city's

A union march in the 1946 steel strike, in which the workers are vilifying three of their enemies (McMaster University, Labour Studies Collection).

policies, giving priorities to such issues as low-income housing, public transportation, urban redevelopment designed to benefit the ordinary citizen, environmental protection and so on.

One of the chief problems facing the NDP in 1970 was that the other political parties refused to accept party politics for city council. Earlier in that year it was thought that the Liberals and possibly the Conservatives would run a slate of candidates but both refused. One person tells the story that when a Liberal organizer suggested to Vic Copps that he head up a Liberal slate the mayor became so angry that he "almost went over the desk at him." The reason is not hard to understand. Party politics that focused the election around issues rather than individuals would wipe out some of the advantages of the incumbent. Party politics would also be particularly dangerous to the business community since it would create polarization at council and bring about consistent criticism of existing programs. In time this could challenge the political domination of business.

The election was a hotly contested affair, with more interest shown in municipal politics than had existed for many years, but afterwards the NDP attempt to create party politics at city hall was declared a failure when all but one of their candidates were defeated. Although the slate did about as well as any other group of new candidates could have done, it did not create the type of political system its organizers had hoped for. By the next election there was a return to the individualistic style of politics that continues to this day.

The political policies of labour in Hamilton in the 1970s continued much as they had in the past: candidates from the New Democratic Party received endorsement from the Labour Council and a small amount of money for their campaigns. However, there has been one important development that could in time change the nature of labour politics in the city. In 1972 the United Electrical Workers were readmitted into the Canadian Labour Congress (CLC) and as a result automatically became members of the Hamilton and District Labour Council. In the days since UE had been expelled from the old CCL the union had been open to raids, but it had been able to retain its membership and in fact had grown in size. By 1972 the United Electrical Workers were a radical union with Communist Party members still at the top levels of leadership, but with solid rank and file support among their membership that was the envy of many unions.

After the UE rejoined the Labour Council it became evident that the labour body would again be polarized as much as it had been in the 1940s.

Speeches in front of city hall during the November 1976 Day of Protest. Bob McKenzie, the NDP provincial member of parliament for Hamilton East, is addressing the crowd (Hamilton Public Library).

For the past few years the largest group in the council has been a group called the "Right Wing," made up of members from the NDP unions in the city and supported by other more conservative locals. The most sophisticated of this group have been Steelworkers staff officers and include such men as Bob McKenzie (now the NDP provincial MLA for Hamilton East), Ben DesRoches and John Morgan. However, they have the broad support of many unions. The "Left Wing" group of the council is considerably smaller, but its members are more politicized. Because they attend meetings religiously and lobby hard for their point of view they can sometimes overcome the drawback of their limited numbers and win issues. The left is led by Hamilton leaders of the United Electrical Workers such as Tom Davidson and John Ball, but they have support from a broad group of unionists who are left-wing New Democrats wanting more radical policies in unions and politics.

The most important issue dividing the Right and Left in the Hamilton Labour Council has been municipal politics. The Right Wing wants to continue the former policy of the Labour Council by endorsing and giving financial support to NDP members running for office. The Left wants endorsement of a broader group of candidates drawn from the labour movement. In this way members of the Communist Party could get labour endorsement and increase their legitimacy in the eyes of the public.

Attitudes around this issue have hardened since the UE rejoined the Labour Council in 1972. On one side, the Right Wing fears that the Left will deny the NDP the political power for which it has worked so hard by splitting the vote, and worse still, by identifying the Communists with the NDP political movement in the eyes of the public. On the other side, the Left Wing views its opposition as a group that is virtually denying it the right to operate as a legitimate political force within the ranks of labour. The politics of the labour group are now so hopelessly polarized that, as in the 1940s, there are very few who are open to being swayed by the debate.

So once a month on Labour Council nights the debates between the Left and Right Wings rage with an intensity that makes any other political forum in the city look pale by comparison. It was here, on the night of November 5, 1976, that Ben DesRoches, one of the leaders of the Right Wing of the council and John Ball, a leader of the Left, finally lost their tempers, and ended up attempting to score points physically that they had failed to make in the debate. The fight was an expression of the frustration of both men but it was also a reflection of all those years of vain struggle for political power by the Hamilton trade union movement.

THE FAILURE OF LABOUR AS AN OPPOSITION GROUP

It has been a full sixty years since labour emerged in Hamilton as the strongest voice of opposition to the business interests who have run the city. But despite the overwhelming size of the working class in the city and the fact that since 1946 they have been led by large and powerful unions, the workers of the city have failed to achieve significant political power or representation on council. The only times, in fact, when labour seriously challenged the interests of business was immediately after World War I, and during World War II. This was not because the Hamilton working class had adopted a radical new ideology at these times, pitting them against the interests of business, but because the social and economic conditions of the day led to militant union activity.

The causes of the failure of Hamilton labour to gain political power are complex. Perhaps the most important basic factor is that the working class in Canada, whether blue-collar or white-collar workers, still closely identifies with the interests of business. The ideal of the independent producer able to own and control his business is still very close to the consciousness of many workers, and politicians have no problems in Hamilton gaining support for projects or policies whose overall intent is to subsidize business interests.[76]

A more specific reason for the failure, however, relates to the divisions within the political leadership of labour in Hamilton and in Canada. With the exception of the 1950s and 1960s, when the Communists were so weak that they retreated into a defensive position simply to survive, the competition between the two wings of labour has been so intense that it has seemed that they saw each other as their major opposition rather than the business political groups who have run the city. There is a tragic strain of self-destructiveness among labour politicians in Hamilton, which has been repeated from decade to decade.

By contrast the business community in Hamilton has always been able to bury its differences in order to achieve its political objectives. This does not mean to say that the business community has been unified. Even at the municipal level there is strong competition among different elements of business, with debates often breaking out into the open, but business in Hamilton has always been unified on one principle: that the chief role of government is to subsidize and help business in any way possible. Their debates are about how best to implement this policy, and who will be the political leaders.

The real problem of labour in Hamilton and the major reason for its failure as an opposition group is that it has never had an alternative to the "ideology of business." The hard truth is that for most of their history in Hamilton the leaders of labour have not seen it as their primary role to be defenders of the working class. It has seemed to them to be enough if they gave support to the objectives of the trade union movement and then, like most other politicians, to continue to support the business interests who have always been the most powerful group in the city. Labour politicians have operated simply as a vested interest group with a limited set of objectives, rather than as a political party dedicated to bringing substantial improvements to the working class and limiting the power of business.

Of course this could change. A beginning would be made if the right and left wings of the trade union movement would enter into a dedicated coalition but even this appears remote. No matter what the prospect for labour, the business community is secure for the forseeable future. Nowhere on Hamilton's political horizons is there an opposition group that could begin to challenge their power.

1. Charles Lipton, *The Trade Union Movement of Canada 1827–1959* (Toronto: New Canada Publications, 1967) p. 29.

2. John M. McMenemy, "Lion in a Den of Daniels: A Study of Sam Lawrence, Labour in Politics," (MA Thesis: McMaster University, 1965) p. 17.

3. See Gad Horowitz, *Canadian Labour in Politics* (Toronto: University of Toronto Press, 1968), for a general discussion of the importance of British immigrants in the Canadian political process.

4. *The Labour News* (Hamilton, Ontario) 16 February 1912.

5. *The Labour News*, 16 February 1912.

6. Martin Robin, *Radical Politics and Canadian Labour 1890–1930*, (Kingston, Ont.: Industrial Relations Centre, Queen's University, 1968) p. 247.

7. Robin, p. 125.

8. Robin, p. 126.

9. Robin, p. 141.

10. M.T. Montgomery, "Stelco Story," *Information* (United Steelworkers of America, August/ September, 1954, Vol. 3, No. 3) p. 5.

11. *The Hamilton Spectator*, 12 June 1916.

12. *The New Democracy*, 22 May 1919.

13. *The Hamilton Spectator*, 8 January 1920. The elements of this story reflect some of the preoccupations of the 1920s. There was widespread belief that "foreigners" were responsible for most crime; the majority of violations of prohibition legislation which was in force in Ontario at the time; and radical political activities. These fears reflect the prejudices of the English Canadians who made up the majority of the readership of *The Hamilton Spectator*.

14. *The New Democracy*, 11 December 1919.

15. *The New Democracy*, 11 December 1919.
16. *The Hamilton Spectator*, 26 October 1970.
17. *The New Democracy*, 1 October 1921.
18. In the late nineteenth and early twentieth centuries there were constant demands by unionists in the Canadian West and as far east as Ontario for the exclusion of all immigrants from the Orient. The reason for this was no doubt in part racist but it also reflected a fear that this group would undercut the wages of Canadian workers. In fact capitalists in the nineteenth century did import Chinese and Japanese workers in the West to work in railway construction, fishing and coal mining for just these reasons. The prejudice was, therefore, based on a realistic fear.
19. *The Labour News*, 16 February 1912.
20. Robin, p. 141.
21. *The Hamilton Spectator*, 16 June 1920.
22. *The Hamilton Spectator*, 14 January 1920.
23. *The Hamilton Spectator*, 20 January 1921.
24. *The New Democracy*, 16 December 1920.
25. McMenemy, p. 33.
26. *The Hamilton Spectator*, 13 December 1920.
27. *The Hamilton Spectator*, 23 December 1920.
28. *The Hamilton Spectator*, 7 January 1921.
29. *The Hamilton Spectator*, 7 January 1921.
30. *The Hamilton Spectator*, 5 February 1921.
31. *The Hamilton Spectator*, 15 April 1921.
32. *The Hamilton Spectator*, 7 January 1921.
33. *The Hamilton Spectator*, 19 February 1921.
34. *The New Democracy*, 19 March 1920.
35. Ivan Avakumovic, *The Communist Party in Canada* (Toronto: McClelland and Stewart, 1975) p. 21.
36. *The Hamilton Spectator*, 1 May 1922. This article is a good illustration of the way demonstrators were treated by the press and the police in the 1920s. They often were called "Reds" or "Bolsheviks" in spite of the fact that at best there would be only a handful of Communists in the crowd, and the bias of the paper is obvious in phrases such as "torrid speeches." The police frequently used excessive force against these demonstrators and the newspapers and public never seemed to raise objections about the abrogation of laws or the violation of civil liberties of the individuals involved. As Stewart Jamieson has pointed out, Canadians view themselves as law abiding and their history as non-violent, but Canadian labour history is marked by incidents of this type.
37. *The Hamilton Spectator*, 25 November 1922.
38. Robin, p. 247.
39. Robin, p., 247.
40. *The Hamilton Spectator*, 12 May 1923.
41. This material on Lawrence's early life was made available in John McMenemy's excellent thesis.
42. McMenemy, p. 6.
43. McMenemy, p. 67.
44. Gerald L. Caplan, *The Dilemma of Canadian Socialism* (Toronto: McClelland and Stewart, 1973) p. 23.
45. Caplan, p. 22.
46. *The Hamilton Spectator*, 11 October 1924.
47. McMenemy, p. vi.
48. *The Hamilton Spectator*, 7 October 1929.
49. *The Hamilton Spectator*, 1 December 1928.
50. *The Hamilton Spectator*, 1 December 1928.
51. McMenemy, p. 37.
52. Caplan, p. 29.
53. Thanks for this quotation to McMenemy, p. 44.
54. McMenemy, p. 50.
55. McMenemy, p. 50.
56. McMenemy, pp. 56–57.
57. McMenemy, p. 70.
58. McMenemy, p. 82.
59. McMenemy, pp. 79–80.
60. Robert McDonald Adams, "The Development of the United Steelworkers of America, 1936-1951," (MA Thesis: Queens University, 1957) p. 130.
61. William Kilbourn, *The Elements Combined: A History of the Steel Company of Canada* (Toronto: Clark, Irwin and Company Limited, 1960) p. 186.
62. *The Hamilton Spectator*, 1 August 1950.
63. McMenemy, p. 37.
64. *The Hamilton Spectator*, 18 July 1946.
65. Kilbourn, p. 194.
66. Kilbourn, p. 192.
67. *The Hamilton Spectator*, 2 August 1946.
68. *The Hamilton Spectator*, 7 August 1946.
69. *The Hamilton Spectator*, 9 August 1946.
70. McMenemy, p. 108.
71. McMenemy, p. 110.
72. Irving Abella, *Nationalism, Communism and Canadian Labour* (Toronto: University of Toronto Press, 1973) p. 139.
73. See Irving Abella's chapter on the Steelworkers in Nationalism, Communism and Canadian Labour for a discussion of these events.
74. Caplan, pp. 157-158.
75. McMenemy, p. 134.
76. Eli Chinoy explores this theme in *Automobile Workers and the American Dream* (Boston: Beacon Press, 1955).

Part II
Organizations

In Canadian society it is organizations rather than individuals that are the vehicles of political power, and to understand political life in Hamilton it is important to focus on key organizations. Henry Jacek's study of the John Munro political machine shows how a group of people have been able to put together an organization to serve their own ends. The study of organized crime in the city describes how a group of men have been able to develop a criminal empire that ruthlessly exploits the public while at the same time having politicians allay public fears by denying its very existence.

The third chapter, focussing on a community organization, shows the possibilities of this form of organization for realizing the potential political power of working-class and middle-class people, and also demonstrates how established powerful interests and organizations can successfully cope with threats of this kind. The study of Hamilton's one newspaper in the fourth chapter illustrates how the policies of a large business organization can lead to a more vigorous and critical local political life, but also how they can stultify public awareness of the actions and policies of powerful organizations and individuals.

John Munro and the Hamilton East Liberals: Anatomy of a modern political machine

Henry Jacek

"Of course there's patronage, and you know it, and everyone knows it . . . Is it wrong to favor a past political supporter over some one else if the two have equal ability? Of course it isn't."

—John Munro,
The Globe and Mail,
July 2, 1974

On September 7, 1978 John Munro, the member of parliament for Hamilton East, and the federal Minister of Labour, was forced to resign his cabinet post. The incident that sparked the resignation involved Julius Butty, a Hamilton developer, apartment owner and supporter of Munro, who had been convicted of assaulting one of his tenants with a hammer. Munro telephoned Judge Albert Marck in the midst of the court proceedings, only moments before sentence was given, in order to give personal testimony for Butty. Clearly this action was a violation of cabinet rules of conduct and when it became public knowledge Munro was forced to resign.

Hamiltonians reacted to the announcement with a show of support for the ex-minister, and there is a certain irony about the event. It had been known for some time that John Munro maintained and enhanced his power by using one of the most effective political machines the country has ever known. Patronage has always been an important part of that machine, and despite the secrecy that surrounds it, several reports about this aspect of Munro's operations had already been published. The incident of Julius Butty that drove him from office was just another example of the use of patronage and by comparison it was a minor instance indeed.

THE PATRON: JOHN CARR MUNRO

It is commonly believed that the classic, old style, urban political machine is dead, or at least that it is an American phenomenon with little relevance to Canada. Quite the opposite is true. For the working-class and predominently immigrant residents of the federal riding of Hamilton East the "Munro machine" is an active force that dominates political life and penetrates the individual lives of many of the constituents. The influence of the machine over the votes of Hamilton East has always contributed to the political power and prestige of John Munro.

At the centre of the machine, doling out favours and receiving political power in return, is John Carr Munro. Munro's political career is one of the most remarkable in Canadian politics. It began in his teenage years, when he was an energetic student politician at Westdale Secondary School. Munro was elected an alderman when he was only 23 years old. In 1957 he suffered the only electoral defeat of his political career; he was trounced in the federal election of that year by Progressive Conservative Ellen Fairclough in Hamilton West. In 1962 Munro obtained the Liberal nomination in Hamilton East and then defeated the sitting member, Progressive Conservative Quinto Martini.

He has won every federal election in that riding since, and the young, ambitious Hamiltonian rose rapidly in Ottawa circles. In 1963 he was appointed parliamentary secretary to the Minister of Citizenship and Immigration and on January 1966, parliamentary secretary to the Minister of Manpower and Immigration. On April 20, 1968 he reached the cabinet as Minister Without Portfolio. On June 28 of that year he was made Minister of National Health and Welfare. In late November, 1972 he was shifted to the Department of Labour, and for nearly three years he was also the Minister responsible for Multiculturalism.

Political success of this type does not happen by accident. It is a reflection of the organization that Munro and the people who work with him have assembled. That organization has more in common with the political machines that dominated cities in the United States, such as Tammany Hall in New York or the Daley Machine in Chicago, than the constituency associations we usually think of in Canadian politics.

A political machine is a complex phenomenon whose characteristics and activities do not apply to most known political organizations. First of all, the machine is well disciplined and tightly controlled from the top, sometimes by a small executive elite, but most often by a single leader. Second, the organization is methodical and permanent: people are chosen or co-opted to perform certain tasks on a long-term basis, and individuals who perform their tasks well are promoted through the machine hierarchy. Third, the political machine commonly exists in areas with a large number of immigrants, either from poor areas abroad or from inside the country itself. The local party leaders often come from these socially disadvantaged groups, with second generation, upwardly mobile individuals providing a major source of machine personnel.

But the key factor to any political machine's success is its ability to grant rewards to its friends. Patronage is important to party workers not only for the material benefits received but also for the social recognition gained, particularly by those sensitive about their ethnic or working-class origins. Even the individual voter benefits from

John Munro, about twelve (Hamilton Public Library).

his loyalty to the party organization, particularly receiving help in his problems with government bureaucracy. In this way the machine is a service organization providing for the needs of both party workers and voters. Because of its importance to the success of the Munro Machine it is necessary first to understand the patronage system.

WHERE THE POWER COMES FROM

Patronage has been a part of Canadian federal politics from its very beginnings but as long ago as Laurier's era the system of regional responsibility emerged.[1] Regional responsibility really means control over patronage appointments, the distribution of federal business contracts without competitive bidding and the making of regionally specific policy decisions, mainly the granting of federal money for public works in a geographical area. Although the prime minister or cabinet minister functionally responsible for a specific administrative area makes announcements of the sort listed above, cabinet ministers have gained control over federal government activity in their regional area. In recent years an attempt has been made to reduce the regional power of

Munro in college politics (Hamilton Public Library).

cabinet ministers and to increase the power of the Liberal Party organization. Three-person advisory groups, composed of cabinet ministers, Liberal caucus representatives and representatives of the party organization, have been set up to give advice on federal regional decisions.[2] It would appear, however, that cabinet ministers have retained the lion's share of power.

In most provinces one cabinet minister has been put in control. In a large province such as Ontario one cabinet minister used to be put in overall control, but because of the vast size of the province three or four regional ministers became involved. In recent times, because of the growth of Ontario's population, the complexity of modern society and the difficulty of producing Liberal majorities since 1957, all cabinet ministers from Ontario have had some regional responsibilities. In this role the cabinet ministers are called political general managers and each minister is assigned a set of federal constituencies to manage politically. By tradition, each federal cabinet minister from Ontario has had a great deal of autonomy.

As a federal cabinet minister, John Munro's responsibilities not only covered the Hamilton-Wentworth-Burlington areas but also the Niagara Peninsula and possibly Cambridge. Altogether he was responsible for fourteen ridings. Although the Norfolk-Haldimand and Brantford areas were not his direct responsibility, some of the key patronage positions based in Hamilton covered all or most of these areas. For example, the chairmen of the local boards of appeals for the Unemployment Insurance Commission are appointed by the federal cabinet. The Hamilton boards have responsibility over a five-county area and they include such cities as Oakville, Brantford and Port Dover. As well, federal citizenship court judges based in Hamilton have responsibilities in St. Catharines, Welland, Waterloo, Milton and Niagara Falls.

Much of John Munro's political clout in Hamilton since 1968, the year he was appointed a cabinet minister, has stemmed from his ability to hand out these various types of patronage positions. After all, political favours are the reward for faithful party workers. Patronage is the grease that lubricates the political machine.

PATRONAGE FOR THE BIG PEOPLE

On July 1, 1974 *The Globe and Mail* published one of the most remarkable stories on political patronage that has ever come to light in this country. In an attempt to clear his name in the Hamilton Harbour scandal that had broken just days before, John Munro made public his files so that the press could be "the people's jury" and judge his involvement in the affair. Unknown to the minister, the papers contained information about contributions to Munro's campaigns and appointments that he had made or recommended. *The Globe* reporters, Jonathan Manthorpe and Peter Moon, analysed the documents and published their findings.

Summing up, the journalists wrote:

More than half the people on a list of recent federal appointees in the Hamilton area drawn up by the riding association of Labour Minister John Munro have also worked for his political organization or given him campaign funds. The list contains 98 names and 52 of them also appear on other confidential political documents as financial distributors or Liberal Party workers.[3]

Here are a few examples. Mr. Dennis O'Leary, a Hamilton lawyer, was appointed by the federal government to the Ontario Supreme Court in 1973. O'Leary had been a member of the Hamilton Mountain Federal Liberal Riding Association, was a former Liberal candidate, and appeared on another list as a contributor of $500 to John Munro's 1972 campaign.

Mr. F.J. Weatherstone, a prominent Hamilton lawyer, gave $500 to Munro's campaign and his law firm gave another $500. On one occasion he ran provincially for the Liberal Party and was a dedicated party worker. In December 1973, he was appointed to the Ontario Supreme Court.

Ed Tharen, later appointed to be the chairman of the Hamilton Harbour Commission, contributed $1000 to the 1972 campaign. He was also, at one

John Munro the lawyer. (Hamilton Public Library).

time, president of the Hamilton Federal Liberal Party.

John G. Langs, described by Munro in a letter as an "elder statesman of the Liberal Party" in Hamilton and one of the principal fund raisers for the party, was appointed director of the Bank of Canada. Langs personally gave $4500 to Munro's 1972 campaign and an entry under his law firm came to a total of $7500. Although the documents did not make clear where this money came from, it is likely that a substantial proportion of it was collected from other people.

Michael Lypka, who was on Munro's finance committee and personally donated $500, was reappointed a director of the CBC.

W. J. Cheeseman, president of Westinghouse Canada Limited, was made both a member of the Science Council and the Defence Research Board. Westinghouse donated $2500 to the 1972 campaign.

The list goes on to mention Munro campaign workers and contributors who were appointed to such groups as the Medical Research Council. Six people from the organization were appointed as arbitrators in labour disputes between the federal government and the unions working for it. Munro even attempted, unsuccessfully as it turned out, to get one of his supporters onto the National Parole Board.

Perhaps even more important for the functioning of Munro's political machine were the lists of people who received lower-level political appointments. The article reported that some forty-three names of Hamilton and area lawyers appeared on Munro's appointment list as having worked for the government, associated with for example, the Veterans' Land Act, the Central Mortgage and Housing Corporation or functioning as Crown drug prosecutors. Of these, eleven appeared on the confidential lists of donors of campaign funds in 1972, others appeared in connection with a testimonial dinner given for Munro and still more appeared in his campaign organization. In all, thirty of the forty-three lawyers appeared elsewhere in the documents.

Even though *The Globe and Mail* article showed the range of appointments that John Munro has made or influenced, they represented only a fraction of the positions he has filled over the years. In the decade that he was a federal cabinet minister, several Hamilton lawyers were given judgeships. Added to this there have been a number of Citizenship Court judges who were appointed in the area, unemployment insurance referees, and Hamilton Harbour Commissioners. Munro had a hand in appointing every one of them.

Previously these people manned the key Liberal offices in the Hamilton area. Some ran for legislative seats, raised campaign funds and organized election campaigns. Others held such offices as president and vice-president of constituency riding associations. Finally, some of these individuals not only raised campaign funds but gave, out of their own pockets as well as on behalf of their law firms, large contributions to John Munro's election expenses.

Over the years other evidence has come to light illustrating the broad powers of a federal cabinet minister and the way John Munro has used them to develop his personal political machine. In 1972 Flaherty Manufacturing, owned by Peter Flaherty, a one-time campaign manager of John Munro, received a $40,000 contract for lapel buttons from the federal department of Health and Welfare. At this time Munro was the minister of the department. It was later revealed that no tenders were ever called on the contract. (For a fuller description of this incident, see in Part III, "Hamilton Harbour: Politics, patronage and cover-up".) Flaherty was later appointed a member of the Hamilton Harbour Commission.

Similarly, it was learned in 1974 that the Department of Labour, while Munro was the minister, gave a contract to the firm of Price, Rubin and Partners Incorporated of Toronto worth $250,000, with a built-in fee of $42,000 for the company. This was an advertising contract and it is well known that almost every level of government in Canada uses political patronage in selecting firms to handle these accounts. Jack Pelech, Munro's law partner at the time and a campaign contributor, was on the board of Price Rubin, and the president, Jack Price, had also contributed money to Munro's campaigns.[4]

The scandal around the CMHC project called York Place on Queen Street North also involved people close to John Munro. It is not known how much the minister was involved in the early stages of this development, but it is known that he sent one of his executives assistants, Ephraim Jonah, to make enquiries of CMHC, a federal agency, to see if they would increase the mortgage. Dominic Morganti, the developer, had donated $1000 to Munro's 1972 campaign and Morganti's lawyer was the minister's law partner and close associate Jack Pelech. (Morganti was subsequently convicted on a criminal charge of bribing a civil servant in relation to his dealings on this project, and further charges are pending.)

There can be little doubt that these few examples represent only a fraction of the patronage given out by powerful federal officials. Much of political life is not open to public scrutiny and decisions of this type particularly are closely guarded secrets. If these incidents are any indication, however, patronage must be a very strong motivation for many people to support politicians with the power to dole out such favours. It is not surprising that there are a number of people, particularly lawyers and businessmen, who are willing to work long and hard for the Munro Machine.

All of this does not imply that the people who were appointed to these positions and the firms selected for certain jobs were not competent or deserving. Many of these individuals have contributed a great deal to various aspects of community life. What should not be missed, however, is the important fact that all of these people have been members of the Liberal Party.

For the most part the key organizers in Munro's machine are personally recruited by Munro himself. He is always on the lookout for potential talent to add to his stable of active followers and shows not the least hesitancy in asking people to work for him. In this way he can carefully control the selection of people to key posts in his organization. Party workers do not volunteer or run for a position in the machine; they are selected for positions.

The lawyers particularly are valuable to the Munro organization. Many are second-generation immigrants from a variety of ethnic groups who speak more than one language. Since they have excellent political skills, important ethnic connections and a willingness to work extremely hard, the rewards of party work are most available to them. There is no doubt that the promise of federal patronage is a particularly strong incentive for these people. Without it Munro would not have the campaign funds and could not get the same quality and number of professional people to make his organization a success.

John Munro demands a great deal from his top people. Often they are called in the middle of the night, and on a moment's notice must drop what they are doing to perform some urgent political task. They put in hours of dedicated work on their own time, collecting campaign funds, running the organization and doing political favours for constituents, but the rewards for their efforts are generous. For the businessman there is always the possibility of government contracts and for a young lawyer struggling to establish a practice, a steady income from CMHC, crown legal work, or government labour arbitration can be welcome.

The extent of the patronage system in Canada is rarely recognized, and this is very much to the benefit of those who dominate political life. Perhaps it was for this reason that John Munro initially panicked when he learned that *The Globe and Mail* intended to write a story about the way he used patronage. "Oh gee," he was reported as saying, "you are going to put that [the appointments] in with the amounts [of donations] next to them? I think I should resign and force a by-election or something — I am finished."[5]

The next day, however, he had collected himself and in a press conference he counter-attacked by saying:

"Of course there's patronage, and you know it and everyone knows it. Is it wrong to favour a past political supporter over someone else if the two have equal ability? Of course it isn't." The voters of Hamilton East must have agreed with him because in the election a few days later Munro was easily returned.

PATRONAGE FOR THE LITTLE PEOPLE

Patronage not only motivates the top people of the Munro Machine, but is also provided to constituents in the form of services that bind them in political loyalty to John Munro. Hamilton East has a large number of disadvantaged people. It is a riding where two-thirds of the working males are in working-class occupations (many employed by the local steel mills, Stelco and Dofasco) and where over half the adult population has no secondary schooling. There are also a large number of immigrants for whom English-speaking Ontario is still an alien land. These people are outside the realm of political power, a fact they recognize all too well. Because they are politically and socially insecure, they are deeply impressed by the federal politician in their midst. Their personal relationship with a friendly power-holder such as John Munro cannot help but make them feel that this association lends them some political significance as well.

Over a third of Hamilton East's population is made up of Eastern and Southern Europeans and French-speaking immigrants from Quebec. Many of these people come from areas where individual government decisions are arbitrary and personalized. The practice of even-handed justice is unknown. Government officials in their home countries are often inefficient and corrupt and the routine handling of government business is done on the basis of extra-legal criteria. For example, to a newly arrived working-class Italian immigrant from Southern Italy or Sicily, the fact that the federal government sends out tax refunds can be amazing. In his experience government officials only take money, never giving it out except to the politically powerful. Little wonder then, that these people have virtually no trust in career government officials whose job it is to help them with their problems.

The partisan political atmosphere of Hamilton East gives people of foreign background very little choice in political matters. The New Democrats and Conservatives are overwhelmingly English in language and culture, but the Liberal organization of John Munro makes a major effort to court the various ethnic communities. The immigrant groups realize that the Liberal Party is the dominant federal party and that it is the federal government which controls immigration and citizenship procedures. If the immigrant wants to become a Canadian citizen, he may be interviewed by a Munro-appointed Citizenship Court judge. If he has trouble with the law, the judge he appears before may be a former Munro worker. And if the ethnic worker has a dispute with the Unemployment Insurance Commission and goes to the referees on the Board of Appeals, the chairman of the board may be a Munro party worker.

But the Munro Machine does more than provide government appointees who are sympathetic to the problems of constituents. It also meets many of the people's immediate needs. The organization provides tangible services to individuals, the most significant of which is its ability to help them cut through the bureaucratic red tape of government services, especially in the social security and welfare fields. People who have successfully dealt with these offices after intervention from Munro credit him rather than governmental procedures in helping their case.

This confusion of Munro's individual power with government structures has helped Munro to get re-elected. Since the language of the government is primarily English, the intervention of bilingual Munro workers is an invaluable aid to Hamilton East ethnic constituents. For the elderly who are baffled by complex tax and pension forms, the services of the Munro worker can produce the appropriate cheques. And if problems arise with law-enforcement officials, some free legal help, especially in minor, routine matters, may come from the lawyers in the constituency organization. As a consequence, many constituents credit John Munro with these services and do not readily see the greater power of the system which provides their benefits through government social security programs.

A particularly important economic service which touches the very heart of working-class life is employment. Many of Munro's constituents are at one time or another unemployed; even if they are employed, they may be looking for a better job. Not only are good permanent jobs a problem, but so are summer jobs for students. A Munro worker can often help. The service is especially appreciated by ethnic groups who expect to experience discrimination. Throughout the 1950s it was not uncommon for personnel directors in some large Hamilton firms to tell an inquiring applicant of Southern or Eastern European origins that the firm did not hire people of his background. Since such a frank admission of prejudice is no longer legally permissible, ethnic discrimination in employment is not practiced openly, but even now when immigrants get jobs in Anglo-Saxon firms they are usually given the most boring, the dirtiest, the most dangerous and the lowest paying jobs. And to make matters even worse, they are also subject to the highest amount of job insecurity. It is no wonder they are grateful for the employment agency function of the Munro organization.

By providing these types of services to constituents the Munro Machine has been able to exploit effectively the severe problems of the working-class immigrant population that makes up a large part of Hamilton East. Munro gains the long-term support and loyalty of many people simply by making use of the failings of the formal governmental structures and bureaucracy.

John Munro as the young Hamilton Alderman (Hamilton Public Library).

THE MACHINE AT WORK

The main objective of the machine is to return its patron John Munro to parliament in every election, but this in itself is not a simple matter. The organizers are aware that if they are to be assured of success they must involve as many people as possible in a well co-ordinated effort that will convince the maximum number of voters of Hamilton East to support their candidate and deliver the voters to the polls on election day. It is in this part of its work that the Munro organization excels.

Election day brings the political machine to a climax of activity. The basic unit of a constituency is the polling division, of which there are 150 in Hamilton East. In charge of each polling division is the poll captain. Under the poll captain is the enumerator, a poorly paid patronage position, who helps establish the list of electors in the polling division. Either the enumerator or poll captain or both (it may sometimes be the same person) canvasses the polling division for the organization during the campaign. On election day the poll organization is often more elaborate. Another machine-appointed government official heads the unit, the deputy returning officer. If the voting occurs in a private home, the owner, usually part of the Munro organization, receives a fee from the government. There is an inside scrutineer who keeps track of which electors have voted, keeping a close eye on whether known or likely Munro supporters, as determined from the campaign canvasses or organization records, have voted. This information is passed on from time to time to the outside scrutineer who calls on likely Munro voters to get them to cast their ballot. The elderly or feeble are offered car transportation, while for women with young children, a baby-sitter may be provided. The obvious goal of this elaborate polling division organization is to get out every possible Munro vote.

The permanent nature of the machine is underscored by the fact that the planning for the next federal election campaign begins the day after the last one ends. At this time estimates are made of the quantity and quality of work done by the various party workers during the campaign. Enumerators who did not do the expected amount of election work are dropped from the list of future enumerators. Poll captains who did not produce the expected number of Munro votes are demoted or dropped and replaced by enumerators who demonstrated campaign effectiveness. Captains who produce what was expected of them or more are kept on, while especially effective poll captains may be promoted to area supervisors if openings are available. The area supervisor is in charge of several poll captains. Some of the area supervisors may also hold posts at a higher level within the organization, for example, members of the riding executive or other riding committees. A typical pattern of promotion may be from enumerator to poll captain to area supervisor to other high posts within the organization. While it is true that a number of people may hold more than one organizational position, during the campaign the organization produces a concerted effort from several hundred people.

Immigrants have their votes solicited in their own language by canvassers from their own group (ethnic committees) who usually include a socially prominent member of that ethnic group. They are bombarded with literature and radio broadcasts in their native language praising the virtues of John Munro. The highlight of the Munro ethnic campaign is usually a series of rallies held in locations associated with particular ethnic groups, such as church halls and restaurants. A nationally known member of the particular community is the main speaker, and this person is sure to tell the assembled how important it is for the group to be represented by John Munro. In the 1974 election, the Italians, French, Ukrainians and Polish received this kind of special attention.

Other functional committees handle such tasks as planning basic political strategy, collecting and spending money, planning social events and constituency meetings, and attempting to attract union support. Another important election activity is putting up campaign signs. The sign crew, with its material loaded on a truck, goes into action as soon as an election is called. This group has a list of sign locations from the last campaign, revised to take into account the residential moves of Munro supporters. This sign crew arrives at a home and if they bother to talk to one of the occupants, they will usually say that John Munro wants to put a sign on their house, lawn or in their window, whatever is most appropriate. Within twenty-four hours of an election call the riding is blanketed with Munro signs. The sign crew ensures the quick replacement of any Munro signs removed and the addition of new ones as canvassers discover new recruits. Munro signs are counted periodically during the campaign.

A more impressive feature of this methodical organization is its record-keeping. Besides the records kept on the workers in the constituency association, systematic records are kept on the constituents over time and on the state of the campaign during election periods. Two major files list all favours done by John Munro and his organization for people, and all services performed by individuals for the association, with the appropriate dates.

The Munro organization is highly successful because it has so methodically penetrated the local community and individual neighbourhoods. Not only does the machine provide services, it solicits business. If someone moves into Hamilton East, the poll captain arrives before all the household furnishings are unpacked and asks whether he (representing John Munro) can help with any problems the new residents may have. Not only is Munro's presence immediately felt but the organization is hoping to set up political obligations. Like a "friendly" loan company, its main objective is to put the client in debt. The "payments" begin at least by the first day of the election campaign when the resident is asked to take a Munro sign, attend a Munro meeting, work for Munro and then cast a vote for Munro. This is the politics of reciprocal personal obligations: rather than something remote and abstract to be decided on the basis of party, party leader or public issues, politics has to do with specific and immediate personal desires and needs in Hamilton East. Voters often need help with the government and Munro needs votes and workers.

In fact the poll captain studiously avoids talking politics between elections. During these times the machine's representative is interested in the individual and his problems. Politics only becomes the topic of conversation during the campaign. The strength of the poll captain is that he builds up a

Munro in the parliamentary library
(Hamilton Public Library).

social and seemingly non-political bond with the voter before the campaign. Then when he calls in his political debts at election time it is hard for a voter to say no to a "friend."

The only explicitly political aspect of Munro's organization between campaigns for the ordinary voter is the annual constituency meeting, which is more of a social than a political event. In the 1970s the rank and file membership of the Hamilton East Liberal Association exceeded one thousand and, at times, over half of these members could be counted on to attend the annual meeting. The meeting usually takes place in an ethnic hall and the business transpires quickly. A short policy speech by "the Minister," formal recognition of important Liberal dignitaries in the audience, such as other area Liberal MPs, Liberal aldermen and the former Liberal mayor of Hamilton, Vic Copps, are a routine part of the meeting. The warmest applause comes when John Munro formally acknowledges his mother. Then after the "election" of riding officers and key committee members (a quick formality), the social part of the evening begins, usually including a dance or at least a cash bar.

As one drifts around the hall, one can hear

John Munro electioneering at the plant gates
(Hamilton Public Library).

at least a dozen non-English languages spoken. One can also notice that many individuals have tags on their clothes indicating they are poll captains of specific areas. And added to all this is the sheer diversity of people in the smoke-filled hall: middle-aged men in expensive suits, attractive young secretaries, smiling students, elderly men and women, and immigrant workers in clean but long out-of-style suits without ties, cap in hand. Diverse groups of people such as these become an efficient political army around the man at centre stage, John Carr Munro.

CLASS AND ETHNICITY

Since Hamilton East is largely a working-class district it is puzzling why the New Democratic Party, with its clear appeal to this section of the population and its alliance with working-class organizations, has done so poorly in federal elections in the riding. Historically, left-wing parties have had strong support in the area. As early as the provincial election of 1883, a labour candidate in Hamilton East won over 20% of the vote. In the provincial election of 1902, Hamilton East produced the first Socialist candidate, L. M. Gordon. The real left-wing breakthrough came about in 1906, when Labour candidate Allan Studholme was elected. The constituency was held by the Independent Labour Party until the incumbent, George B. Halcrow, was ousted by John Munro's grandfather, Leeming Carr, in 1923.

By 1934, the provincial riding had returned to labour by electing Samuel Lawrence, the candidate for the Co-operative Commonwealth Federation (CCF). His tenure in provincial office ended with the Hepburn Liberal landslide of 1937. The CCF got back into power in 1943, lost in 1945, won again in 1948 only to be defeated again in 1951 and 1955. Since 1959, however, the CCF-NDP has been in firm control of Hamilton East provincially. There have also been, over the years, a number of other working-class candidates under various labels such as Soldier-Labour, Communist, Labour-Socialist, Socialist-Labour, Independent-Labour, Labour Progressive and Labour Progressive Party. One can add to these numerous municipal victories of working-class candidates over the years in the Hamilton East area, so that the traditional popularity of labour candidates can easily be demonstrated.

Since John Munro was first elected in 1962 his major opposition has been the New Democratic Party, but they have been unable to mount a serious challenge. One reason for this is that the NDP in the area is very badly divided and poorly organized. The party's permanent organization follows provincial ridings, so that for every federal election the Hamilton East organization has to be reconstituted out of the two provincial NDP associations of Hamilton East and Hamilton Centre. For many years a bitter feud has divided the leaders of these two associations into rival camps who find any form of co-operation very difficult. As a consequence of this, the federal NDP effort in Hamilton East has been very weak and in the last four federal elections Munro has faced four different candidates.

However, the real reason why the Munro Machine is so successful is that it has played down the importance of class differences and has worked hard to gain the support of ethnic voters. Class structure is an important factor in politics and it is essential for Munro that it does not become a liability. The Conservatives have a clear-cut middle-class orientation while the New Democratic Party, backed by a number of important unions, projects itself as the defender of the working class. This class cleavage is most salient to the population with a British background but if it were to spread to the ethnic groups it could wreck the Munro organization.

Munro and his chief lieutenants project an image as friends to all, rich and poor, businessman and trade unionist alike. Their dilemma is clear:

Tom Cherington, one of Hamilton's best known media personalities, talking about John Munro on CHCH/TV news (Hamilton Public Library).

for continued success they need the votes of the workers and their families, campaign contributions from the business and professional community, and party organizational work from both. Munro's organization deliberately attempts to play down the class tensions in society, arguing that class is not an appropriate way to understand society. Their ideology is that people can improve their economic conditions through their own efforts and that when they have temporary economic problems not of their own making, help from the Munro organization is just a phone call away. Economic problems are individual and personal; present government policies are inadequate to provide the basic economic protection that everyone needs.

Sometimes, however, the Munro Machine will adopt a pro-labour stance, a position which is more symbolic than substantive. If there is an important strike going on in the constituency, especially during an election campaign, as happened with the Firestone strike in 1972, Munro and his workers will make sympathetic statements on the strikers' plight that have no tangible effect on the course of the strike itself. Munro is fond of saying that the trade union movement should have input into the governmental process yet he carefully avoids endorsing the concrete, specific goals of the labour movement. For these reasons, most of the major trade union leaders in the city have refrained from supporting John Munro. They want politicians who will speak clearly for them in the government, without trying to reconcile workers' aims with business policies: union leaders want political spokesmen, not brokers of diverse interests.

Clearly, Munro's connection with the labour movement presents a great opportunity, yet it is fraught with many difficulties. If John Munro were able to detach the trade union organizations from the NDP and move them into the Liberal Party, he would accomplish a Liberal goal unfulfilled since the time of Laurier. As early as 1963 he attempted to develop support from labour, and went as far as to set up a Liberal-Labour group in the city to attract dissident unionists.[7] The problem with this strategy, however, was that Munro ran the risk of alienating the upper-middle-class professionals and businessmen who have given him so much support in the past.

This issue is far from settled. Some Munro lieutenants believe that labour must be weaned away from the NDP. Although the labour-NDP alliance has not been successful in the past there are those in the organization who still fear that this opposition coalition is potentially too powerful to be left alone. Others are satisfied with the string of Munro victories; their strategy is to cultivate assiduously the traditional support base of John Munro.

The basic strategy of the machine still remains to downplay class and to emphasize continued ethnic solidarity. While the NDP and the Conservatives remain primarily Anglo-Saxon organizations, the Munro Liberals attract people from every imaginable ethnic group in the area. Electorally this has paid handsome dividends. In an election when the Liberals are relatively unpopular, as in 1972, Munro can count on a little less than one-third of the vote from voters of British background. When majorities from the various ethnic groups are counted a Munro victory is produced. Of course, when the Liberal fortunes are up, as in 1974, Munro receives a larger proportion of the vote across the board and can get a clear majority of the vote despite the fact there are two major parties opposing him.

Should class conflict set in among people of non-English-Canadian background, even to the extent that Munro would have his ethnic majorities reduced to pluralities, then he could come dangerously close to losing in a period when the Liberals are unpopular. For this reason the ethnic lieutenants in the organization are very important. They must keep a close hold on the different groups and pay special attention to the ethnic workers. Otherwise, the latter may seek help from union officials who will encourage a class vote for the NDP.

POWER AT WORK

A 1968 *Globe and Mail* article, summarizing the qualities in John Munro that would lead to his rise in federal politics, said "Munro is every inch a politician. Politics is his occupation, vocation, and recreation. He has no outside interests... and no inclination to do anything except practice the art of politics in his own rough and tumble fashion."[8] In the more than ten years since those words were written little has changed. Munro remains a fiercely ambitious man who has created an organization loyal to himself, rather than the Liberal Party, in order to achieve his ambitions.

If personal ambition is the motivating force for the patron the same is true for those working within his organization. For businessmen the rewards are the possibilities of government contracts; the lawyers find substantial profit in the patronage that is given to those willing to dedicate themselves to hard work; and even ordinary voters find personal advantages in supporting John Munro. For these people politics is not a struggle to achieve some abstract ideological goal; it is a way of receiving tangible rewards.

A political machine of this type represents a set of reciprocal relationships between the political boss and his workers and constituents. The politician receives money to run his campaign, willing and dedicated campaign workers, and votes at election time; in return he gives patronage in the form of appointed positions, a variety of different types of grants, and services to the constituents.

The fact that John Munro tried to intervene in the judicial process on behalf of Julius Butty is not surprising. He was simply providing services for one of his supporters as he had so often done in the past. It is also not surprising that Hamiltonians should have been astounded that Munro was forced to resign over the incident. They have long grown accustomed to their most powerful federal politician providing services of this kind.

The resignation of Munro from the cabinet was potentially disastrous for his organization. With Munro cut off from his power to distribute significant patronage, would it be difficult to motivate people to perform all the chores necessary for the smooth running of an effective machine? Apparently not, in the 1979 election campaign. Again Munro's people were hard at work, putting out signs, canvassing households, and getting out the vote. Supporters believed the rumours that their patron's absence from the cabinet was only temporary and that soon it would be business as usual. Election day saw him re-elected with a comfortable majority, the only Liberal from the Hamilton area.

The defeat of the Liberal Party in the 1979 election, however, may prove more of a threat to the machine than Munro's resignation from the cabinet. It is difficult to see how an organization nurtured almost solely on the ability of the patron to distribute the rewards of office can survive once this power has been cut off. Only the future will tell whether Munro can find new ways to motivate his followers but clearly the organization must be radically revamped if it is to continue to deliver its impressive string of electoral successes. No matter what happens in the future, for ten years the Munro Machine was a truly remarkable organization. It is hard to believe that anyone will easily replace John Carr Munro in Hamilton's political life.

1. For a good description of the federal Liberal pattern of assigning regional political responsibilities to specific senior cabinet ministers see W. A. Matheson, *The Prime Minister and the Cabinet* (Toronto: Methuen, 1976) pp. 205–211.

2. A good description of this process can be found in Robert Jackson and Michael Atkinson, *The Canadian Legislative System: Politicians and Policy-Making* (Toronto: Macmillan of Canada/1974) p. 46 and Matheson, p. 210.

3. *The Globe and Mail,* 1 July 1974, pp. 1–2.

4. *The Hamilton Spectator,* 20 December 1974.

5. *The Globe and Mail,* 1 July 1974.

6. *The Globe and Mail,* 2 July 1974.

7. The earliest record of this strategy to woo the trade unions into the Liberal Party is a *Spectator* article of 24 January 1963. By 1966 this was an active policy of Munro and his group. In that year he edited a monthly Liberal newsletter aimed at influencing Canada's labour elite and 5000 copies were distributed (*The Hamilton Spectator,* 28 July 1966). At about the same time he tried to ally himself with the members of the Autonomy Group, a nationalist rank-and-file group operating within Local 1005 of the Steelworkers. The leaders of this group had been suspended from union activities and Munro offered them legal help, but ultimately they refused. This strategy to try to win the alliance of labour to the Liberals for Munro relates not only to his attempts to hold onto Hamilton East and influence other Hamilton ridings but also to his ambitions as a contender for national leadership of the Liberal Party. If he were to succeed and the Liberals won the support of labour there is no doubt that he would be viewed as a possible future leader of the party and prime minister of the country.

8. *The Globe and Mail,* 22 April 1968.

The Hamilton Mob and the politics of organized crime

Bill Freeman

From 1975 to 1977 the Quebec Police Commission inquiry into organized crime heard from witnesses who described how the underworld in that province operates. Their testimony detailed how the Mafia, or Cosa Nostra as it is sometimes called, imports narcotics, controls gambling and loan sharking, operates prostitution rings, launders money, infiltrates legitimate business and influences politicians. The relationships among the Montreal Mafia and the families in other parts of Canada and the United States, and the complex chain of command through which the organization is administered were revealed.

The reaction in Ontario and the rest of Canada was to ignore the importance of the findings of the Commission or to claim that they had no relevance for other parts of the country. Federal Justice Minister Ron Basford, on June 13, 1977 said that a Royal Commission into organized crime in Canada was not justified. "Such enquiries were best conducted by provincial attorney generals who are responsible for administering the criminal code."[1] The position taken by the federal government denies the evidence, which points to the national and international aspects of organized crime. It also ignores the fact that the RCMP has exclusive jurisdiction over narcotics enforcement, one of the major rackets of the Mafia. In fact, the federal force has long claimed that it alone should be given responsibility for dealing with organized crime in Canada.

Ontario's Attorney General, Roy McMurtry, following a long tradition set by his predecessors, on February 2, 1977 ruled out a public enquiry into organized crime in the province because he claimed it would interfere with ongoing investigations. As recently as November 2, 1976 he even told *The Globe and Mail* that "loose associations of criminals operate in Ontario" but that he did not think they had a Mafia structure.

It is difficult to know whether Canadian politicians outside Quebec make these statements out of simple ignorance or from a desire to cover up the activities of organized crime. The evidence is overwhelming that the Mafia has operated for years in Canada and that year by year it grows stronger and more prosperous, assuming increasing control over public life. Statements claiming that the Mafia is weak or non-existent allay the fears of the public while aiding organized crime. Nothing contributes more to their power, in the long run, than being ignored by public officials.

Hamilton public figures have also followed this policy of denial and yet there are few places in all of North America where the Mafia operates more openly. In 1963 the then-head of the police commission, Magistrate Walter Tuchtie, stated categorically that organized crime did not exist in Hamilton or any part of Canada;[2] in 1970 Police Chief Lawrence declined to talk about organized crime in the city.[3] In the political life of the city no one mentions the Mafia, and not once since the days of prohibition has the existence of organized crime become a political issue.

Those who are wise in the city's street life are amused by this situation. The fact is that "the Mob" is a permanent organization that has existed in Hamilton since the beginnings of Prohibition. Since the Second World War the Mafia has become increasingly large and complex so that today it operates a huge illegal empire almost with impunity.

PROHIBITION AND THE ROCCO PERRI GANG

Organized crime as it is known in Hamilton began with Prohibition. In 1916 the Ontario government, with support from the powerful Temperance Movement, forbade the sale of liquor, supposedly in an attempt to increase productivity for the war effort. When the United States began its Prohibition on January 16, 1920, virtually the entire North American continent was dry. In spite of the legislation, the production of alcohol in the province boomed. In total six distilleries and twenty-nine breweries continued in operation in Ontario throughout the entire Prohibition era and sales were at an all-time high.[4]

During Prohibition it was quite legal in Canada to produce spirits for the export trade. Permits were given to distilleries and breweries and the alcohol was openly transported by rail and truck to docks in places like Hamilton and Windsor. There it was loaded aboard boats destined for places where spirits could still be legally consumed, such as the Caribbean islands or the French islands of St. Pierre and Miquelon in the St. Lawrence.

It was then that the bootleggers took over. While Prohibition lasted in Ontario, from 1916 to 1925, fast boats would leave docks like the ones in Hamilton, sail out into the lake and then, under cover of darkness, come back into shore to rendezvous with trucks and souped-up cars. These vehicles had special compartments under the seats, hood and luggage sections where up to 250 gallons of alcohol could be stored.

Prohibition was in effect in the United States from 1920 to 1933. During this time Canadian liquor was in great demand because it was of bonded quality. Hamilton bootleggers would load up fast boats with legally manufactured alcohol and race across Lake Ontario to meet their American partners. The next morning they would be back in harbour — in spite of the export licence claiming that they had delivered the liquor thousands of miles away.

Prohibition made millions of dollars for people in Ontario daring enough to take the risks. Not

Rocco Perri, about 1925 (Hamilton Public Library).

long after Prohibition legislation was passed in 1916 the bootleggers had become well organized. One of the most powerful was Rocco Perri. For ten years he was the "king of the bootleggers," in the Toronto-Hamilton-Niagara region. He was Hamilton's Al Capone: as colourful, boastful and ruthless as any of the bootleggers who ran the liquor trade in the American cities in the 1920s.

Rocco Perri was born in Regio Calabria, Italy in 1890 and came to Canada via the United States in 1903.[5] He worked for a time in a Dundas stone quarry and later as a construction worker on the new Welland Canal. In 1912 Perri boarded in Toronto with a Jewish family by the name of Starkman. He became involved with Bessie Starkman, and soon they began living together in St. Catharines.

In 1913 a depression struck Canada and life was difficult for the young couple. Rocco did not have enough money for shoes and Bessie had nothing but tattered clothing. Just before the war broke out Perri worked for an Italian macaroni manufacturer in St. Catharines, and in 1915 things began to get better when the couple moved to Hamilton and opened a small grocery store on Hess Street North that specialized in Italian goods. Once prohibition started, in 1916, the Perri store became a bootleg joint where whiskey was sold for 50 cents a shot.

75

The rise to prosperity for Rocco and Bessie was remarkably swift. In 1920 they bought a huge house in Hamilton at 166 Bay Street South, and from there they ran one of the biggest bootlegging operations in the province. Perri had scores of men working for him, owned a fleet of fast boats and cars and is alleged to have bribed large numbers of police, politicians and customs officers.

Perri bragged that there was no violence in his organization, but people living near the lake, from Hamilton to St. Catharines, often heard the chatter of machine guns as the police tried to catch up with the bootleggers' fast boats. In 1924 there were two murders in Hamilton related to illicit trafficking in liquor: in November 1924 the body of Joseph Boytovich, a jitney driver, was found at Albion Mills, and in the same month Fred Genesse was found dead at the bottom of a cliff east of Stoney Creek.

These murders prompted Perri to give a remarkably candid interview to *The Toronto Star* on November 19, 1924. "While I admit that I am king of the bootleggers," he said, "I can assure you that I have nothing to do with these deaths ... I only give my men fast cars, and I sell only the best liquor, so I don't see why anyone should complain, for no one wants Prohibition." He was quoted as saying that his expenses for the previous year were $80,000, "so you can see I do a big business. Some days I handle 1000 cases for my customers and the very best families are my customers." The interview was a sensation that caused near riots at newsstands and by late in the day copies were selling for $2.00 each.

A group of Hamilton ministers was horrified at these confessions. They demanded Perri's deportation, but they were told by police that, "a boast is not proof of guilt. There must be sufficient evidence of the illegal sale of liquor before any action is taken."

It is not surprising that many came to feel that the "king of the bootleggers" had protection in powerful places. Perri spread his money around, often openly paying the fines of the men who worked for him. He was both a friend of Canada's "public enemy number one," Mickey MacDonald, and of cabinet ministers and powerful businessmen. He gave freely to charity, making donations to both Catholic and Protestant churches. Once he gave $30,000 to the "Drys" in their campaign on behalf of Prohibition. This was a sensible business decision since it was Prohibition legislation that kept him in business. He was a big spender and many Hamiltonians can still remember Rocco Perri digging into his pocket with a broad smile on his face to give them a big tip.

The Perris lived in a style that only the very wealthy could afford. They brought one of the first radios to Hamilton and had their house beautifully decorated. Rocco drove sporty cars, wore pork-pie hats, fashionable race-track outfits, hand-tailored business suits, and smoked expensive cigars. His wife Bessie dressed in beautiful gowns, and wore jewellery worth thousands of dollars on every-day occasions.

It is not surprising that they were able to live like this. Throughout much of Prohibition the Perris ran a tight organization that handled about 1000 cases of 60 proof whiskey a day, bought at $18 and sold at $80 a case. The profits in this operation were enormous.

However, by the mid 1920s things began to get more difficult for Perri and his gang. In 1925 35 people were thought to have died from alcohol poisoning in the Hamilton, Toronto, Oakville and Brantford areas and a Royal Commission was set up to study the problem. At that enquiry it was revealed that Rocco Perri, who called himself a "macaroni salesman" and an "export and mailorder businessman," in 1926 had only paid $13.30 in income tax. Bessie Perri was officially listed as supporting her husband and she paid $96.43 in taxes. Bank officials showed, however, that she had as much as $500,000 on deposit in eight Hamilton banks, and at one time had deposits totalling $945,000.

In 1928 the newspaper interview Perri had given to *The Toronto Star* landed him in jail for six months when he told a court that he had never given it. After Prohibition was ended in Ontario the Perri gang was forced to rely on the American market. This became more difficult after 1930, when Canada refused port clearance to suspected rumrunners. Four of Perri's men were convicted for manslaughter in the wood-alcohol poisoning of a number of people, and it was widely rumoured that the gang had been forced to branch out into the narcotics trade.

The climax of the lives of Rocco and Bessie Perri came suddenly on the night of August 13, 1930. The couple had been visiting the home of Perri's cousin in the city's North End and at about 11:00p.m. they drove home in their coupe. They came south along Bay Street, turned into the alley behind their home and maneuvered into the darkened garage. The couple got out on either side of the car when:

... the terrifying, deafening report of the first gun was heard. Perri screamed and lunged towards his wife. But the second gun was fired and by that time there was so much smoke in the garage that he could not see whether or not she had fallen. In terror he rushed for the garage door, and was in the doorway when the third shot was fired.[6]

Perri fled down the street "breathless and distraught" until he met a man out walking his dog. Then, after he had collected his courage, the two men went back to the garage and found the bleeding body of Bessie, still wearing thousands of dollars worth of jewellery, torn by two shotgun blasts fired at close range.

Clues to the murder were scanty. Police found discarded license plates and a carton containing nine unused shotgun shells a few blocks from the Perri home. The shells were creased so that they would scatter once they were fired. Altogether three shots had been released. Two of them had struck Bessie Perri.

An inquest found that Bessie had been killed "from gunshot wounds inflicted by a person or persons unknown." Rocco offered a $5000 reward for the arrest of the gunmen, but the murder was never solved. Speculation pointed towards some internal gangland war, and most thought that the real target was Rocco. Others claimed, however, that Bessie was the power behind the throne of the "king" and that the gunmen had hit the right target.

The funeral of Bessie Perri was an unprecedented spectacle for the citizens of Hamilton. The streets were lined solid along the route from Bay Street South to John and Arkeldun to the Olev Zedek Cemetery on the Caledonia highway. The service, held in the Perri home, was:

...interrupted several times by the noise of the huge crowd of people milling about the street in front of the house. The disturbance caused by the shouting throng, and the noise of the motor cars striving to force a passage through the crowd, caused the undertaker to come out and call for order from the verandah on two occasions. Verandahs in the neighbourhood were crowded with trespassers. Usually rational people invaded private property to stand on porch railings for a better view. The way for the funeral procession was cleared by motorcycle police. Because Bessie Perri was a Jewish woman who had left her husband for a man of another faith, she was buried on the fringe of sacred ground. At the cemetery, the milling about and the shoving were so great that it was feared some would be pushed into the grave as hundreds sought to catch a glimpse of the expensive [$3,000 silver-trimmed] casket and the sorrowing king of the bootleggers.[7]

With the death of his wife Perri fell on hard times. In 1932 police arrested two of his gang and sent them to jail for operating a 26,000 gallon distillery in the home of a former judge on Concession Street. A number of legal suits, said to be gambling debts, took much of Perri's money and in 1933 he spent ten days in jail for inability to pay a $20 car repair bill.

But soon he was back in the money again as head of a new bootlegging gang. From 1937 to 1939 he ran a private brewery on Fleet Street in Toronto, but was not once arrested for the offence. In 1938 he was important enough to have two attempts made on his life. On March 20, 1938 two or more sticks of dynamite were tossed under his front verandah. They blew up; however no one was injured. This may well have been a warning, because a second attempt was much more serious. On the night of November 23, Perri was seated in his car after a card game, talking to two friends who were standing on the sidewalk. When he switched on the lights and pressed the starter there was a tremendous explosion under the car which blew a three foot hole in the pavement and somersaulted the auto, tearing and twisting its body and setting the gas tank on fire. The two men standing on the sidewalk were seriously injured, but Rocco Perri was thrown clear, and, as other people came rushing to help, they found him unruffled, dusting off his pant cuffs.

When the war came Perri was interned in Petawawa detention camp as an enemy alien. (In spite of his wealth he had been unable to get Canadian citizenship) In 1943 he was released and he went to work in Toronto as a janitor in a Bloor Street theater. On April 23, 1944 he was in Hamilton visiting a cousin. He complained of a headache, took two aspirins and stepped out for a little air. He was never seen again. Some speculated that Perri had gone to Mexico, but an RCMP officer claimed that he was certain that Perri had been "taken for a ride." "Informed underworld sources had told him that Rocco was murdered, his body encased in cement, and dumped into Hamilton Bay."[8]

For the next two years violence wracked the Hamilton underworld as several factions struggled for control of organized crime in the Hamilton-Toronto-Buffalo area. Paul Doneff, a shoeshine parlor operator, disappeared a year after Perri. Soon after, John Durso, a restaurant owner, was reported missing. His car was later located in the Old Welland Canal near Thorold, but his body was never found. Louis Wernick, a narcotics runner from Buffalo, and a good friend of Rocco, was found in a snowbank at Toronto's Long Branch race track with five bullets in his body.

Rocco Perri's death appears to have been part of a series of killings that marked the end of the control of organized crime by the men who came to power in the days of Prohibition. They were replaced by a much more tightly knit group of criminals who brought a new style of organization to crime. It was the Italian Mafia who eliminated Perri and his associates and inherited his territory.

Although the era of the bootlegger may reflect a more colourful age, it would be wrong to think that organized crime during Prohibition was less ruthless than it is today. There were enormous profits to be made in bootlegging and people were willing to kill to get them. Although Perri was a big tipper to messenger boys, courteous to ladies, and always conscious of his public image, he was also believed to have been responsible for seventeen gangland murders and had the reputation of running a strictly disciplined operation.

Politically, Rocco Perri and his gang were relatively unsophisticated. The evidence indicates that payoffs were made to various officials, and it is likely that there were "contributions" to political

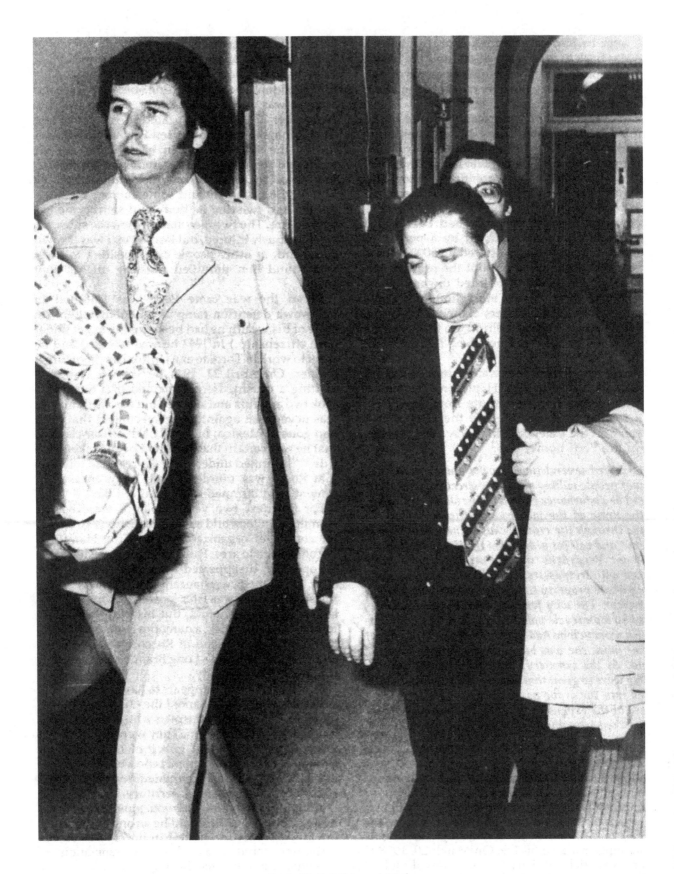

Paolo Violi (*Globe and Mail*).

groups other than the "Drys," but it does not appear that Rocco Perri systematically infiltrated the political process in order to achieve his objectives.

The main reason that there was not a sustained effort to stamp out bootlegging was that there was little public demand for this to be done. Prohibition legislation was not popular in the cities, and particularly in a working-class centre such as Hamilton. As a result, Rocco Perri and people like him were viewed more as colourful local characters than as the dangerous criminals they were.

The enormous profits from bootlegging gave organized crime in North America the opportunity to develop into the sophisticated organization known today. By the 1930s and 1940s the criminal gangs had organized themselves across the continent, co-ordinating their efforts to exploit the population. They had tremendous financial resources, considerable political power, and although bootlegging was quickly fading as the chief money maker, the legislators had left a variety of illegal activities which could be easily developed.

THE MAFIA AND JOHNNY PAPALIA

The Italian gangs that took over control of organized crime in the 1930s and 1940s in the United States and Canada were very different from the groups that operated during prohibition. The bootleggers usually ran loose organizations of criminals commanded by one person. Mafia gangs operate on a strict hierarchical chain of command, in which the decisions of the man at the top become law, but there are two levels within a Mafia organization. First, there is an inner circle of men surrounding the leader who are almost invariably of Sicilian background and usually interrelated by blood or a history of close family ties. It is this small group, probably no more than 5000 in all of North America and 500 in Canada, that is the real Mafia. Second, working for this group in a variety of different rackets are associates of virtually all ethnic groups, whose number have been estimated at somewhere around 50,000 in North America.[9]

There are real advantages to running illegal activities with a structure of that sort. The biggest problems facing all criminal gangs are secrecy and loyalty to the group. This distinction between an inner circle of Mafia figures who give absolute loyalty to the organization, and the outer circle of ordinary criminals who run the individual rackets, makes it difficult for the police to get much information on the overall operations of the organization. At best they can close up one racket run by the mob and possibly arrest one or two Mafia members, but they have never been able to destroy the whole organization. Even when top leaders are arrested other members are quickly moved in to take their place, and a lucrative racket is reopened soon after the police close it down. Of the twenty-four Mafia families said to be operating in North America, not one has been dismembered in the forty or more years of their existence.[10]

The Mafia group in Hamilton that eliminated Rocco Perri and his gang came to be called the "Three Dons" because it was led by three men. Tony Sylvestro was the best known of the group; another ran a real estate business as a front and the third owned race horses. All three men were first generation Italians who did not operate easily in an English-speaking milieu, but they commanded great respect and their power, particularly in the Hamilton area, was undisputed.

The "Three Dons" were the Ontario branch of the Magaddino family in Buffalo, and they took their orders directly from Don Stefano Magaddino. As bootlegging decreased in importance, the major rackets dominated by the Mafia were gambling, the narcotics trade, loan sharking, prostitution and extortion. The Mafia also became involved in legitimate business. The Hamilton Mob was involved in all of these rackets in the 1940s and 1950s, but it also controlled the heroin trade for the Ontario market by bringing the drug in from Buffalo.

The Hamilton group was the first sophisticated Mafia operation in Ontario, but it was not until the mid-1950s that it moved to take over organized crime in the entire province. The man who set out to do this was Hamilton-born John Papalia — or "Johnny Pops" as he is known on the street.[11]

Papalia's father, Anthony Papalia, emigrated from Italy to Hamilton in 1900 and raised his family of six boys and one girl on Railway Street in the city's low-income Italian neighbourhood. Anthony Papalia was involved in rum running and was a close associate of Tony Sylvestro. John, born in 1924, dropped out of school in eighth grade, dodged the draft in World War II, and became involved in petty theft, bootlegging and breaking and entering. He said that he operated out of an old ice house still standing on the corner of Railway and Mulberry Streets. It was at this time that he developed a reputation as a person who enjoyed the violent side of crime.

In 1949, when he was 25, Papalia was selling drugs in Toronto when police caught him with several capsules of heroin near Union Station. He was sentenced to Guelph Reformatory for two years less a day. In 1951, when he was released, he went to Montreal and worked for the powerful Galente organization as one of their enforcers. In these next four years Papalia completed his apprenticeship and was accepted as a full member of the Mafia.

When he arrived back in the Hamilton-Toronto area in 1955 Papalia already had good connections with the Mafia families in Buffalo, Montreal and New York, as well as blood and friendship ties with all of the important organized crime figures in Hamilton. He was only 5'8" tall, but he was a powerfully built man, intelligent, controlled, fearless and violent. The Mafia had decided to take over organized crime in Ontario and "Johnny Pops" was the man brought in to do the job.

At that time much of organized crime in Ontario was still independent. There were a number of gambling operations in Cooksville and Toronto making a large profit, and Papalia's first move was to go to each of the operators to tell them that he was going to take a cut of those profits.

The gamblers were powerful men in their own right, and they were determined that the Mafia would not control their operations. At the instigation of Max Bluestein, the biggest gambler in the province at the time, they arranged to have two men from Detroit come in to "rough up" Papalia. It did not work. When the Detroit enforcers discovered Papalia's connections with the Mafia families in Montreal, New York, Buffalo and Hamilton they immediately backed off and even lent their support to his move. Soon all the gambling operations in the Toronto-Hamilton area, with the exception of Max Bluestein's, were paying protection to Papalia. The Hamilton Mafia was well on its way to dominating the entire Ontario organized crime network.

That same year, 1955, Papalia began to branch out into a number of different operations. In 1949 an old friend, Danny Gasbarrini, had been given a sentence of seven years in Vancouver for conspiring to traffic in narcotics. He was released in 1955 and returned to Hamilton. Like Papalia he was well connected to the earlier generation of Mafia figures and had married the daughter of the old Don, Tony Sylvestro.

Gasbarrini and Papalia set up a gambling operation called the Porcupine Mines Social Club at fifteen and a half John Street North, just a block away from the city's Central Police Station. Years later Gasbarrini told the press: "For two years the police never bothered with us although they knew it was going on. But we never paid anyone off. It was just that we ran an honest game and had some of the best people in town coming to it." It was closed, he said, when the police "stopped looking the other way."[12] Why the police started looking in their direction is not known.

By 1958 Papalia had moved into Hamilton gambling operations in a big way. In July of that year a raid uncovered a large sports betting operation run by Red LeBarrie, Joe and Dominic Papalia, John's brothers, and Tony Pugliese, a brother-in-law. Later Angelo and Rocco Papalia, two other brothers, were implicated in Hamilton gambling.

In the same year Papalia became involved in legitimate business by starting Monarch Vending Machines, still located on Railway Street in Hamilton, and entering into partnership with another Mafia figure, Alberto Agueci, in setting up the Star Vending Machine Company in Toronto. Police later claimed that Papalia's vending machines were often put into the businesses of people who owed gambling debts and that store owners who would not accept the machines occasionally were threatened. Not long after these companies were set up a number of railway cars and transport trucks filled with cigarettes were hijacked. Police were certain that the goods ended up in Papalia's vending machines but could not prove it.[13]

In the late fifties loan sharking became another major activity of John Papalia and his associates. This particularly lucrative operation deals mainly in small loans to low-income people, but the profits are huge. The usual terms of the loan are that the borrower must repay $6.00 for every $5.00 borrowed within one week. These enormous rates of interest are often collected by violence. Victims have had their legs broken by baseball bats for debts of as little as $200. Papalia was rumoured to have become something of an expert in this field.

Extortion from businessmen who themselves were involved in shady business deals was another of Papalia's specialties. On one occasion he beat up a Toronto stock promoter with a blackjack in front of his secretary and a room full of customers. Similar things happened when Papalia went to collect gambling debts for the Mob. Often a businessman was faced with the choice of paying the debt immediately or signing a part of his business over to the Mob.

By 1958 Papalia was the most important organized crime figure in Ontario, and the Hamilton Mafia operated widely across the province. The one major operation that continued to be independent, however, was Max Bluestein's gambling organization in Toronto. Bluestein was a big man, who was known to be a daring and clever operator. By this time he was wealthy from his legitimate investments, but he still operated the biggest gambling operation in Ontario, with over 200 runners working for him. When the other gamblers in the province had capitulated to Papalia in 1955 Bluestein had resisted and was powerful enough to get away with it.

In January 1958 Bluestein was asked by Papalia to a meeting at the Westbury Hotel. When he got there he found representatives of all the Mafia families who had interests in Ontario, including people from the families in Montreal, New York, Buffalo and Detroit, as well as Papalia's Hamilton gang. He was given the message that he was to merge his operation with the Mafia gambling syndicate and give them a percentage of the take. Bluestein considered his options and refused.

The pressure on Bluestein to capitulate to the Mafia was intense over the next three years. There were police raids on his operations and in turn he gave information to the police on Papalia's gambling outlets. Finally, another meeting between the two parties was arranged on March 21, 1961 in the Town Tavern.

On that night over 100 people were in the popular Toronto dining spot. Most of them were Papalia's people, who had been invited especially to watch him intimidate the last major independent organized crime operation in the province. Both men came in and sat with their own circle of associates. After some time Papalia sent a waiter over to Bluestein's table with a drink. The Toronto gambler knew that if he accepted it, it would be a sign that he had agreed to become part of the Mafia's organization. If not, there would be open war.

Bluestein was well aware of the situation he was dealing with. Papalia was the most prominent Mafia figure in Ontario, and he was operating in conjunction with organized crime figures across the continent. It was a powerful organization that could not be resisted for long, but Bluestein had always been independent. He had come to discuss terms, not to capitulate, and he waved the drink away.

To Papalia this act of defiance was an insult that could not be tolerated. For much of the rest of the evening things went on as normal in the Town Tavern. Bluestein grew more confident, and his friends gradually drifted away when he assured them that he was safe. However, at 1:00 a. m., as Bluestein was about to leave, Papalia and six of his men suddenly confronted him at the door. Bluestein pulled a pocket knife and stabbed one of them six times, but iron bars swung on short ropes smashed his skull and cheek bones, brass knuckles gouged his face and eyes. When he fell to the floor a broken bottle was shoved into his mouth. The gambler was left unconscious in a pool of blood.

Over 100 people witnessed the beating, but they were held back from intervening by Papalia's men. The next day when police tried to find a witness no one would come forward. It was only after Pierre Berton wrote an article in *The Toronto Star* decrying the state of lawlessness in Toronto's supposedly peaceful streets that the police gave the incident any priority.

For a time after the Bluestein beating Papalia disappeared, but this new publicity seemed only to increase his notoriety and power. For the next two years he continued to operate Ontario's Mafia from his Hamilton base without interference. The first major trouble that he came up against resulted from heroin smuggling.

The main market for heroin until the mid-1960s was New York City. Most of the narcotic that was used in the trade was grown in Turkey and with the help of the Sicilian Mafia it was smuggled to Marseilles where it was refined. From there it came into North America. Much of the heroin entered directly into New York through the hands of the Mafia-controlled longshoremen. Another heroin route was via the Vic Cotroni gang in Montreal;

John Papalia (*Globe and Mail*).

a third was controlled by the Magaddino family in Buffalo and routed through Ontario. Papalia, the leader of the Mafia in the province, was an important link in this trade.

Vincent Mauro, a New York Don, had organized the "Ontario connection" in the mid-1950s. The chief operators were Alberto and Vito Agueci, recent Italian immigrants who had good contacts with the Italian end of the operation, but Papalia was involved in setting up and running the trade. The heroin came into Ontario in false-bottomed trunks belonging to Italian immigrants, often without their knowledge, and then was shipped from Ontario to New York in a variety of ways.

In 1960 an emergency arose when one of the trunks went astray. The Ontario group rushed about trying to find it. Alberto Agueci sent telegrams to Sicily while Papalia travelled to New York and Buffalo to assure the Dons that everything was under control. But things were not under control. Police had the heroin and they were able to trace the movements of the two Agueci brothers and Papalia. In the spring of 1961 the three men and one of their couriers, Rocco Scopelletti, were arrested and charged in New York with a conspiracy to import $150 million worth of heroin.

The men were freed on bail that summer and by November Alberto Agueci was dead. He apparently went to see Don Stefano Magaddino in Buffalo, the chief organizer of the trade, and threatened him because he felt he had not received the promised legal protection. His horribly charred and mutilated body was found beside a highway near Rochester, New York. The investigation concluded that he had been tortured, perhaps for months, before he died because his body was fifty pounds lighter than its normal weight.

Papalia and Vito Agueci chose another way to deal with the incident. They used every legal device possible to fight the charges but when they were convicted in 1963 they went to jail. Agueci received a sentence of fifteen years and Papalia a sentence of ten years in prison. At the time Robert Kennedy, then the Attorney General of the United States, said that the successful conclusion of the case represented the deepest penetration into organized crime that had yet been made. This gives some indication of the respect American authorities accorded the Hamilton branch of the Mafia.

After 1963 organized crime in Ontario and the Hamilton Group that controlled it appeared on the surface to be in serious difficulty. Its most important leader, John Papalia, was in jail and the heroin traffic, one of the group's most lucrative lines of business, appeared to have been stopped. But this was far from the case. The Hamilton Mafia carried on as if little had changed. The heroin traffic was quickly resumed, in conjunction with the Montreal and Buffalo families. The lucrative rackets of gambling, loan sharking and prostitution, and the extension into legitimate business continued much as before. Even though he was in jail, Papalia was still the head of the Hamilton organization and his interests were well protected.

Altogether Papalia spent less than five years of his ten year sentence in jail. In January 1968 he was released by the parole board in New York on humanitarian grounds because he was supposedly suffering from an advanced stage of tuberculosis. When he returned home his health recovered miraculously, and he soon re-established his dominance over the Hamilton Mafia that was operating across Ontario.

But there had been changes while Papalia was in jail. The Hamilton group missed its Don's ruthless leadership and gradually the Toronto rackets, which had never been firmly under its control, grew more independent. By the time Papalia was released there were two other Toronto Mafia groups running their own operations and the Hamilton group was unable to reimpose its supremacy. Since that time there has been no single group dominating Toronto's organized crime network.

In Hamilton, however, the Papalia gang was firmly in control. By 1970, when *The Spectator* did a series of articles on organized crime in the city, journalists found the Mafia operating in its traditional areas of gambling, loan sharking, and prostitution, while increasingly shifting its operations into legitimate business.

The Spectator has learned that the Mafia owns or directly controls a vending machine company, several entertainment establishments catering to the public, a specialty sales firm, two auto-body repair shops, and several contracting companies. It is also involved in investing in local real estate ... One large firm catering to the public in the city is being bought by Cosa Nostra connected men who were formerly earning $150 a week and now have acquired a $100,000 payment for the business.[14]

Papalia's old friend and gambling partner Danny Gasbarrini seemed to be one of the major figures moving into legitimate business. In 1963 he had been publically linked to the Mafia at the U.S. Senate Sub-committee hearings in Washington and had been named as being involved in supplying narcotics to Stefano Magaddino in Buffalo. By 1970 Gasbarrini was president of eight Hamilton firms, owned a number of apartment buildings and had investments as far away as North Bay.

In retrospect, 1970 appears to have been an important year for the Hamilton organization. That was the year of the Clinton Duke judicial inquiry, in which it was shown that senior Ontario Provincial Police officers stationed in Burlington were friendly with Duke, a one-time criminal and businessman, who was on very good terms with such figures as John Papalia, Danny Gasbarrini and the gambler Donald "Red" LeBarrie. The publicity, monopolizing the Ontario media for months, focused on the activities of the Hamilton Mafia.

The second incident of major importance for the future of the Hamilton Mob was a meeting held in Acapulco, Mexico on February 24, 1970 to discuss the laundering of money. This meeting of several American and Canadian Mafia families was organized by Meyer Lansky, the legendary Mafia financial wizard, and Benjamin Kaufman of Montreal. The Hamilton participants included Rocco Papalia, Red LeBarrie, Richard Perrin, Dominic Ciarillo, Jack Donnelly and Jack Pettigrew.[15] As a result of the agreements reached at these talks, Hamilton became one of the major centres for the investment of money gained through organized crime across North America, and the Hamilton Mafia became important in the laundering of money gained by illegal means. (One of the major problems of organized crime is to convert money gained illegally into funds that can be accounted for to the authorities. The various techniques used to do this are called "laundering.")

These events indicated that the Hamilton Mafia would have to change if it were to continue to dominate organized crime in the area. The Duke affair showed how an obscure set of events could escalate to the point where a full-scale public enquiry was reviewing the activities of the Mob. As the Mafia increasingly became involved in legitimate business and the laundering of money, it was more important than ever that the public remain ignorant of its activities. Otherwise the Hamilton Mob was inviting public demands that it be eliminated.

This situation faced the Hamilton Mafia with real problems. John Papalia was an old-style chief who loved the show and violence of his trade. He had seized power when his major assets were family contacts and a ruthless use of force. He did not adjust to the new style of crime, which called for the leader to have the ability to work in both the legal and illegal worlds, and he had no ability to supervise complicated financial deals.

Even after 1970 Papalia operated with the daring openness that was increasingly deprecated by many of the Mafia figures. At this time he controlled Diamond Jim's, a popular Hamilton night spot, and he often ran his rackets from there. One person with an intimate knowledge of the Hamilton scene claims he would often see him there:

It was just like in the movies. "The man" [Papalia] always had a table reserved for him up front centre. He'd arrive in his big car and first his boys would go in and check out the place. Then Papalia would come in, dressed in a flashy suit, sunglasses, his hat pulled down. He'd sit down at his table with his boys around him, and he'd deal right there. He was that brazen about it. You'd see the guys come up to him — mainly young guys dealing in street drugs. He'd talk to them, money would change hands, they'd go away and someone else would come. That was Papalia's style. He never gave a damn about anybody.

It was that style which ultimately led to the end of Papalia's leadership of the Hamilton group. Vic Cotroni, head of the Montreal family that now controlled Hamilton, told him that he would have to change, and when it became obvious that he would not or could not change, a new leader was selected. For a time Papalia began gathering a group of young men around him and it appeared as if there might be a power struggle, but at a meeting Cotroni and the new Hamilton Mafia leader told him to back off or take the consequences.

Papalia considered the options and then accepted the order. He knew enough to withdraw while he still had the opportunity. The organization was offering him an honourable way of stepping down. He could still run his own rackets, he controlled a number of legitimate businesses, and he would be given the respect of a retired chief, but he was no longer the head of the Hamilton mob.

THE NEW MAFIA AND ITS DON

The new leadership of the Hamilton Mafia is radically different today from the way it was in the past. Papalia was an old-style crime boss who loved the action of the business; he dealt directly with the men on the street who ran the rackets, and was reputed to have inflicted beatings with his own hands. By contrast the Mafia today is careful to keep a low profile by moving into respectable business. Real estate is a good way of laundering money that is made in the rackets. The objective of respectability has been so effectively achieved that organized crime is barely talked about any more, yet it is far more powerful today than at any time in the past.

The new leader is a well-known businessman who owns a number of apartment buildings and is prominent in the real estate industry. He comes from a large Italian family and grew up in a poor area of the North End. His rise to prominence as a developer came in the boom times of the 1960s but few people know that he used Mafia money to finance his projects.

In personality he is a gregarious, likable individual who maintains close ties with his family. He has a broad circle of friends among politicians, business men and ordinary citizens of virtually all ethnic groups, and if he has any weakness it is his love of beautiful women and a driving ambition which compels him to deal in organized crime in spite of his considerable wealth. Unlike the retired chief he does not surround himself with body guards and often can be seen driving his cadillac alone through the streets of the city quite secure in the knowledge that he is protected by his absolute control over the Hamilton Mob and the anonymity that he maintains.

In the last few years the Hamilton Mafia has moved increasingly into legitimate business. The police now estimate that the Mob controls over 100 businesses in the area. These include vending machine companies, the Home Juice Company (ownership of this company once changed hands in a Detroit crap game), a number of restaurants, and some construction companies. The most concentrated area of Mafia ownership is in the real estate industry.

Real estate is particularly important in the laundering of money and after the Acapulco meeting of 1970, Hamilton became a major centre for the investment of money from the American Mafia families. Experts claim that it is almost impossible to trace money as it comes into the country. Often the funds come into the country through lawyers, and are then invested in legitimate businesses in the United States. In Hamilton it is rumoured that the most common method of laundering money is for the Mafia to

Vic Cotroni (*Globe and Mail*).

provide funds to a front company or individual who erects an apartment building. Once the building is completed the front turns the profits over to the criminal. Another advantage of this technique is that the company can claim consistently high levels of profits, which in fact have been earned from criminal activities. Another simple technique is for an American Mob figure to buy a piece of land for a nominal amount, perhaps $25,000. It is then purchased by a Canadian for the inflated figure of $500,000, with funds brought in from the United States. The profit of $475,000 can then be taken back as legitimate money. For involvement in these transactions the Hamilton Mob receives a healthy fee, providing money for its expansion into legitimate business.

Gambling is still the most lucrative operation for organized crime in the city. Every day of the week thousands of people lay bets with Mafia outlets on horse races or sporting matches. This represents millions of dollars every year. This Mafia racket is virtually immune from prosecution. In 1971, for example, the Ontario Provincial Police anti-gambling squad had only a total of 71 arrests for the entire province. A total of $8,125 was paid to courts as a result of these prosecutions and only two people went to prison. Of a total of $7,531.88 seized during raids, only $1,066.21 was forfeited to the Crown. This level of prosecution is hardly a deterrent to anyone, let alone an organization as sophisticated as the Mafia.

The drug trade has changed considerably in the last few years but the Hamilton Mafia is still deeply involved. There is some heroin coming via Turkey, Marseilles and Montreal through the Wellington Street Docks but this has been reduced to a trickle since the Europeans closed down the Turkish and French part of the operation. Today most heroin comes through Vancouver from the Golden Triangle in the Far East via Hong Kong, and the trade is controlled by a small group of Chinese. The street traffic in Hamilton, however, is still controlled by the Mafia. They get their supply from Vancouver and distribute it to dealers, often members of motorcycle gangs, who sell it on the street.

In recent years the Hamilton Mob has specialized in chemical drugs. Some speculate that the city has become the centre for Canada, and possibly for the Eastern seaboard of the United States as well, in supplying drugs such as speed, LSD, and other "happy" pills. There are alleged to be laboratories and warehouses in the city in which the drugs are manufactured, and from where they are smuggled by an elaborate transportation system that distributes the chemicals across the continent. The former owner of a large Ontario pharmaceutical firm is believed to be the brains behind the organization but all aspects of the operation are financed and controlled by the Hamilton Mafia.[16]

And prostitution has once again become big business for the Mob. One informant claimed that Mafia-linked men are always on the lookout for young girls and boys to be recruited and, usually, sent to other parts of the country to work. Their new front has become body-rub parlors and dating services, but many still operate from bars. One report claims that the Hamilton Mob controls a string of prostitutes who are regularly sent through Northern Ontario and Western Quebec.[17]

All of this indicates that organized crime in Hamilton is much more sophisticated than ever before. Now members of the Mob dress in business suits, join the Rotary Club and Chamber of Commerce and take an active interest in politics. Although they still deal in the traditional rackets of gambling, drugs and prostitution, they are also adept at financial manipulations which are so complicated that they baffle normal police methods.

But in spite of this change in the methods of operation, secrecy and violence are still at the heart of the Mafia's control of crime in the city. The people "muscled" are not ordinary citizens. That would simply invite retaliation, and rarely are they members of the Mafia inner circle. Almost invariably they are the small operators who run the rackets for the Mob. Occasionally one of them will get over-ambitious and try to take too large a slice of the profits, or sometimes one will attempt to set up an independent operation. Rarer still is the one who becomes a police informer. All these people represent a threat to the Mafia which must be dealt with summarily if the organization is to survive.

Whenever an emergency of this type occurs a decision is made by the top person in the organization "the Man" as he is called on the street. First a warning is given, then a beating, which may result in a broken arm or leg. If the individual persists his friends will find him dead from an overdose of heroin or from alcohol poisoning, or he will simply disappear. His body may end up in the bay or encased in concrete in the foundation of a building. When this happens people rarely lodge a complaint with the police. Often, the individual is a drifter and is simply assumed to have moved on, but those involved in the organization know that he has been murdered. It is still important in the control of the Mafia that the lower level men operating the rackets know that the leaders are willing to use violence to maintain discipline. Otherwise their domination of crime in the city could slip from their grasp.

The success of the new-style Hamilton Mafia can be judged by the incredible growth in its operations since the new Don took control, but it can also be seen in the virtual immunity of the Mafia from prosecution. The arrest of John Papalia in 1975 shows the contrast between the two styles of leadership. Papalia, along with Vic Cotroni and Paolo Violi, leaders of the Montreal Mafia, and Sheldon Swartz, a Toronto operator, were arrested and charged with conspiracy to obtain $300,000 by the commission of an indictable offence. In the trial, evidence showed that Papalia had threatened two Toronto stock promoters, saying that he would reveal that they had made money fraudulently unless they paid $300,000. Originally all four men were convicted but later, on appeal, the charges against Cotroni and Violi were dismissed. Papalia was given a sentence of six years. (Violi, the one-time head of the Montreal Mafia, was murdered in January 1978.)

It is inconceivable that the new leader of the Hamilton Mafia would be involved in an offence of this type. An added irony is that it was believed by many of the police and by the public that the most important figure in the Ontario Mafia had been arrested. Nothing could be further from the truth. Papalia's arrest on this charge, in fact, reflects how low his fortunes have fallen in recent years. Organized crime continues to thrive in Hamilton and there is no indication that its power is about to be broken or that the politicians have any desire to try.

THE MAFIA AND HAMILTON POLITICS

The details in the story of organized crime in Hamilton and the leaders who have ruled it remain sketchy. The very nature of all crime is that it is a conspiracy demanding secrecy, and libel laws in Canada make it difficult to name names and write about incidents unless events have been clearly proven to have happened by reliable informants or court evidence. Nonetheless, the picture that emerges is of a permanent Mafia-styled organization existing in the city at least since the 1940s, with roots that can be traced to the beginnings of Prohibition in 1916.

How has organized crime been able to exist for so long without inviting retaliation by the community? A number of factors are involved. One is the two-tiered structure of the Mafia, with its inner core of criminals bound together by their ethnic background and family connections, which makes the organization virtually impenetrable by the police. It is interesting that the Chinese group that specializes in the importation of heroin into Canada follows a similar pattern, with an inner circle bound by ethnic and family ties. The Canadian police are finding this group as unassailable as the Mafia.

Another important reason for the survival of organized crime is that it specializes in activities in which there are no victims in the traditional sense. Rum running, gambling, prostitution, drug trafficking and loan sharking are all crimes in which the criminal and the victim enter into a conspiracy to break the law. Because of this no one is likely to complain to the police.

In most of its operations, organized crime deals mainly with the poor and the working class. Gambling, for example, the most lucrative of the Mob's activities, is engaged in mainly by the disadvantaged in our society. For people over forty on a low income, the dream of winning a large amount of money through gambling and retiring in luxury is often a central part of their lives. Despite the fact that people are constantly reminded that the odds against winning, especially in a Mafia-run game, are very remote, they only become more convinced that perhaps they will be the lucky ones to strike it rich. Since the politically powerful middle and upper classes usually do not become involved in gambling, loan sharking, prostitution, narcotics and so on, organized crime in our society tends to be ignored or underestimated.

Police officers and others often explain the lack of prosecution of organized crime figures as a result of legislation that protects the civil liberties of the accused, which allows Mafia leaders to insulate themselves from prosecution. This was an argument which led to greater police wire-tapping powers in the early 1970s. The Mafia is, however, much too

Monarch Vending on Railway Street (Bill Freeman)

sophisticated to be found discussing its plans on the telephone or in a room that might be bugged.

Basic to organized crime's freedom to operate in a city like Hamilton is its ability to protect itself from police intervention and prosecution. An American report on organized crime comments: "Today's corruption is less visible, more subtle, and therefore more difficult to detect and assess than the corruption of the Prohibition era. All available data indicate that organized crime flourishes only where it has corrupted local officials."[18] The Quebec report on organized crime pointed out that criminal organizations had millions of dollars with which to corrupt public officials, and commented: "The unanimous opinion is that it would not be possible for organized crime to entrench itself, develop and prosper without a measure of co-operation on the part of the administration of justice. The principle is bluntly enunciated by stating that there is no organized crime without a measure of corruption."[19]

The extent to which corruption exists in Hamilton is not extensively documented, but in the last few years there have been two incidents which have been publicly reported in which John Munro, the powerful former federal Liberal cabinet minister, has been linked to convicted criminals.

In the Hamilton Harbour scandal, a political associate of Munro's turned out to have criminal convictions in the 1940s on charges of bookmaking and gambling. Joseph Lanza, a one-time Hamilton alderman, was twice a campaign manager for John Munro. He was appointed through Munro's efforts to the Hamilton Harbour Commission where he served from 1964 to 1975, and he was later Munro's executive assistant in charge of riding affairs. The National Parole Board has refused a request from Lanza to pardon him for his former criminal record.

In the second case, a series of newspaper articles by Jim Travers of *The Spectator* and a subsequent RCMP investigation sparked by those articles, revealed that close associates of Munro were involved in using political influence to help a small-time local developer in dealing with a federal agency, the Central Mortgage and Housing Corporation. The case involves a complicated set of financial deals which show not only the way apartment developers sometimes operate but also reflect Munro's political patronage system.

In September 1968 Jack Pelech, then the law partner of John Munro, entered into an agreement to buy the Tuckett Tobacco property on Queen Street North, owned by Imperial Tobacco, for $275,000. In July 1969 Pelech assigned his interest in the property to a Mr. Frank Martin, in return for Pelech's legal fees of $3500. Martin finally purchased the four-acre site for $275,000, the same amount that originally had been offered by Pelech.

The property, located in a low-income neighbourhood north of York Street, was thought to be appropriate only for some type of subsidized housing project. After Martin bought it, three different developers made offers on the land contingent on receiving CMHC funding, but all

York Place, in a neighbourhood of working class homes (Marsha Hewitt).

of them failed to get approval from the federal agency. Finally in January 1972 Dominic Morganti received approval from CMHC for a $5.7 million, low-interest mortgage for construction of a twin-towered, 467-unit project on the site, to be called "York Place."[20]

There were a number of peculiar things about this loan. CMHC requires that a builder must be able to demonstrate that he is capable of completing a project before being given funds. In the late 1960s Morganti had been able to get enough money to finance and build a large apartment building called "Main Place" in the city's west end, but at the time of the CMHC application this project was still under construction. More interesting than this is the fact that the price of the Queen Street North property had been jacked up well above its market value before Morganti purchased it. In April 1969 Imperial Tobacco had the site appraised by an independent firm at approximately $210,000 and not more than $230,000. Despite this Martin bought the property for $275,000. A little later in 1969 CMHC appraisers set their own value on the land: $569,100. Nevertheless, when Martin sold the land to Morganti its cost was $700,000 and this amount was approved by CMHC. In little more than two years the value of the land had increased by $425,000, or more than 150%.

It is also interesting that Jack Pelech, John Munro's law partner and close political associate, was involved in all stages of the development of this property. In 1972, when the land was sold to Morganti, Pelech did the legal work on both sides of the transaction, and Pelech handled Morganti's application to CMHC through the law firm of Munro and Pelech. Since then Pelech has remained deeply involved with York Place as Morganti's lawyer. There are fascinating sidelights to this story. First, Stanley Dudzic, a one-time city alderman, a long time political associate of John Munro and an executive member of Munro's Hamilton East riding association, handled the legal work for CMHC in this transaction. Dudzic admitted "he is on a list of Liberal lawyers who have work allotted to them by CMHC."[21] Second, John Munro at one time admitted that in the 1972 federal election

87

campaign he received donations of $1700 from Jack Pelech, $500 from Stanley Dudzic and $1000 from Dominic Morganti.

It is also interesting that three developers could not get CMHC support to develop this site, but that Morganti, working through Jack Pelech, John Munro's partner, was able to get the subsidized mortgage despite the great increase in the cost of the land. How this was arranged is not known. It is known, however, that when Morganti's York Place project fell into financial difficulties in the spring of 1973 Jack Pelech visited his law partner, John Munro, who at that time was still a prominent federal cabinet minister, and after that discussion Munro sent one of his executive assistants, Ephraim Jonah, to CMHC with inquiries about increasing Morganti's mortgage. As Jonah remembered it: "I do not recall that he [Munro] said 'don't push too hard because of my association with Pelech.'"[22] Shortly after this visit CMHC took the unusual step of increasing the mortgage, first by $480,000 and later by another $1 million. In total the mortgage finally amounted to $7.18 million. Munro later terminated his partnership with Jack Pelech, and in 1974 he explained that this had been because of the relationship with Morganti.

In spite of these substantial subsidies York Place was never finished. In 1976 Morganti's project was forced into receivership, but this was not before a number of incidents occurred which illustrated that the owner was not the usual kind of developer. Morganti moved residents into the building before it was finished, and living conditions were so bad for them a tenant's union was started. An organizer working for the Family Service Agency, trying to help tenants with their problems, was seriously beaten by unknown assailants, while another was later called into Morganti's office and in the presence of three other men was grilled about his activities with the tenants. Later Morganti was convicted of bribing a public official, when it was proven in court that he had given one of CMHC's building inspectors a motor boat worth several hundred dollars. The developer served three months in jail on this charge. More recently, in November 1978, the RCMP charged Morganti with defrauding CMHC of more than $450,000 by diverting funds to another project.[23]

The story of York Place illustrates how easily a business like real estate can combine illegitimate methods — in this case bribery — with the legitimate practices of ordinary business, and how easily politicians can get drawn into complicated and messy involvements. John Munro's assistance to a developer later convicted of bribery of a federal official left him in a very compromised position politically.

Ironically, one of the most important objectives of the Mafia at the present time is to promote the interests of the business community. With its increasing investments in real estate, restaurants, construction companies and other legitimate businesses, the Mafia shares with other businessmen the need to have a group at city hall that will support private enterprise, and particularly promote the development industry.

But, by far the most important political aim of organized crime is simply to be ignored. If there are only a few police officers dealing with gambling, loan sharking, narcotics, prostitution, and so on, there will not be many arrests. If there are politicians who deny or downplay the importance of the Mafia and who refuse to talk about it publicly, because it may antagonize the Italian community, or because it may upset the Tory image of Ontario as a safe, crime-free province, then organized crime will have licence to do pretty much as it pleases.

To judge the political success of organized crime in Hamilton it is only necessary to reflect on the fact that for sixty years various groups of criminals have operated very profitable illegal empires virtually unchallenged by any civil authority. Today the Mafia is more powerful and protected from arrest than ever before.

These documented connections between politicians and criminals are probably representative of a larger pattern. Organized crime today is increasingly involved in the political life of Hamilton. The new Don takes politics very seriously. Money and organizational help have been given to Liberal and Conservative candidates at both the provincial and the federal levels, and at the municipal level the Mob has made very significant inroads. Some candidates for civic office have been almost entirely financed by organized crime, and others have received heavy donations. The result is that it is almost impossible to find a line where local political life ends and where criminal life begins. The two realms interconnect in many ways, and a hidden web of alliances, deals, corruption and protection has emerged which has an unseen influence on many of the policies and decisions of governments not only at the local level but in Queen's Park and Ottawa as well.

1. *The Globe and Mail* 14 June 1977.

2. *The Hamilton Spectator*, 17 October 1963.

3. *The Hamilton Spectator*, 3 June 1970.

4. Gerald A. Hallowell, *Prohibition in Ontario, 1919–1923* (Ontario Historical Society Research Publication No. 2, 1972) p. 117.

5. Information on Rocco Perri comes from interviews as well as the following two articles: The Hamilton Review, 25 March 1944, and *The Hamilton Spectator*, 31 August 1946.

6. *The Hamilton Spectator*, 31 August 1946.

7. *The Hamilton Spectator*, 31 August 1946.

8. *The Hamilton Spectator*, 31 August 1946.

9. Report of the commission of enquiry into the administration of justice on criminal and penal matters in Quebec, Crime, *Justice and Society*, Vol. 3, (Quebec: Government of Quebec) p. 20.

10. Crime, Justice and Society, p. 21.

11. The information on Papalia comes from a number of interviews and newspaper reports. The following article was particularly helpful: Alan Phillips, "Organized Crime's Grip in Ontario," *Maclean's*, 21 September 1963.

12. *The Hamilton Spectator*, 18 October 1963.

13. A. Phillips.

14. *The Hamilton Spectator*, 3 June 1970.

15. *The Hamilton Spectator*, 6 June 1970.

16. Vic Phillips, "Is the Mafia Making Us All an Offer We Can't Refuse," *Quest*, November 1976, p. 66.

17. V. Phillips, p. 66.

18. *The Federal Effort Against Organized Crime*, Hearings held before a subcommittee of the committee on government administration, Part 1, Washington, D. C., 1967.

19. *Crime, Justice and Society*, Vol. 3, p. 50.

20. *The Hamilton Spectator*, 16 November 1976.

21. *The Hamilton Spectator*, 16 September 1976.

22. *The Hamilton Spectator*, 27 October 1976.

23. *The Hamilton Spectator*, 4 November 1978.

Independence or control: Ten years at *The Spectator*

Marsha Aileen Hewitt and Bill Freeman

"*The Spectator* is the best paper in Canada."
— *John Muir, Publisher*

The Spectator, with a circulation of 140,000, is the only daily paper serving a population of 500,000 people in Hamilton, Burlington and surrounding areas. Its monopoly of the local market gives it tremendous social and political influence on the area, beyond that of any other comparable media or business organization.

Public opinion is very much shaped by media treatment of events. The amount of space an item receives in a newspaper, the page on which it is featured, the size and wording of the headlines and the consistency with which a story is reported are all elements that contribute to the view people take of that event. If more than one newspaper exists in a city, people may have the luxury of reading about a given event from differing perspectives. In cities where there is only one newspaper, however, that paper becomes the single most important vehicle in shaping opinion about local matters.

The liberal standpoint on the role of the press in society is that it is a watchdog defending the public interest. The ideal newspaper, in the liberal view, shows aggressive political independence. Reporters must have time to cover stories in depth, they must have the talent to know what is relevant and they must know how to get to the essential issues. Most important for the realization of the ideal is that management encourage and support this type of reporting and provide funds to see that it happens.

There are very few such newspapers in Canada. Newspapers are businesses whose primary aim is to make a profit for their owners. Tough, aggressive reporting in a paper that has achieved saturation of its market, like *The Spectator*, may not increase sales and may in fact decrease them. More important, this style of journalism can offend the paper's big advertisers who are its major revenue source. In 1978 an employee in *The Spectator* advertising department noted that two major local stories had been "toned down" in an eight-month period because they criticized two heavy advertisers. One case concerned a company that had large-scale plans for investment in Hamilton. *The Spectator* was running stories critical of its business practices. On the insistence of the company the stories were modified and the investments went ahead. Most newspapers are sensitive to the political views of their advertisers, who are hardly enthusiastic about an aggressive style of reporting that uncovers the stories behind the news. They fear that they could find themselves under attack.

All newspapers have their own styles. Some go to great efforts in an attempt to achieve the liberal ideal, while others are content to represent the conservative bias of business. *The Spectator* in the 1960s and 1970s reflected first one and then the other of these totally divergent styles. The reason for the transformation can only be explained by the completely different approaches of its two publishers in this period: Tom Nichols and John Muir. A study of how *The Spectator* changed under the direction of these two men not only reveals the politics of the newspaper itself but also the powerful influence of a news media organization on its city.

THE NICHOLS YEARS AND JOURNALISTIC INDEPENDENCE

The Spectator is owned by the Southam Company, which owns a number of the largest and most influential newspapers in English Canada. This company until the late 1970s had a policy of appointing publishers from members of its senior staff and decentralizing decision-making to allow each of them the right to determine the editorial policies of their own papers. Though this has not yielded radical or even unconventional publishers, since the Southam board of directors promoted publishers who shared their own basic political views, the result of this decentralization is that Southam papers vary considerably from city to city, and in different periods, depending on their publishers.

Tom Nichols, the publisher of *The Spectator* for most of the 1960s, developed a newspaper that emphasized coverage of community news. The statements that he made in his 1970 submission to the Special Senate Committee on the Mass Media reflect this. Said Nichols: "Our paper in Hamilton relies for success, I think, almost overwhelmingly on the local news we give to the people . . . We run on an average through the year about 24 solid pages of (local) material a day." Nichols went on to emphasize that he believed "our news should be divorced completely from the editorial page," and denied that in its news coverage *The Spectator* represented any one particular point of view. He believed that a newspaper should try to maintain objectivity on the issues and that it had an obligation to its readers to cover current issues as the reporters and editors saw them. Finally he commented: "A newspaper is itself an organ of dissent. It is full of dissent. Most people complain there is too much dissent in it — too much criticism."

Nichols was publisher of *The Spectator* for most of the 1960s, but it took until 1968 before the type of newspaper that he wanted had emerged. His belief that a paper should focus on community news was a major contribution to the style for which the paper became known, but there were a number of other factors. One factor of real importance was that the publisher had been a reporter himself and had the newsman's sense of pride when his paper was carrying stories that were thoroughly researched and well written. But reporters who worked under him pointed out that he appointed editors and reporters in whom he had confidence and let them get on with the job. One editor described him as an aloof "absent-minded professor" who never made an attempt to control what went on in the newsroom and in fact had little idea of the stories his staff was working on, but who gave his people support when they needed it. This support was crucial in giving them confidence to tackle controversial stories.

One of the first pieces of investigative journalism undertaken by *The Spectator* illustrates the interplay of these factors. In the mid-1960s Hamilton's St. Joseph's Hospital had lost its accreditation. A new chief of staff had been brought in to establish new policies and more careful procedures. The hospital gained back its accreditation but not long afterwards an incident occurred that again threatened their position. A woman who had been scalded was admitted to the hospital. The doctors, who had failed to note that the patient had a heart condition, planned a skin graft operation. The woman was given three pints of blood. Her weakened heart could not handle the transfusion and by morning she was dead. The coroner, in a misguided effort to ensure that the hospital would not be threatened by loss of its hard-won accreditation, falsified the death certificate.

An aggressive young Spectator reporter, Gerald McAuliffe, learned of this incident, wrote it up and submitted the story to the paper. It went first to the senior editor, Tom Farmer, who demanded to know his sources. When the journalist refused to divulge them, the decision about whether to print the story was turned over to Nichols. The publisher called in McAuliffe and again asked the sources of his information. Again the reporter refused but assured Nichols that the story was accurate.

Everyone involved knew that an article of this kind was sensitive. It was possible that the publicity would again result in the loss of accreditation for the hospital, and at the very least it would further damage its reputation at a time when it was struggling to demonstrate to the public that things had improved. To make things even more difficult for Nichols, he happened to sit on the board of the hospital and knew many of the people implicated. This did not influence his judgement, however, and he decided to "go with the story."

As far as the public knew, the results were that there was an inquest into the woman's death, and that St. Joseph's Hospital was criticized but did not lose its accreditation. However, the most interesting event occurred behind the scenes: a meeting was held between the board of the hospital and the publisher and editors of *The Spectator* so that St. Joseph's could "smooth out press relations," as one person put it. The meeting was at times angry. At one point Warren Barton, the new city editor, bluntly attacked the chief medical officer for trying to cover up the death. At another time one of the doctors said that Nichols' chief responsibility in this affair was to the hospital because he sat on the board. On the spot, the publisher took out a sheet of his beautifully embossed stationery and wrote out his resignation.

There was no real resolution to the meeting but the incident is revealing because it illustrates the editorial policy that would dominate the Nichols era. Good journalism would be supported and encouraged, even if it provoked objections by those with power and influence in the city. It also shows the degree to which the publisher supported his editors and journalists. Nichols' policy, in effect, was one of decentralization. He appointed his staff and gave them the authority to do the work as they determined it.

The publisher was not the only person who contributed to *The Spectator*'s spirit in this period. The newspaper was fortunate in having two young, aggressive editors who played a role in determining what stories would be covered and the approach that would be taken on them. They were Warren Barton, the city editor, and Paul Warnick, who was responsible for the rest of the district. Barton was a particularly tough, uncompromising newsman. He had come to the paper in 1962 as a young reporter, and by the time he took over as city editor in 1968 he had already decided on the kind of journalism he wanted. *The Spectator* never consciously followed a policy of investigative journalism, Barton claims, but he and others like him wanted to write stories that followed right through to their conclusions. "You've got to probe," he maintains. "If you ask the really good questions the story will write itself." The one rule he insisted on was that all the different aspects of the story had to be covered and explained; the rest would be for the public to judge.

Barton was also determined that he and his reporters would never be compromised. When he came to Hamilton he did not join any of the clubs in the city and recommended that the journalists working under him do the same. His firm policy was that reporters must refuse various perks that were offered to them because these could easily lead to favours being given to some group or individual. In his characteristically tough way of putting things, Barton said: "I wasn't going to play their game. There was no way people could get at me. I was not going to be compromised."

Paul Warnick, the district editor, was a different type of journalist. By nature he was more cautious than Barton and at times he was critical of the latter's aggressive style, but journalists working under him often characterized him as a fine newsman with a sure sense of what made a good story. Warnick had the ability to get the best out of his reporters.

The other ingredient that made *The Spectator* a good newspaper between 1968 and 1970 was the quality of the journalists themselves. In part this was because the newspaper paid above-average wages and had good employee relations. More than anything else, though, it was because the journalists in the newsroom, working under editors with high standards such as Barton and Warnick, thoroughly learned their trade, and were encouraged to excel in an atmosphere that demanded tough and comprehensive reporting. In his 1970 submission to the Senate Committee on the Mass Media, Nichols pointed out that morale at the newspaper was very high. *The Spectator* had not lost a journalist to another paper in two years. This is a remarkable record when it is remembered that at that time there were many jobs available for experienced reporters.

The issues tackled by *The Spectator* in those days included every imaginable aspect of the city's life. Peter Calamai and later Tom Coleman covered the city's Civic Square urban renewal project. Between them, they uncovered a mass of detail which often conflicted with the information put out by First Wentworth, the developer, and the city's negotiation committee, Vic Copps and Jack MacDonald. Their articles made clear that the city representatives were deeply compromised by the political power of the Pigott family, who were the owners of First Wentworth, and their work played an important role in creating and sustaining a citizen's group called "Save Our Square," which in a short time became a powerful political force in the city.

Paul Mindale and Peter Moon covered organized crime in the city. They were able to show that a Mafia-styled organization had existed in Hamilton for some years and that this group was increasingly moving into legitimate business. All of this investigative work was accomplished with virtually no co-operation from the police.

In March 1970 *The Spectator* published an article by Tom Coleman on the Hamilton Harbour Commission that was the first critical look at its operations. This article was the culmination of many months of work. At first the Commissioners refused to give *The Spectator* any information on the sale of water lots. Warren Barton threatened the Commissioners with court action if they refused. Del Hickey, the chairman of the Harbour Board, phoned the publisher, trying to head off an investigation, but Nichols supported his staff and finally the information was released. Coleman's article brought the harbour issue to public attention. Soon citizens' groups were talking about public access to the harbour, the pollution hazards of filling water lots and the use of the Lax landfill site in the west end of the harbour.

The Spectator was also one of the most important elements in sparking a judicial inquiry into the construction of the new city hall in 1970–71. Persistent questioning by reporters on the paper revealed that the marble facing on the new building had begun to fall off almost from the time it was put in place. Because of political influence, the contractors, Pigott Construction, had been able to

Picketing in front of *The Spectator*, during the 1946 International Typographical Workers strike (McMaster University, Labour Studies Collection).

avoid responsibility, and in the ensuing inquiry the judge was very critical of then Controller (and later mayor) Jack MacDonald. (See "The New City Hall Saga 1955–72," by Marsha Hewitt, in Part III.)

One story that caused problems at *The Spectator* during this period concerned events surrounding the murder of a city police officer, Sergeant J. Cameron McMurrich, on December 22, 1968. McMurrich had been killed in a fight with a gang of criminals. There was tremendous public sympathy for his family and outrage that the crime had occurred. *The Spectator* started a fund for McMurrich's children and donated a large sum of money.

However, while covering the case, Stew Brooks, *The Spectator*'s court reporter, was given information that the police had been harassing the men who took McMurrich's life by deflating the tires of their cars, pouring sugar in their gas tanks and dropping metal shavings into a truck crank case. On the night of the killing some of the members of the police squad, including McMurrich, had been drinking. The police reports on the activities of the evening of the murder did not accord with the known facts. When Judge Robert Morrison banned the press from his court for the preliminary hearings, the first time this had ever been done in a capital murder trial in Canada, Brooks became convinced that there was a major cover-up of the facts, in order to save the reputation of the Hamilton Police Department.

All this information was reported in *The Spectator*. Brooks was given time away from his regular duties to research different aspects of the case, but he came dissatisfied with the support that he was receiving from the publisher and editors of the newspaper. Finally he became convinced that *The Spectator* itself was involved to some degree in the cover-up, when some of his stories on the case were rejected. He approached Maclean's magazine to do a story on the issue. The editorial accompanying that article contended that Brooks faced "a surprising degree of indifference on the part of his own newspaper. *The Spectator* never took a stand on aspects of the case ... and he received little editorial encouragement for his views."[1]

This was a hard judgement of Nichols and his editors. Brooks could never have followed this story if his newspaper had not given him encouragement, and all of the information contained in the Maclean's article had been published in the paper at various times. The only thing lacking was an editorial condemning the police and judicial practices that had been revealed by the case. Newspaper editorials are, however, considered the prerogative of the publisher, and at any rate do not have the impact of actual news coverage.

The best known and perhaps most important story dealt with by *The Spectator* during the Nichols years was Gerald McAuliffe's uncovering of what came to be called the "Clinton Duke Affair." After a lengthy investigation, McAuliffe was able to show that Clinton Duke, a man with a criminal record dating from the 1920s and later the wealthy owner of a Burlington lawn-equipment business, was given special treatment by the Halton County court system after he was charged with threatening a woman with a gun. The case was not handled in

The Spectator office on King Street East (Hamilton Public Library).

the regular Provincial Judge's Court but was given an *in camera* hearing in the Family Court. Duke was allowed to wait in the judge's chambers while the case was being heard. After he admitted his guilt he was simply ordered to keep the peace and his gun license was lifted for six months.

In the course of his investigations McAuliffe was able to uncover much more about the questionable relationships of this Burlington businessman. He showed that Duke had a very close friendship with several senior Ontario Provincial Police officers and because of this had been given lenient treatment on several driving offences. He also had a close relationship with a number of well-known Hamilton Mafia figures. He had held parties with Danny Gasbarrini, John Papalia and Donald "Red" LeBarrie. He had even shared an apartment with John Papalia at 255 Bold Street, a building owned by Gasbarrini and his wife, using the alias of Clinton Jones.

The Duke affair was one of the most remarkable pieces of investigative journalism ever carried out in Canada. It sparked a judicial inquiry, which in turn led to a reprimand of several senior OPP officers. At that inquiry Mr. Justice Campbell Grant ordered McAuliffe to divulge his sources of information but the reporter resolutely refused. For a time it appeared that McAuliffe would be jailed for contempt. He was prepared to accept this consequence of his silence because he felt that it would destroy his ability to guarantee anonymity to his informants if he were to do otherwise, but in the end Justice Grant backed down and a contempt charge was never laid.

Throughout the entire difficult period, while he was collecting material for his story and during the judicial inquiry, McAuliffe was given full support by the editors of *The Spectator* and particularly by the publisher. After it was over *The Spectator* gave him a $600 bonus and some time off for a holiday. As a final show of support for his efforts Nichols, in the last editorial he ever wrote for the paper, said that McAuliffe had done a service to every journalist and to the public by refusing to divulge his sources.

These are some of the more outstanding cases of investigative reporting covered by *The Spectator* in the Nichols era, but it would be inaccurate to leave the impression that the newspaper excelled only on such issues. Generally, all of the local news was well reported during this time. City hall news was thoroughly covered, council meetings were reported in depth, the work of most committees was followed, and there was a regular education reporter. Political issues that arose in neighbourhoods were consistently reported, and journalists were often sent out of town to cover stories of special interest to Hamiltonians. McAuliffe was in California for several weeks covering the death of a well-known Tiger Cat football player, and Tom Coleman once followed Mayor Copps and Controller MacDonald all the way to Germany and Paris to report on their efforts to raise money for Civic Square. During this period *The Spectator* was an excellent paper.

However, in spite of the corps of journalists and editors dedicated to high quality news coverage in Hamilton and the district, it was not long before all this was to change. On January 1, 1971, Tom Nichols retired and John Muir was appointed to replace him. A notice went up on the bulletin board in the newsroom announcing the change and saying that editorial policy would remain the same, but all the employees knew things would be different; their only uncertainty was what direction the change would take and how quickly it would come.

JOHN MUIR AND THE NEW POLICY OF EDITORIAL CONTROL

The most significant difference between Tom Nichols and his successor, John Muir, is that Nichols was a newsman before becoming a publisher, while Muir was always a businessman. For almost 20 years before he became publisher, Muir had managerial posts in both the advertising and business departments of the paper. What he brought to his new position, therefore, was a businessman's point of view. This has had discernable effects on *The Spectator* in the 1970s.

In a 1978 interview Muir was asked about his attitude toward investigative journalism. He immediately rejected the term "journalism" on the grounds that he "doesn't like the word," but preferred the term "newspapering." In Muir's view, investigative "newspapering" is "very dull work. It isn't popular with those (newsmen) who do it. Besides there is the constant risk of lawsuits against the paper or jail terms for reporters." He went on to say that, in his opinion, since the Watergate scandal in the United States, investigative journalism had "become a fad."[2] Many reporters at *The Spectator* still joke about Muir's ordering the withdrawal of the Doonesbury comic strip because the publisher admired former President Nixon and felt that the Doonesbury strip was too critical of him during the Watergate period. This incident reveals a lot about the personal control Muir has exercised over his paper. Muir's negative attitude to investigative journalism, coupled with his control, has meant that very little of this type of reporting has appeared in *The Spectator* in recent years.

Not long after Muir took his position as publisher in 1971, he began to implement his new policy of editorial control. Shortly before he took over he called Warren Barton, the city editor, and Paul Warnick, the district editor, into his office for a talk. This is the way Barton explained what happened:

Muir said what he wanted to see in his senior people was compassion and responsiveness. He wanted us to tread more easily — to back off. Well I wasn't going to play that game for him. That's not my style of journalism. People may get hurt — their careers may suffer — I realize that, and I have compassion for them too, but the public has the right to know what's going on in their city and they should be able to look to their newspapers to find it.

A clash between Muir and some of his editors and journalists became inevitable. As Barton expressed it, Muir wanted his people to "back off," while many in the newsroom wanted *The Spectator* to inform the public of what was going on in their city in an uncompromising way. A fundamental difference of this sort could not be resolved. Muir was the publisher and he had the power to make *The Spectator* into his kind of paper.

Warren Barton said of this period: "I was not winning battles any more. They found ways to head me off." It became increasingly difficult to carry on the aggressive style of journalism that they had thrived on under Nichols: stories that were critical of some aspect of the city's life were being killed on the publisher's desk. For Barton things came to a head over a story on a drinking-driving

John Muir (Bruce Macaulay).

charge against Mo Carter. Carter was a prominent Conservative, owner of a large automobile franchise and, perhaps most important, a big advertiser in *The Spectator*. When Carter was to appear in court, Muir told his city editor that he was not to run a story on the incident. Barton was incensed that he was being censored and the story was slipped into the Saturday edition. After this, working conditions became impossible for the city editor and within a short time he left the paper to become an editor with *The Globe and Mail*. (In this position Barton was responsible for some of the most outstanding investigative reporting *The Globe and Mail* ever undertook.)

In the years after Muir took control many journalists encountered obstacles to their work. Said former reporter Gary Smith:

It wasn't that you were told "No, you can't cover city hall," in order to pursue, say, the harbour scandal. Rather, they said "Go ahead — but remember the ladies' bazaar this afternoon, the dog show tomorrow," stuff like that. After covering all that stuff there was no time to follow up on any good stories.

Muir's style was reflected in the way he controlled the editorial page. Nothing went into it which Muir did not personally approve. Once he took control of the paper he held a meeting every

Gerald McAuliffe.

morning at 10:15 with his executive editor, general manager and editorial page editor to discuss the editorials. At these meetings Muir selected current issues he felt strongly about and conveyed his views to his top staff. The editorials faithfully reflected these views. Asked about possible differences of opinion that might arise between himself and his editorial editors as to the paper's stand on a particular issue, Muir replied that such occurrences were "a very rare thing."

With a middle management staff who were sensitive to the publisher's views, and who themselves gave no encouragement to investigative reporting, it was not surprising that the news pages reflected Muir's tastes in "newspapering." "Stories aren't actively censored at *The Spectator*," said one former reporter. "It's just that stories you think are good, critical stories might be edited in such a way that they are confusing or not as tough, or they are buried on a back page with an obscure headline."

After Warren Barton resigned, Paul Warnick was promoted to the senior position of managing editor. Warnick, along with Gordon Bullock, the executive editor, attempted to act as a buffer between Muir and the reporters in the newsroom. This created problems. Muir wanted things done his way, and Warnick and Bullock were still doing a little to encourage the old style of journalism.

For a time at least, however, there was little Muir could do.

There was one journalist, however, who was just too prominent and controversial for John Muir to accept. In the time that he had been at *The Spectator*, Gerald McAuliffe had developed into an outstanding investigative journalist. After Muir's appointment he carried on his work but soon met with opposition. In 1971, shortly after Muir's appointment as publisher, McAuliffe did a story on a company selling a machine which produced an electrical field that supposedly arrested cancer. There was absolutely no medical evidence that this machine was effective, but in spite of this, at the request of a patient, one of the machines had been installed at the Oakville-Trafalgar Hospital.

McAuliffe's story in *The Spectator* brought about an inquest, and warrants were ultimately issued for the arrest of the salesman of this machine on a medical malpractice suit. But rather than being pleased that his newspaper had performed a public service, Muir was furious. He had been away on holiday when the story had appeared, and on his return he let everyone know that this type of journalism had to be stopped. He is reported as saying that this story "appealed to the lowest common denominator of readers."

McAuliffe continued to get into difficulties. By the fall of 1971 he had been taken off his investigative reporting work and was being given regular assignments, usually in Burlington. During the provincial election campaign, in September and October of 1971, he was assigned to cover the riding of Halton, where Conservative cabinet minister George Kerr was running for re-election.

While covering the election McAuliffe wrote three stories that were an embarrassment to Kerr, the Progressive Conservative Party and *The Spectator* management. The first began in a press conference, when the cabinet minister pointed out that there was a real need for public housing in Ontario. McAuliffe knew that most of Kerr's campaign team, including the then Mayor of Burlington George Harrington, was opposed to public housing of any sort, and he wrote an article pointing out this contradiction.

The second story grew out of an address to a group of high school students, in which Kerr told them that the Ontario government would create a 1,300-acre provincial park in Halton County. McAuliffe was at the meeting and wrote up the story. Afterwards, Kerr realized that this news should have been saved for later in the campaign when the Premier was planning to make a special announcement about it. Kerr tried to get McAuliffe to cancel the story. When the reporter refused, Kerr approached *The Spectator* publisher. According to McAuliffe, Muir was sympathetic but apparently felt he could not intervene.

Finally, near the end of the campaign McAuliffe was responsible for a piece reporting how George

Kerr had gone to a meeting of the congregation of a Dutch Calvinist Church and had promised them government support for their separate schools much like that received by the Catholics. The issue of support for religious schools was important in that election and here was Kerr, a cabinet minister, making an appeal to a special interest group by promising them a policy that had never been (and never was) announced by the government. If this had become public information it would have caused real embarrassment to the Conservatives. McAuliffe, who knew of the meeting and knew he would be recognized, arranged to have a junior reporter cover Kerr's speech. When the reporter's article reached Muir, the publisher tried unsuccessfully to get in touch with George Kerr. Then, eight minutes before press time, he killed the story and it never appeared.

Much of McAuliffe's work was thwarted by Muir and the new editors appointed by him. He worked for many weeks on a story about a Grimsby alderman named Peter Preston, who was promoting an institution called "Lake Erie Boy's Town." Preston claimed to have had the endorsement of a number of senior Hamilton police officers and church leaders in the area and claimed to have options on land for the project. On the basis of these claims a number of high school students went out collecting public donations for the Boy's Town. McAuliffe was able to show that the scheme was a fraud, that the options had never been taken out, that money had disappeared, and that people on the so-called board of directors were not aware of how their names had been used. This was a straight piece of investigative reporting which could have been verified by anyone interested in checking the facts. A variety of objections to the piece were raised by management, however, and it never appeared in The Spectator. Finally, out of frustration, McAuliffe quit the newspaper and joined Barton at The Globe and Mail. The Boy's Town story subsequently received full-page coverage in the Toronto newspaper.

As time went on, problems increased for Paul Warnick and other editors and journalists who wanted to produce a comprehensive paper stressing community news. Muir often wanted to have meetings with his staff in order to explain his approach, but Warnick tried to keep them to a minimum. "Those meetings were disastrous," Warnick remembers. "Muir wanted a paper that does not offend anyone. A family paper that just reported good news. His version lacked any positive thrust and it tended to dishearten the journalists."

Warnick knew that if his reporters pursued certain stories, and especially if they carried out any investigative journalism, an argument with Muir was bound to result. Still he and his immediate superior Gordon Bullock told reporters to cover the stories. As Warnick put it: "We were prepared to take the can in order to see some good journalism done." Nevertheless, morale in the newsroom

Tom Nichols (Gerald Campbell).

sagged. Tom Coleman, Peter Moon and Malcolm Gray went on to *The Globe and Mail*; Stew Brooks, the crime reporter, quit and later went back to England; and others scattered to various papers.

By 1972, little investigative reporting of any type was being done by *The Spectator*. There was virtually no reporting on issues involving the Board of Education or urban redevelopment. Even city council news was reduced to the covering of council meetings and a few of the important committees. The emphasis of the newspaper had decidedly shifted, from an attempt to uncover the stories behind the news, in order to make the city's life intelligible to its inhabitants, to a superficial reporting of events.

Often Muir did not replace reporters as they quit. Many of the new managers that were brought in were Scottish, and did not know the Canadian and Hamilton political scene. Often they were chosen because their views were similar to Muir's. One experienced reporter commented that when he was with *The Spectator* he wrote stories for editors who had very little idea about the issues or even the places he was writing about. "I worked for bosses who didn't even know where Cayuga is . . . Once *The Spectator* even rented a bus to take the reporters around to see the countryside. That's how ignorant they were."

It is of course impossible to estimate the stories that *The Spectator* missed as a result of Muir's new policy. A newspaper with aggressive reporting becomes a center of information and ordinary citizens with stories to tell seek out reporters because they see this as a means of bringing issues to public attention. As Warren Barton puts it: "When you get a climate of tough reporting you start getting people talking to you." The opposite is also true. People will not go to a newspaper that ignores social issues because they know it will have no effect.

The Spectator has certainly avoided a number of important issues since 1971. The paper failed to report on the single most important political failure in the city's history: the collapse of the commercial section of Civic Square (The Lloyd D. Jackson Square). This grandiose project, which has left acres of land in the heart of the city sitting vacant for years, has not been given the serious treatment it deserves since the days of Tom Coleman and Peter Calamai.

The Hamilton Harbour affair, certainly the biggest scandal to rock the city's political life, was covered by the newspaper. There were, however, a number of issues that were ignored, such as the disappearance of some important log books from the Harbour Commissioner's yacht, the Seaport; the political support of Kenneth Elliott on city council; and the alleged relationship between organized crime and the Commissioners. On a number of occasions *The Spectator* suffered the indignity of being scooped by news organizations from out of town.

A number of other local issues were ignored by *The Spectator*: the prevalence of air pollution in areas adjacent to the big steel mills, and the peculiar contradictions in information available about the Mount Hope airport expansion. Even human-interest stories focusing on the plight of the poor, often grist for the mills of newspapers across Canada, are bypassed by *The Spectator*.

Of all the issues ignored by the paper, the one that best illustrates the conservative bias of the newspaper's policies is that involving Hamilton's former federal cabinet minister John Munro. In the midst of the spring 1974 federal election, the Hamilton Harbour scandal broke. Five men were charged with a number of offences, including fraud and uttering forged cheques. Information available pointed to a conspiracy to set dredging prices that involved some of the most prominent business interests in the country.

Not long after the charges were laid, New Democratic Party leader David Lewis came to the city and, in an off-the-cuff remark to reporters, stated that John Munro had impeded the investigation of the harbour commissioners' activities. Munro was furious and said that the NDP leader was guilty of a character smear. A number of charges and counter-charges were then made by both NDP and Conservative candidates.

This was clearly an important political controversy, which could well have had a bearing on the outcome of the election in Hamilton. *The Spectator* decided not to print any of it. They even refused to report on a 30-minute television interview between Munro and Paul Kidd, one of their own reporters, in which Kidd showed that the RCMP investigation of the scandal had indeed been delayed. In response to criticism that *The Spectator* was smothering the news, the management of the newspaper claimed simply that they had been advised by their lawyers that they might be in contempt of court if they printed stories about the harbour. "As a responsible newspaper," an article in the paper said, "*The Spectator* has to make sure that the rights of other people who are not involved in this debate are not prejudiced."[3] Meanwhile, virtually every other newspaper in the country was covering the story. In spite of frustrated claims by both the Conservative and NDP candidates that news was being controlled at this important juncture in the city's political life, the newspaper refused to change its policy. Citizens of Hamilton who relied on *The Spectator* for their news learned absolutely nothing of the issue.

Less than a month later *The Spectator*'s coverage of another issue showed even more clearly how its inherent conservatism has led to the covering up of important information. In a resourceful piece of investigative journalism, *The Globe and Mail* was able to show that John Munro used the political patronage system to help him retain political power. Using Munro's own records, *The Globe and Mail* proved that a number of federal appointments had been given to people who had made heavy financial contributions to Munro's previous election campaign. Out of 98 federal appointments that had been made in the area in the previous two-and-a-half years, 52 had gone to people who had worked for or contributed a substantial amount of money to John Munro's previous election. *The Globe and Mail* article went on to name names and the federal positions they held.

This article showed that Munro, Hamilton's most powerful federal political figure, relied heavily on political patronage, and by implication shed light on the way Liberals maintained power across the country. At any time this was important news, but a few days before a federal election it was potentially explosive. *The Spectator* did not report directly on the findings of *The Globe and Mail*, nor list the Hamiltonians who had benefitted from patronage, but it did cover a press conference at which Munro and two of his close associates defended the patronage system.

Instead of reading how political campaign contributions led to federal appointments, Hamiltonians read a story buried on the back pages which was a simple defence of the status quo. "Of course there is patronage," the newspaper quoted Munro as saying. "You know it and everyone knows it. Is it wrong to favour a past political supporter over somebody else, especially if the two have equal ability? Of course it's not wrong."

Prominent Liberals such as Mayor Copps were reported by the paper as defending Munro's use of patronage and John Agro, a well-known Conservative, was at the press conference to lend his old friend his support. Agro said that he was on a Conservative patronage list and added the revealing comment: "How else does a party gather supporters?"[4] (Interestingly, Agro was later given the plum political patronage position as the Chairman of the Hamilton Harbour Commission.)

By the late 1970s, Muir's control of the newsroom was almost complete. In 1976, after a brief power struggle between editors, Paul Warnick, the last holdout of the Tom Nichols era, was forced to resign. A number of people were promoted to middle management positions who were quite happy with Muir's style of running a newspaper, and the morale of the journalists again fell to a low ebb. The senior reporters resigned in the summer of 1978. The editors in control were now so totally loyal that, as one person put it, they seem "dedicated to a life of touching their forelock whenever John Muir goes by."

THE SPECTATOR AND HAMILTON POLITICS

The contrast between the Nichols and Muir styles of journalism could not be more striking. It would have been unthinkable for the team of Nichols, Barton, Warnick and the journalists working at *The Spectator* between 1968 and 1970 to ignore the Hamilton Harbour and political patronage scandals in the midst of an election. Muir and his staff, on the other hand, now have a paper that contains virtually nothing that makes any established interest in Hamilton uncomfortable.

Decisions made at the management level of *The Spectator* have had clear implications for the political life of the city. When Nichols was the publisher there was a different flavour to Hamilton politics. To some extent at least the paper tried to understand and explain what was going on in the city. No politician was actually defeated as a result of the paper's aggressive style of reporting, and the paper never threatened the business interests that dominate Hamilton's political life. Still, politicians were forced to explain and justify their positions on a number of issues, citizens' groups emerged in a variety of neighbourhoods, and people talked about the major issues facing local government. This was a considerable accomplishment.

After 1971, when Muir implemented his style of journalism at *The Spectator*, Hamilton political life was again characterized by a lack of controversy and citizens' groups became far less important. *The Spectator* was not the only factor behind these changes. There is no doubt, however, that *The Spectator* was important both in creating controversy and in stultifying it, according to the type of coverage it gave local events.

If newspapers are judged only as a business and success is measured by profitability alone then it is likely that *The Spectator* was less successful under the control of Nichols than Muir. Investigative journalism is expensive. It takes talented reporters and they must be given time away from more routine assignments to work on their stories. Legal fees alone can be very expensive. The Duke inquiry and the subsequent legal fees arising from a suit Danny Gasbarrini launched against the paper cost *The Spectator* thousands of dollars. But a newspaper must be judged on much more than its profit-and-loss statement. Papers have a social responsibility to provide information to the public about the issues of the day. This responsibility is particularly important for a newspaper which holds a virtual monopoly in its city.

If there is no organization that seeks out and reports the news, then there can be no informed political debate and politicians cannot be held accountable. This has been the situation in Hamilton and its surrounding area for some years and there is no indication that it is about to change.

1. *The Hamilton Spectator*, 2 July 1974.
2. Interview with Marsha Hewitt, July 1978.
3. *The Hamilton Spectator*, 6 June 1974.
4. *The Hamilton Spectator*, 2 July 1974.

Selling out: The story of the Victoria Park Community Organization

Bill Freeman

This is the account of the Victoria Park Community Organization* one of the few Alinski-styled groups set up in Ontario. And it is a personal account. I was employed by an organization closely affiliated with Victoria Park for a year, and I have followed it with interest since then. Certainly not all community organizations in Canada have followed the same road as the Hamilton group, but the evidence suggests that other groups may be similarly co-opted by depending on grants that have very obvious strings attached.

The project began innocently enough. In 1969 the Reverend Gordon Hume, the minister of Zion United Church, located in the north-west section of the city, decided that something had to be done to help the low-income residents in the area. A massive urban renewal project which promised to remove hundreds of working-class families was still on the books and there were a number of low-income families suffering real poverty. To Hume and his middle-class congregation, the solution seemed to be found in an Alinski-styled organization which could bring the people together and help them help themselves.

THE EARLY YEARS

Hume's group was drawn primarily from United Church ministers and the congregation of Zion United Church. Their first priority was raising money. The United Church committed approximately $4,000 annually for three years and the Presbyterians gave a small amount, but that was the extent of the private funding. Hume and his group then went to Hamilton city hall and obtained a grant of $7,000 a year for three years.

The contradiction was immediately apparent to many observers: a community organization by its very nature would have to oppose some city policies, and yet the major portion of the organization's funding was to come from the municipal purse. Many city politicians were aware

---

* *The organization was later called the Victoria Park and Northwest Community Organization and now goes under the name of Strathcona Community Project.*

Gary Quart (*The Spectator*).

of this paradoxical situation, but after much debate they approved the grant application.

Once the "Board of Directors of the Victoria Park Community Organization," as they called themselves, had the money, they set out to hire an organizer. With little difficulty they found a young United Church minister by the name of Gary Quart, who had a small church in the east end of the city. Quart's qualifications were impressive: he had spent a year working and studying in an Alinski-styled organization in Chicago, and, more important to the group, he was part of the United Church.

By far the most attractive qualification was his belief that, in order to be successful, a community organization needed a person with the vision to know where the group should be going and the organizational skills to make it happen. He saw the organizer as the real power behind the group, and the community members as followers.

The issues were of secondary importance to Quart. The most important thing, he often said, was to develop a powerful organization capable of defending the interests of the community. Any issue which brought people together was acceptable. For example, in Chicago in the mid-60s, he had been involved in organizing groups of white property owners to keep blacks out of their neighbourhood. The organizers ignored the ethical considerations and saw the issue only as a vehicle for galvanizing the community into group action.

Quart's basic tactic in those early days, was something he called "creative conflict," a term he derived from Alinski. Real change in a society, he used to say, occurs through conflict. By creating confrontation, an active, politically-aware community group could focus attention on issues that were important to the community and force politicians to adopt workable solutions.

During his first two years in Hamilton's Victoria Park community, these tactics achieved some success. Once on the street distributing leaflets and talking to people, Quart discovered a number of issues that concerned residents. The two most important issues were the plight of York Street merchants, who were being displaced by urban renewal, and the treatment of welfare recipients by the local welfare office.

To deal with the urban renewal issue, Quart organized meetings of residents and merchants in which they could express their opposition to the project and develop into a cohesive group to oppose the project. As it happened, the federal government withdrew support for urban renewal at about that time and much of the neighbourhood was saved from demolition. But the widening of York Street was still on the planning books, and the York Street merchants were being forced out

John Munro, the patron of the Victoria Park Community Organization (C.P. Wirephoto).

of their shops with inadequate compensation from the city. In the summer of that year, the community organization hired Ray Harris, an activist law student. He organized the merchants into a group to pressure city hall and after a number of political skirmishes, the city offered the businessmen a much fairer settlement.

The problems facing welfare recipients, however, were quite a different matter. Few people knew what benefits they were entitled to, and often the administrators treated them badly. A welfare recipient might wait for his cheque for hours at the office, and if his turn had not come by closing time, he would have to return the next day. If it was a Friday he had to struggle through the weekend as best he could. Quart's confrontation tactics proved to be very effective here. He organized some welfare recipients to force the administrators to keep the office open until all those waiting had received their cheques, and this group then fought a number of cases in which individuals had not received maximum benefits. Through the spring and summer of 1970, the welfare group had a number of successes, and it quickly grew in size and confidence.

However even during that first summer of 1970, Quart began to withdraw from an active involvement with the community organization in order to direct his energies towards what he saw as its most serious problem: its lack of a secure financial base. It was obvious that the group's funding was very precarious. A substantial proportion of the money came from the city, and, as the organization's attacks on city agencies and politicians increased, it appeared unlikely that the grant would be renewed.

Quart approached a number of foundations and government agencies for money, and finally, by the end of the summer, his efforts began to bear fruit. At that time the federal Minister of Health and Welfare was John Munro, a native of Hamilton who believed in channelling some of the rewards of office to people in the local area. At that time too, there was considerable talk of "participatory democracy" and "the just society" in the new Trudeau administration. A grant of money to a low-income group appeared to be beneficial to all involved. Gary Quart wanted a firm financial foundation for his struggling community organization and John Munro and the federal government saw political gains to be made by funding such a group. It was not long before a grant application was submitted by the Victoria Park Community Organization and the submission was accepted by Health and Welfare.

HAMILTON WELFARE RIGHTS ORGANIZATION

The Health and Welfare grant of $35,000 a year for three years did not go to the Victoria Park Community Organization. During negotiations Munro insisted that the money should be designated to develop a group which would confront the welfare system in the city. Since welfare was administered on a municipal level, the new group would have to be a city-wide organization. Quart had put together a small group calling itself the Victoria Park Welfare Committee which operated out of the larger community organization. To meet Munro's demands he simply renamed it the "Hamilton Welfare Rights Organization."

From the beginning the group's terms of reference were quite clear to everyone involved. Welfare Rights was to be an Alinski-styled organization, designed to challenge, through confrontation, the administration of welfare in the city. Although it was expected that the group would provide some services for recipients, it was to be essentially a political group, organized so that welfare recipients could effectively change welfare policy.

Structurally, the Victoria Park Community Organization was very closely tied to the Welfare Rights group. Gary Quart was to carry on as the community organization's employee but he would also receive part of his salary from the Welfare

Rights grant. In addition some of the grant money was paid to Victoria Park for office space and other services and part of it was to be used to pay a second organizer. On Quart's recommendation, I (Bill Freeman) was hired.

Not long after the money arrived in January 1971, the Hamilton Welfare Rights Organization successfully made welfare a major political issue in the city. The so-called "Poor People's Conference" was held in Toronto (again supported by Health and Welfare), and one of its resolutions was the decision to designate Monday, January 25, as a day of protest against the conditions of the poor. Welfare Rights responded by organizing a demonstration of about 60 people who went to Hamilton city hall for speeches, and then on to the welfare office to begin a sit-in for the right to dispense information to recipients at a table in the welfare office. The evening concluded with a teach-in about welfare.

For three days the group occupied the welfare office, giving out information to recipients and occasionally representing them in the role of advocate with welfare administrators. Then, after a fierce debate in Hamilton's Board of Control, the group was ordered out of the office. Once it was learned that city council would debate the issue of whether Welfare Rights should be allowed to keep the information table, the group agreed to leave.

It took over a month of political wrangling before the issue was resolved in council. In the end Welfare Rights lost. But the group did make major gains during this period. Almost every day *The Spectator* ran news accounts of the welfare issue, and the radio hot lines were alive with callers wanting to discuss it. Although the backlash against welfare recipients was evident everywhere, the point was successfully made that the conditions under which welfare recipients lived were dreadful and that the administration of the welfare program was inadequate in the extreme. Hamilton Welfare Rights came to be seen as a powerful, militant group, willing and able to take on important issues. Within three months of its formation, over 600 welfare recipients had become affiliated with the organization. Although the politicians voted against an information table at the welfare office, the more enlightened realized that they would have to bring about major reforms in the welfare system or invite serious political trouble.

Within the first three months of the three-year project, the Hamilton Welfare Rights Organization had achieved its most important objective. By comparison, the activities of the group after March were anti-climactic. Welfare Rights attempted to design projects that would involve people who had expressed an interest in the organization. The most successful of these was the creation of an advocacy service, located near the welfare office, to advise and help people in their appeals. But almost all of the other projects disintegrated as soon as they were formed. The problem was that projects such as co-op stores and clothing exchange shops, were simply beyond the administrative and financial resources of the group. After several failures, enthusiasm began to wane and participation faltered.

Throughout this early period, many of the activities of the Welfare Rights Organization had been given full coverage in the Hamilton news media. Although this focused publicity on the inadequacies of the welfare system, it also identified the organization in the public mind as little more than a militant group defending "welfare bums." More than anyone else the publicity affected John Munro. Since his ministry had funded the organization, its unpopularity spilled over onto him. To make matters worse, Welfare Rights operated in his riding, and his constituency office received many complaints about the group's activities.

The pressure on Munro must have been intense. In the summer of 1971 he ordered Welfare Rights to tone down their activities, and in early December the grant was terminated. The excuse given by Munro to the press was that Welfare Rights was "widening the already polarized public opinion on welfare." But this was not the reason: a federal election was expected the following spring and the organization had become a political liability.

Most of the people involved in Welfare Rights were outraged that the money should be withdrawn for doing what the grant originally had proposed. Welfare Rights could do little more than force a confrontation with Munro, hoping to embarrass him publicly, and demand an explanation. Some members of the group met with him and, after a bitter exchange, the delegation called a press conference where it condemned Munro and the federal Cabinet.

The failure of Welfare Rights was inevitable from the start. Munro appeared to encourage the group and endorse its Alinski-style tactics when he first funded it, but when a serious attack was mounted against the welfare system, and particularly when Munro's political popularity in his own riding was threatened by his apparent sponsorship of this radical organization, the grant was quickly terminated.

While the Hamilton Welfare Rights Organization did make some important and long-lasting reforms in welfare procedures, the history of the group illustrates once again how politically powerless poor people's groups actually are. Canadians and their politicians expect the poor to be humble and grateful for what they get, and anyone daring to ask for anything more is dismissed as a troublemaker.

Although political differences and personal animosities had divided the Welfare Rights group, when Munro cancelled the grant, the members rallied around a new cause. But Gary Quart, the person who had developed and fostered the confrontation tactics that the group used, was conspicuously absent. It finally emerged that Quart was attempting to make a deal with Munro. In fact, on the very

The V. P. C. O. office at 448 York Street, with the new name of the organization in the window (Marsha Hewitt).

same day that Welfare Rights had had their angry confrontation with the cabinet minister, Gary Quart met with Munro and Father Ed Hinsberger, a priest from the Cathedral of Christ the King, to discuss how the money from the Welfare Rights grant could be redirected to the Victoria Park Community Organization.

Quart's interest was one of survival. He saw that the withdrawal of money from Welfare Rights would soon lead to the collapse of the whole organization. The fact that Munro had acted unjustly toward Welfare Rights and that the group needed Quart's support seemed to matter little to him. He was willing to make any compromise to save himself and his community organization. In the meeting with Munro, Quart and Hinsberger promised that, if the money was redirected to the community organization, Victoria Park would be much more moderate in its actions. As the organizer of Welfare Rights, I was given the blame for the group's now-problematic "radicalism."

From Munro's point of view, Quart's proposition must have had a lot to offer. Welfare Rights had put him in a tight spot. He had been criticized for funding the group in the first instance, and now he was being attacked (particularly by The Globe and Mail) for cutting off the funds. By shifting the money to the Victoria Park Community Organization (in return for a promise of no more "creative conflict"), he could counter the criticism that he was reneging on his duties to the poor and thus maintain his liberal image. In any event, the leadership of the groups would be irreparably split, a further insurance against any resurgence of political activism.

Before agreeing to grant the money, Munro insisted on two guarantees: Welfare Rights must be killed and confrontation tactics must be rejected. It was when Quart accepted these stipulations, in late 1971 or early 1972, that we can date the beginning of the new, and totally co-opted, community organization.

COMMUNITY DEVELOPMENT

In order to justify his actions, Quart had to espouse an entirely new approach to community organization. He now told everyone that Alinski-styled organizations had outlived their usefulness, and that the new tactic to promote meaningful social change was "community development." The organizer's job, he claimed, was to provide community services and get people involved in community projects, not to create conflict. He seemed to be oblivious to the fact that community development, which does things for the people in the neighbourhood, is the antithesis of community organization, which tries to get people in the neighbourhood to do things *for themselves*. One approach encourages passivity, while the other encourages people to be the agents of their own change.

Quart's change of approach caused a devastating division among the people involved in the two organizations. The members of Welfare Rights tried to carry on as best they could without funding. Money was solicited from local trade unions to keep the office open, and the welfare advocacy program was maintained on a volunteer basis. But Quart let it be known that he wanted the organization to die and those who were loyal to him deserted it. Others were forced to take jobs; some were co-opted by a Victoria Park LIP grant; the United Church gave money to hire the most outspoken member of the group, John Morris, as a lay lawyer; and finally, in the summer of 1972, the last hold-out was given an organizer's job by Munro in another part of the province.

Meanwhile, the Victoria Park Community Organization limped along on funding from various sources. The organization still had money from the United Church and the city, and, with Munro's help, it was able to get a Local Initiatives Program grant. However, in spite of the promises of Health and Welfare, a major grant did not materialize for some time. Quart had to demonstrate to Munro that Victoria Park had become politically trustworthy before the Liberal Cabinet Minister would gamble his reputation again.

During the early part of 1972, Quart had some success in changing Victoria Park over to a community development style of organization. By hiring some people who had been involved as volunteers with Welfare Rights, he was able to develop a welfare advocacy service which expanded into unemployment insurance advocacy. However, workers were instructed by Quart to challenge the administration's policies, but to restrict themselves to fighting individual cases.

Quart ran into his first serious problems during these attempts to expand community services. In the spring of 1972, John Buttrum, a social work student, prepared a proposal for an Opportunities For Youth grant to operate out of Victoria Park. With the help of Quart and Munro, Buttrum got the grant, but soon after the group began work in May, a serious conflict developed between Quart and the students. The OFY group wanted to be involved in action that would produce social change, while Quart, because of his deal with Munro, wanted nothing to do with conflict.

The first problems arose over a high-rise, low-income development called York Place that was being built in the Victoria Park neighbourhood with federal funds. There was considerable local opposition to the project, and an OMB hearing was scheduled to review the objections of neighbourhood residents. The hearing was suddenly cancelled because the objections were withdrawn by letters bearing those same residents' signatures. The withdrawals were forgeries and one of them was traced to a real estate agent involved in the deal. When the community organization would take no action on this issue, Kate Hohler, one of the OFY workers, took the matter to the NDP Riding Association and a leaflet opposing the project was prepared and distributed in the neighbourhood.

When Quart learned of it he was furious. He criticized Hohler for lack of loyalty and the NDP for meddling in the community. Later it was learned that Quart and Rene Wyatt, an executive member of the Victoria Park Community Organization, had been meeting privately with Dominic Morganti, the developer, apparently in an effort to get him to build community facilities into York Place. Quart made no effort to capitalize on the strong opposition to the project presumably because he thought that his community development techniques would achieve great benefits for the neighbourhood. In the end the developer refused to include any community facilities whatsoever and the project was imposed on the community. Since it has been built York Place has been plagued with financial problems and has turned out to be one of the worst examples of low-income high-rise that can be found anywhere in Ontario. Dominic Morganti ultimately was convicted on bribery charges in connection with this project.

The year 1972 was a difficult one for those involved in Victoria Park. The organization struggled along with little money and the bitterness of the Welfare Rights experience and constant arguments over tactics produced serious divisions. Finally, at the end of the year it was confirmed that Health and Welfare would supply more funds and on January 1, 1973 Victoria Park started another three-year project.

Quart knew exactly what he wanted to do with the money. He intended to provide various types of social service facilities and possibly do a little organizing around "safe" local issues. Above all, he wanted to use the money to try to get the organization on a firm financial footing.

The only practical way of doing this, Quart concluded, was to develop various profit-making projects whose surplus funds could be plowed back into the organization. Although it may sound strange to use a federal Health and Welfare grant to turn what had become essentially a community self-help project into a profit-making organization, in terms of Quart's new community development theory it made perfect sense. As he pointed out, the purpose of the organization was to provide community services. What could be wrong with having some of these services make a profit?

Three major money-making projects were started, but none were financially successful. A print shop was set up in the basement of the Victoria Park office to print church and social agency

A widened York Street (Marsha Hewitt).

bulletins, but the wrong kind of press was leased, and operations only limped along.

A second project was the publication of a regular community newspaper. As early as 1971 a small tabloid-sized newspaper called *Community Forum* had been published periodically by the community organization to publicize its activities. It had always been hoped that the paper might break even through advertising, but this had never happened. In April, 1973, Quart approached Kate Hohler, the same person he had had problems with over York Place the previous summer, to become the editor of an expanded newspaper.

For six months the paper operated under the auspices of Victoria Park Community Organization, and although there were problems, it established a crusading style that made some politicians and citizens take notice. On more than one occasion it exposed slum landlords by detailing grievances and revealed some vicious blockbusting. It even tried to report on wider community issues, such as city politics and disputes within the trade union movement.

In spite of the fact that the newspaper was gradually gaining more support through subscriptions and advertisements, in the fall of 1973 the executive of Victoria Park, on Quart's recommendation, cut off its funds. It is not difficult to understand why. Quart wanted to promote community development and the newspaper, under Hohler's editorship, took a strongly reformist stand. This alone was an embarrassment to Quart, but the newspaper also showed there were many issues that needed immediate attention and the community organization was doing nothing about them. An attempt was made to keep the newspaper going, but without financial support it soon folded.

By far the most ambitious project was the Community Home Improvement Program (CHIP). The project was started to provide rental units for low-income families by borrowing money to buy deteriorating houses and fixing them up. As the property increased in value, new homes could be bought by using the existing property as collateral. To get the project underway, the United Church funded Victoria Park with a $4,000 interest-free loan and a $1,000 straight grant. With this downpayment, a number of homes were purchased.

On paper the project looked good, but Quart drastically overextended the organization's resources. By the time four units had been purchased, virtually no money was left to do any repairs, and tenants had to be moved into the houses immediately in order to keep up the mortgage payments. To make the financial picture even worse, in the spring of 1973 the community organization bought a three-unit row-house on Woodbine Crescent. The houses had to be repaired before they could be rented because they had been condemned by the Board of Health. The community organization had no funds for renovations, so Quart directed staff members to contribute their labour and took money out of the federal grant to hire a contractor and buy materials. The money was replaced later when the houses

York Place, in a neighbourhood of working class homes (Marsha Hewitt).

were completed and he could raise a mortgage on them. When the three units were finally finished in September and families moved in, the units were still unfinished inside. Rubble was heaped in the front and back yards and the units were overrun with mice and rats.

Ironically at the same time that most of the CHIP houses were in a dilapidated condition, a great deal of money was being put into remodelling the community organization office. New heating and air conditioning systems were installed, the inside of the building was remodelled, gold carpets were laid, panelling was put on the walls, and expensive office equipment was purchased.

In spite of Quart's emphasis on profit-making schemes there *was* money in the new Health and Welfare grant for a community organizer. Doug Branigan, a young local resident who had been involved in the organization, was hired and within a few months, he became active in a number of important issues. Branigan helped organize the residents of York Place into a tenants association. He put considerable effort into organizing senior citizens on a city-wide basis, and he was the only one who tried to put together a community group to resist the widening of York Street.

But at literally every stage of Branigan's work, Quart attempted to restrict his actions. It became very clear that Quart feared that, if allowed freedom, Branigan would promote confrontation, and this would reflect badly on Victoria Park. Friction between the two men increased until it became obvious that they could not work together. Finally in May 1974, Branigan was asked to resign. Although there was money in the grant for an organizer, no one was ever hired to fill the vacancy.

It seemed to those who had been involved that Victoria Park was gradually becoming more and more of an embarrassment. Many who had been inspired by the concept of community organizing left. Those who remained consisted of a handful of staff and executive members who remained loyal either because they still believed in Quart, or because they knew he had the money and they had to co-operate with him. But as each month went by the crisis seemed to become more and more serious.

THE CONVENTION

The dissension that wracked the organization finally came to a head around the community convention. Nominally Victoria Park was a democratic organization. In May, 1971, a founding convention had been held at which members elected an executive, passed various policy resolutions, and adopted a structure that called for a yearly convention to review all aspects of the organization. In spite of these requirements, between 1971 and 1974 no convention was held, and to make matters worse the original executive had been reduced to a mere handful.

As a result of pressure, a convention committee was appointed in the spring of 1974, but soon it became obvious that Quart would not give it his co-operation. Any convention in the community was bound to bring together people who would criticize him and his patron, John Munro, and he was determined to stop this from happening at all costs.

But as he manoeuvred to block the convention, a group emerged to ensure that it went ahead. The pro-convention group, calling itself the "Committee to Reform Victoria Park," had influence over the convention committee through its chairman, Tom Moerman. They used this control to block Quart's efforts to cancel the convention and made every effort to get their supporters to attend. When Quart saw what was happening, he tried to get his people to attend as delegates. Quart and his supporters claimed something like 25 delegates from both Christ the King and All Souls churches, although only one of the church groups had ever been involved in the community organization and then only briefly. A group called the "Queen Street Resident's Association" claimed 95 members, but no one had heard of the association before. Incredibly the Victoria Park Welfare Committee claimed to have 868 members and registered 26 delegates even though no one had ever heard of its existence since before the days of Welfare Rights.

The wrangling became intense. The reform group challenged the credentials of Quart's delegates, and finally on the day of the convention, Quart and his supporters marched out of the hall, leaving the reform group in control of the proceedings. Resolutions were passed condemning the inadequacies of the previous executive, the problems surrounding the properties were explained, motions were passed committing the group to a set of organizing principles and a new executive, headed by Tom Moerman, was elected to carry out the reforms.

GRANTSMANSHIP AND SURVIVAL

When the convention was over, the new executive tried as best they could to take over the organization, but that proved to be more difficult than it appeared. The Victoria Park office was registered in the name of a corporation, and most of the staff were paid out of the federal grants over which Quart and the old executive had signing power. They stubbornly resisted all challenges.

The new executive responded by writing to all of the funding bodies — the federal government, the United Church and the City of Hamilton — requesting that the payments of all grants be suspended until the issue of who controlled the community organization was clarified. Surprisingly, within a matter of weeks, the federal Department of Health and Welfare announced that it was withdrawing support from the organization. (By this time John Munro was no longer the Minister.)

For a while it seemed that Quart's control over Victoria Park was over. A sign appeared in the window of the community organization office urging people to "Help Keep Victoria Park Open — On Feb. 28th This Place May Close" and asked people to sign a petition opposing the withdrawal of funds. But it was not long before Quart had developed a new strategy: he simply created a new organization. On April 22, 1975, the founding convention of a group called "The Strathcona Community Project" was held at Zion United Church. It was not an open meeting and only selected people showed up. An explanation of some of the services that had existed at Victoria Park was given and a new executive was elected. This new executive was virtually identical to the old one except for the addition of Doctor George Morrow, the father of Hamilton City Controller Bob Morrow and a prominent United Church member.

Some interim funding came from the United Church to keep the organization afloat (Quart is still a United Church minister), and within days after the new group had been formed, Quart was at city council asking for $10,000, which he got with little effort. This was enough to keep the organization going for a time.

Not long after the Victoria Park convention, some of the issues around the housing project came to a head. By this time, the community organization owned seven houses. Three of these had had extensive repairs, but the other four had been in bad condition when they were purchased and no money had been spent to improve them. By late 1974 they were in a deplorable state.

Doug Branigan, the former Victoria Park organizer, began meeting with the tenants of the houses and helped them form a tenants group in an effort to improve conditions. Their complaints were identical. They claimed that over and over again Quart had made promises to fix up the homes, but nothing was ever done. Finally, on December 1, 1974, the day after the community convention, three of the tenants began a rent strike.

The group notified Quart of their action and, like any other landlord, he began legal proceedings against them. The cases dragged through the courts until finally, on April 23, 1975, the issue was heard by Judge William Warrender.

The Spectator news report gives the best summary of the events:

Violet Stunden, of Ray Street North, whose husband is disabled, testified that their home was rented nearly two-and-a-half years ago for $125 a month. She testified that the Ray Street home was in disrepair and filled with

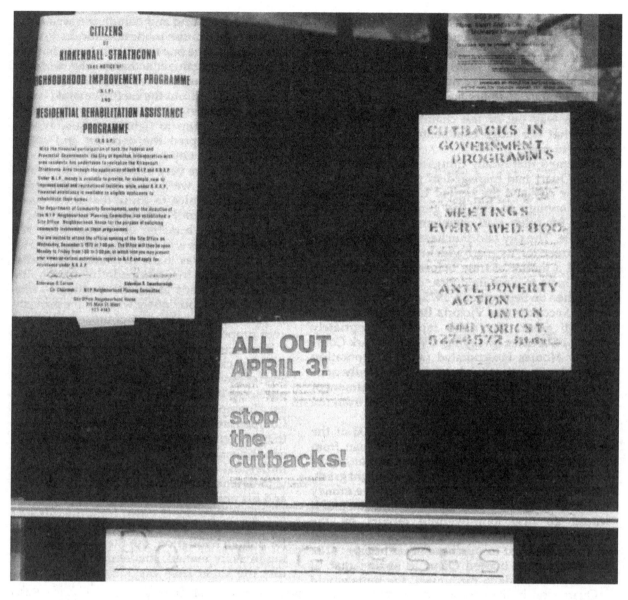

Notices in the window of 448 York Street give the impression of activity (Marsha Hewitt).

garbage when the move was made and that Mr. Quart was going to have the needed repairs made, but he has not done so.

Of needed repairs in the Stunden home, the judge asked Mr. Quart: "Why don't you do something about it? You got her a house — do you want her to live like a pig?"
He asked Mrs. Stunden: "If things are dangerous there, why stay?"
"Because he [Quart] has promised he's going to get it fixed," she replied.
Judge Warrender dismissed the application "By reason of the fact Mr. Quart got the house [for the Stundens] and after a considerable length of time has done nothing despite complaints."
Pat Buzza, who rents the second and third floors of a Wood Street duplex, said that she rented the premises from Mr. Quart for $155 a month . . . She said that rotten roof rafters are covered with green moss and that water leaks down to the floors below."Three floors need new ceilings."
"I've heard of animals being treated better," said the judge. Miss Buzza said that she needs low-rent accommodation and that Mr. Quart had inspected her home many times."He just looks at it and goes home." In dismissing the application, Judge Warrender found that Mr. Quart "steered" Miss Buzza to the dwelling after she answered an advertisement, but permitted conditions of disrepair to continue."If ever there was a deplorable state of affairs this is it."

(On his way out of the chambers, the reporter noted that the judge commented, "Man's inhumanity to man.")

It seemed that finally things were about to collapse. Quart had managed to get some funding from the city and the United Church, but it was hardly enough to pay his generous salary and money for other staff members was simply not available. The city had purchased the office at 448 York Street for its road-widening project, and it seemed a matter of time before the organization would have to close its doors.

But then on September 8, 1975, it was announced in *The Spectator* that Victoria Park had received a $120,000 grant. The news report appropriately started its articles by saying: "Victoria Park Community Homes Incorporated (a new corporation created by Quart) which has been repeatedly criticized by Provincial court judges for its treatment of tenants, has received more than $120,000 from the Federal Government."

The article went on to say that $95,000 of the grant was a $25,000-a-year, 8 per cent loan from Central Mortgage and Housing Corporation, and a total of $25,551 was in the form of an outright grant. Although it was not clear exactly what the money was to be used for it seemed likely that some of it would go into long-overdue repairs on the organization's rental properties and some would probably be used to purchase other houses. (*The Spectator* report quoted Quart as saying that, if repairs were made to the houses, the rents would have to be raised.)

Then in September and October, 1975, it was announced that Victoria Park would get an $18,000 LIP grant and another $10,000 from the Hamilton-Wentworth regional government. In December the Hamilton Presbytery of the United Church voted to renew its sponsorship of the project to the tune of $16,000. This would pay for the Reverend Quart's salary, living expenses and travel allowance for the next year.

Quart won in the end because he was able to survive. However, judging from what happened to the organization and what was accomplished in the community, it is difficult to see what he has achieved. The Victoria Park Community Organization was started to give the residents some power over the political decisions that were being made for their community. But it seems to have done just the opposite. It actually co-operated with the developers of York Place, a project that was clearly opposed by the majority of the community residents. In another part of the community, some nasty blockbusting and demolition was going on, but the organization made no effort to do anything about it. And the one issue that should have been a community organizer's dream, the widening of York Street, was accepted with virtually no fight. Typically, Quart and the executive hired lawyers to oppose the street widening, rather than develop a community group to fight the issue. When they lost, they accepted the decision and sold their property to the city as quickly as possible. In reality, except at the very beginning of the project, no real organizing went on in the community.

It would be nice to think that there was more organizing around individual complaints, but if true, it is only a matter of degree. After Welfare Rights, the focus was on trying to help individuals, but no effort was made to change the welfare or unemployment insurance administration, and no attempt was made at collective action to improve housing. (That obviously would have proven to be an embarrassment in view of the condition of their own properties.)

The focus of the group seems to have been on fighting cases for individuals wronged by some level of government. This is important work, but in one sense it is relatively easy to do. Welfare as well as Unemployment Insurance and Workman's Compensation have appeal procedures built into their structures and to fight a case an individual need only ask that it be reviewed. The real need for individual advocacy in low-income communities is to defend people against slum landlords. Quart and his organization virtually ignored this type of problem. Two doors down from the office an old couple lived for a year in conditions not only unfit for human habitation, but illegal, and a family living in a city-owned, condemned house almost across the street from the Victoria Park office was attacked by rats and not even a protest was voiced.

What happened is a classic case of co-optation. Because the organization needed money to survive, Quart entered into an alliance with John Munro and the federal Liberals and with the Liberal and Conservative members of city hall. The alliance netted the organization three major federal government grants as well as a host of smaller grants from LIP, OFY, the city and the churches. More than anything else the case of the Victoria Park Community Organization shows the very political nature of grant-giving in Canada. After his experience with the Welfare Rights group, Quart learned this lesson very well, and, in order to keep the money, he transformed his community organization into a conservative agency of social control which created more divisions and caused more problems in the neighbourhood than any other group could conceive of doing.

Part III
The uses of power: Case studies in city politics

All politics involves promoting the interests of one set of people at the expense of another. It is, therefore, by examining the programs and policies of government and analyzing who benefits from these programs that we can see political power at work. No amount of sociological analysis of "the power structure" or statistical studies of the back-grounds of those who are said to hold power can replace the detailed analysis of the political decision-making process in action. The following chapters, focusing on development in Hamilton in the sixties and seventies, demolish the myth that the city's government equally represents all the people. They amply demonstrate that the interests of business are generally put first by the politicians. It has been this way since Hamilton was founded early in the nineteenth century, and it continues this way today.

The new city hall saga 1955–1972

Marsha Aileen Hewitt

"It is contrary to the interest of public policy if contractors, like feudal barons of ancient times, are permitted to have responsible public servants posturing as if they were personal lackeys."
— Kenneth Rouff, City Solicitor, in his submission to Judge Theo McCombs, June 25, 1971.

In the early 1950s, Hamilton politicians decided that the city needed a new city hall. The old James Street North municipal building, erected in 1889 at a cost of $26,000, was an elegant structure in the French Romanesque style, built of Newcastle stone, resplendent with graceful arches and towers. Its illuminated clock was set in the high tower that dominated the building. The ponderous striking of the hours could be heard in the far corners of the city. Ultimately, the building was demolished, and the land it sat upon sold to a private company for development.

The building of the new $10-million city hall[1] is a story of how powerful private interests seized an opportunity to plunder the public purse. The new building turned out to be a poorly constructed and costly enterprise for the city. The ensuing political problems brought about a judicial inquiry which gave the public a tantalizing glimpse of the private backroom dealings between the city and some of its leading corporate citizens.

EATON'S GETS THE OLD CITY HALL

The first phase of the new city hall project involved a subsidy for the T. Eaton Company. The old building and its site were sold to Eaton's in 1955 for a total price of $800,000. The city hall was to be demolished to make way for a new Eaton's store. The city agreed to be out of the James Street location within five years. But at the time of the sale the city had no site for a new city hall. The city thus found itself scrambling around town for a site upon which to build a new city hall so that Eaton's could have the old city hall site for an expansion of its department store.

The land was not purchased by public tender and many aldermen felt that the city was probably not getting the best possible price. As it happened, the city ended up paying close to $2 million for its site, and acquiring the land involved expropriating residents and stores.

The construction contract for the new city hall was awarded to the Pigott Construction Company Ltd., the same firm that had built the old city hall some 70 years before. In the 1950s Pigott was the biggest contractor in Hamilton and one of the largest in the country. Three generations of the Pigott family had been builders and they had put up some of the largest and most complex structures in the city.

Not only were the Pigott family the owners of one of the most successful construction companies in the country, but they also had considerable political power in Hamilton. The family is Catholic, and family members are leaders in the Knights of Columbus, one of the most influential political clubs in the city. More important, the Pigotts are Tories, and through the party they had influence upon powerful local political figures such as then-Controller Jack MacDonald. This connection proved extremely valuable to the Pigotts during construction of the new city hall.

The new city hall was beset with construction

Laying the cornerstone of the Old City Hall (Ontario Archives).

problems from the very beginning, primarily with respect to the marble cladding that covered the exterior of the building. Huge 450-pound slabs of imported Italian marble kept falling off the building. City politicians did nothing about it until 1970, when Controller Anne Jones and her chauffeur were nearly killed by two falling slabs which crashed to the ground as they were entering the building.

The politicians could no longer ignore the problem; it was in fact the sixth time the marble had fallen off their new city hall. Since 1970 was an election year, several appropriately embarrassed city politicians seized the opportunity to make a campaign promise that they would press for a judicial inquiry into the situation. The falling marble, together with perpetually leaking roofs, cost the taxpayers of Hamilton $1 million in repair bills over 10 years.[2]

THE JUDICIAL INQUIRY

The mandate of the judicial inquiry conducted by Ontario Judge Theo McCombs, which began February 15, 1971, was to investigate and report on "the conduct and actions of city council members, city employees and outside contractors or consultants with respect to carrying out the construction of the new city hall."

One of the first witnesses to testify at the inquiry was city architect Alex German, who took over the office in 1960, shortly after former city architect Stanley Roscoe, designer of the new city hall, left to enter private practice. German testified that by the time of the inquiry at least six marble slabs had fallen from the building's exterior walls, and that on other occasions the marble cladding had been in the process of either caving in or bulging out. German sent seven letters in 1961 to William Pigott, president of the construction company, outlining the various faults in the workmanship of the building. Some of the deficiencies he listed (there were 39 items) included:

- the marble cladding in the 18 decorative first-floor columns was broken and falling (the columns were later removed altogether because the damage was so extensive that it was cheaper to remove them than do repairs);

- water was leaking through the roofs of the garage and the main building;

- daylight could be seen through the council chamber floor due to faulty insulation and leaky pipes; and

- water leaking through the roof of the main building was causing damage to the marble, stainless steel and glass in the building.

Pigott's reply to this letter was that the "construction was completed according to contract."[3] On another occasion in reply to complaints from German, Joseph Pigott wrote that "most of the items on these (deficiency lists) have turned out to be matters of maintenance rather than deficiencies."[4] Throughout the inquiry Pigott's counsel blamed both faulty maintenance on the part of the city and Roscoe's design for the problems of the city hall.

When the first marble slabs fell from the building during its construction, the City Hall Building Committee (formed by city council to oversee the construction) recommended to council that it pay half the $20,000 bill for repairs. This decision was made in July 1960, four months before the city moved into the building. The Controller responsible for persuading the committee to recommend this cost sharing plan was Jack MacDonald, later mayor of Hamilton.

The council did not see fit to call in an outside consultant to assess the condition of the marble or to find out why the slabs fell from the partially completed building. This negligence on the part of the Building Committee meant that it had no idea if the fall was an isolated incident or if it was indicative of the overall quality of the construction. However, unknown to most people on the city hall committee except MacDonald, the Pigott firm retained its own consultants, Edgar Cross and Associates, to inspect the marble.

The report submitted by Cross stated that the condition of the 450-pound slabs was "frightening" because the bronze manganese anchors holding them in place were defective. According to the report, "one cannot depend upon any of the anchorage system of the marble as now hung." The Cross report further recommended in May 1960, months before the city moved into the building, that the slabs should be re-hung, since there was "no other alternative."[5] The Pigott firm decided to keep this report private and ignored its recommendations.

The inquiry also heard testimony indicating that others were aware that the anchors were faulty during the construction phase. Frank Burman, a former employee at C. C. Parker, a consulting engineering firm under contract to the city for general supervision of construction, said that early in the construction of city hall he had recommended to someone in the city architect's office that the city scrap all the original anchors for the marble slabs because they were of such inferior quality that he was able to break them in half with his own hands. "At the break I could see a cross-section of the anchors. Only 25% to 30% of each one was solid; the rest was hollow."[6] Why this information never got beyond Burman is unclear, but the inquiry was able to determine that at least Pigott Construction and, possibly, others knew of the dangerous state of the anchors before all the marble was hung.[7]

The inquiry also found that the condition of the anchors was known to Controller Jack MacDonald. When the Building Committee made its recommendation to share the cost of repairs of the marble with Pigott Construction in 1960, no one on the committee except MacDonald knew of the Cross report's existence. During questioning on the witness stand by Ken Rouff, the city solicitor who was legal counsel for the city, MacDonald admitted that he had "knowledge" of the report but "I couldn't swear to whether or not I had seen it, but I must have seen it because I am familiar with the general content [of the report]."[8]

During the inquiry, all other members of the former Building Committee stated, under questioning by Rouff, that it had been Jack MacDonald who recommended that the city split the cost of the repairs with the contractor:

Ada Pritchard: *Well, it was broached by . . . the one Controller . . . and I went along with it because we had no idea and it had to be done.*

When asked by Counsel for Stanley Roscoe for the name of the Controller, she replied "Controller MacDonald."[9]

Joseph McLaren: *Controller MacDonald was negotiating with some of the committee and Pigott.*[10]

Margaret Standen: *MacDonald did put forth a very strong argument as to why we should absorb half the costs.*[11]

Dave Lawrence: *The Controller [MacDonald] came to the committee and he was the vocal person; my understanding was that he was watching this job very carefully.*[12]

So MacDonald knew of the existence of the Cross report, which claimed the anchors were defective and had to be replaced, and it was through his influence that the city's Building Committee agreed to share the cost of repairs with the contractor. City solicitor Ken Rouff suggested to the inquiry that MacDonald was in "special confidence" with the contractor.[13] MacDonald said that he recommended the cost-sharing scheme because of the difficulty of determining who was responsible for the falling marble, even though it was falling during construction.

MacDonald's connections with Pigott go back a long way; MacDonald used to be a plumbing contractor in Hamilton, and on occasion did subcontracting work for the Pigott company. Ramsay Evans, counsel for Pigott, was MacDonald's campaign manager when he ran for Board of Control.

In the early 1960s, though city architect Alex German was ignorant of the Cross report, he was aware that the marble cladding on the building was defective and was engaged in a losing battle to have Pigott Construction make the proper repairs. He provided Pigott with a deficiency list in March 1962 which noted that 50% of the slabs on the patio deck had slipped one inch and that the marble was broken in various places. Nothing was done. German fought Pigott Construction over an 18-month period during 1961 and 1962, sending them a total of seven deficiency lists, and trying to get the firm to correct construction defects.

While Alex German was wrangling with Pigott Construction, the company's buyer, Ramsay Evans (himself a former city alderman), was trying to get the city to pay the company the $100,000 "holdback" money, the balance owing on the construction contract which the city had not yet released. The payment of this money, along with the architect's final certificate, would help limit the company's further liability for defects in the building. German claimed he was present at a meeting between Evans and former city solicitor Foster Rodger to discuss this payment. German argued that the money should not be paid until the building's construction flaws were corrected. Evans replied to this by sending city council a letter saying that he no longer wanted to deal with German, who was "being difficult." German testified in 1971 that "I imagine Mr. Evans was trying to get the money released as quickly as possible and I was not co-operating until certain parts of the contract were fulfilled."[14] In spite of his recommendation, council chose to pay out the $100,000. Nevertheless, the repairs were never made.

Why the politicians gave in to the contractor over the protestations of the city's own architect has never been properly explained. Alderman Mac Cline, chairman of the Building Committee at the time, tried to discredit German's competence when he testified at the inquiry that "We [the committee] didn't receive any advice from Mr. German in which we placed any reliance."[15] Yet neither Cline nor anyone else on the committee gave any concrete reasons for doubting German's competence. Ken Rouff explained the city's action by saying it "was prepared to bail out the contractor."[16] Board of Control minutes made no explicit reference to the falling marble until two years after all payments had been made to Pigott Construction.

Alex German was not the only city employee to challenge Pigott Construction. The testimony of Victor Dukeshire, the city's Clerk of Works from July 1958 to June 1960, while the new city hall was under construction, highlighted another serious problem in the workmanship — the leaking roofs. The roofs, like the marble, began to show serious defects well before the building was completed.

Dukeshire had kept diaries on the job site while he was supervising construction for the city. In his testimony to the inquiry, he used these to recall that he ordered LaBarre Roofing Company to halt work on the roof because the work was "of the poorest quality."[17] Dukeshire claimed that he issued 45 to 50 "stop work" orders during construction because, in his view, the contractor was continually violating building specifications.

Reading from his diaries, Dukeshire provided information that:

- the roofing on the eighth floor was improperly applied;

The Old City Hall (Hamilton Public Library).

- the second-floor waterproofing membrane was laid over wet concrete and would not bond, an action contrary to the specifications that all materials must be free of dust and moisture before they would bond to the concrete (because of this defect blisters formed on the garage roof); and

- the flashings on the roof were improperly installed so that water just "ran down behind the roof."

Over the objections of Pigott Construction, Dukeshire ordered water tests taken of the repaired roof and found that it still leaked. Water had penetrated the eighth- and second-floor roofs, and had filtered into the duct system, running into the basement. Dukeshire claimed that the water was running into the basement for two days and that no attempts were made to stop it: "You could hear [water] dripping in the duct works." All these problems were reported to the contractors on the building site.

With regard to the marble, Dukeshire testified that in May and June of 1959, he issued four complaints to Pigott Construction about the marble facings in the building, which had only been up one month. At that early date, they had already

An aerial view of Hamilton's downtown area, showing the Old City Hall and Eaton's immediately behind it
(Hamilton Public Library)

shifted three-eighths of an inch and the mortar joints were cracking and falling out.

Dukeshire had a continuous long-running dispute with Pigott Construction over changes the company made in the specifications from the time construction began in 1958. He quoted from his diaries that "the superintendent . . . of Pigott Construction is constantly making changes without permission . . . co-operation is very poor. The superintendent's . . . work is one mistake after another."[18]

In February 1959, Dukeshire was summoned to a meeting at the Pigott Building in downtown Hamilton at which were present Joseph Pigott, Jr.; William Pigott; former city architect Stanley Roscoe, the city hall designer; and the city hall Building Committee chairman, Alderman Mac Cline. It appears that Dukeshire was summoned to this meeting so that he could be persuaded to be more co-operative on the job site. According to Dukeshire, Joseph Pigott said: "A job of this magnitude is like a ball team — there can only be one coach."[19] When Dukeshire replied "Did you ever see a ball team without an umpire?" he was asked to leave the meeting with no protest coming from Alderman Mac Cline. In fact, Dukeshire said that Cline and other city hall officials had chastised him for trying to make Pigott follow building specifications. In the inquiry, Cline denied he attended the meeting.

When Dukeshire received no support from Stanley Roscoe during that meeting, he resigned. Roscoe then apparently asked him to return to the job, but when Dukeshire complained that it was improper that he had been summoned to the meeting at the Pigott Building, Roscoe's reply was, according to Dukeshire: "It's bad enough that I have to fight the city hall Building Committee without having to fight you."[20]

Without the support of the city politicians, people like Victor Dukeshire and Alex German did not have sufficient power to protect the city's interests. After the holdback money was paid to Pigott there was little the city could do to force the contractor to make the necessary repairs.

Nothing was done about the falling marble until 1968, when the city engaged Douglas Stiles of the firm Cross, Stiles, and Brown (formerly Edgar Cross and Associates) to make a report on the problem. This was the same firm that had been hired by Pigott Construction to report on the problem with the falling marble in 1960. Edgar Cross himself had found at that time that the problem was caused by faulty pins and recommended that all the slabs be

The New City Hall under construction (Hamilton Public Library).

re-hung. But Stiles did not tell the city of the previous study and in fact had apparently approached the city for the consulting job after hearing about it from William Pigott.

In his report Stiles told the city what Pigott Construction had been asserting all along: that the problem occurred as a result of Roscoe's "faulty design" in the building specifications. Stiles asserted that the constant expansion and contraction of the marble as temperatures changed caused the anchors to break. During the inquiry Ken Rouff, the city solicitor, pointed out that this finding was inconsistent with the report done a few years earlier by the same firm. He also suggested that Douglas Stiles was "possibly unethical"[21] in accepting the consulting job for the city in 1968, since his firm had done the same kind of work on the same subject for the contractor.

It was only on the last day of the inquiry that the story of the anchors was finally told. It was disclosed that Pigott Construction had originally subcontracted the manufacture of the bronze manganese anchors to Mills Steel, but later switched to a company called Central Ornamental Ironworks Ltd., who in turn subcontracted to Fergusson Foundry of Dundas to make the anchors. Pigott Construction made the switch to obtain a cheaper price. The owner of the J. R. Fergusson Company Ltd. testified that he knew nothing about the chemical composition of metals in his foundry and that he had on his own initiative increased the tensile strength of the anchors from the specified 65,000 pounds per square inch to 90,000, not knowing that this made the anchors more brittle.

A volunteer witness at the inquiry, Hamilton professional engineer Joseph Leitersdorf, said that he was "horrified" and "shocked" at the "deplorable conditions" under which the bronze anchors were manufactured at the foundry.[22] Mr. Leitersdorf added that in his opinion the general contractor should be responsible for making sure the anchors were the proper strength and quality.

THE JUDGE'S REPORT

In their final submissions to Judge Theo McCombs, Pigott Construction's lawyers, Ramsay Evans and Earl Cranfield, condemned the city for its handling of maintenance and repairs to the roof of city hall since the completion of the building, even though

the roof was already leaking during construction. They also tried to shift the blame for the falling marble onto Roscoe's design. The city solicitor, on the other hand, argued that "it was the general contractor's responsibility to ensure that the material and workmanship used in the construction of the city hall were of the highest quality and in this respect Pigott Construction Company failed."[23]

In his 465-page report Judge McCombs held the construction company responsible for the falling marble because of the poor quality of the anchors. According to the judge, a contractor must "deliver a building constructed in a workmanlike way, of workmanlike materials in accordance with specifications."[24] Regarding the water-damaged roofs, he blamed the city for its failure to inspect the roofs regularly. He also criticized the general inertia of city hall officials, who had failed to make themselves aware of the problem, and had not asked their own employees to inspect the roofs and contact the contractor, even though buckets were sometimes required to catch water leaking into the council chamber during rainstorms.

In criticizing the role of city politicians the judge noted that the maintenance staff had never been given a standing order to inspect the roofs regularly. He noted further that the garage roof had leaked continually from 1961 and that this had been reported by a consulting engineer to Alderman Mac Cline. Despite this the final construction payment of $25,000 was paid to Pigott Construction. In a condemnation that included the Board of Control and city council, the judge said that "there was a failure on the part of the city hall committee as a whole to call a formal meeting forthwith ... for the purpose of launching an organized investigation into the extent and causes of the problems at city hall."[25]

Curiously, Judge McCombs went on to blame city architect Alex German for "disassociating himself" from the problem of the roof during the years 1963 to 1968. A review of the facts shows that, in fact, German waged a solitary war with the contractor on behalf of the city's interest with complete lack of support from the politicians. Even his recommendation to withhold the final payment to Pigott Construction was rejected.

The judge condemned the fact that Victor Dukeshire and Stanley Roscoe were asked to leave the meeting in the offices of the general contractor: "This alone — aside from everything else — indicates Mr. Roscoe did not enjoy the confidence of his employers which the magnitude of the project and his own competence would require."[26] Moreover, the judge found that in no way did Roscoe's design contribute to the faulty anchors. This, he ruled, was the responsibility of Pigott Construction.

Finally Judge McCombs accepted the testimony

of the former Building Committee members regarding the importance of Jack MacDonald's role in the decision to share the cost of repairs with Pigott. In his report he stated that:

Controller MacDonald performed . . . a most noticeable if not dominant role . . . it appeared that not only did Controller MacDonald assume the effective role I have described but there was a recognition of his greater familiarity with the problem which influenced them [the Building Committee] to accede to his suggestions.[27]

MacDonald's involvement was the most significant revelation to emerge from the inquiry. He protected the interests of Pigott Construction and sacrificed those of the people of Hamilton when he recommended the cost-sharing plan for the repairs. From that moment on, he called into question the company's responsibility to make the repairs by persuading the city to accept a part of that responsibility. The precedent was set, thus protecting the company from paying damages to the city in the future. The payment of the holdback money clinched the company's immunity from being forced to make repairs to a building of poor quality.

AFTER THE INQUIRY

When the inquiry was over and the judge had handed down his report in May 1972, city council asked its solicitor, Ken Rouff, for a report on the possibility of launching a lawsuit against those responsible for the problems with the marble cladding on the building. City council hoped it could obtain damages for the costly repairs to the walls and roof.

In a 10-page legal report, Rouff advised the city against a lawsuit, pointing out that they had themselves to blame, because in February 1962 the city had issued the final certificate to the contractor waiving all future claims for remedial work on the building. Rouff quoted from Article 26 of the agreement between the city and Pigott Construction, which said that "the issuance of the final certificate shall constitute a waiver of all claims," meaning that the city indicated by issuing the certificate that it was satisfied with the contractor's work.[28]

In response to this report, Controller Jim Campbell, who had been highly vocal in calling for the inquiry, demanded the city solicitor's resignation. No one else on council supported him. A rightly embarrassed Campbell, who had been one of those singled out for ignominious distinction in the judge's report, argued that Rouff should have known about Article 26 before the inquiry, and should have recommended against it. Campbell said: "I submit his action has placed council in the most ridiculous position it has been in during my 12 years here."[29] In fact it was Campbell who was in the ridiculous position; while getting ready to woo the voters of Hamilton, he had seized on the falling marble issue more than anyone else, and he had done this for his own political ends.

The inquiry did not lead to a lawsuit against Pigott Construction, nor did it lead to a reclaiming of the tax dollars spent on repairs. It did, however, provide a glimpse into a rather shoddy form of municipal subsidy to business. Rouff was correct when he likened the contractor to a "feudal baron," to whom city politicians indeed postured "as if they were personal lackeys."

1. *The Hamilton Spectator*, 9 September 1970.
2. *The Hamilton Spectator*, 9 September 1970.
3. *The Hamilton Spectator*, 16 February 1971.
4. *The Hamilton Spectator*, 17 February 1971.
5. *The Hamilton Spectator*, 18 February 1971.
6. *The Hamilton Spectator*, 25 March 1971.
7. *The Hamilton Spectator*, 4 May 1971.
8. Inquiry Report on Hamilton City Hall, submitted by former Senior County Judge Theo McCombs, p. 412.
9. Daily transcripts of the McCombs Inquiry, vol. 27, p. 4372.
10. Ibid., vol. 27, p. 4438.
11. Ibid.
12. Ibid., vol. 29, p. 4775.
13. *The Hamilton Spectator*, 4 May 1971.
14. *The Hamilton Spectator*, 23 April 1971.
15. *The Hamilton Spectator*, 23 April 1971.
16. *The Hamilton Spectator*, 23 April 1971.
17. *The Hamilton Spectator*, 29 March 1971.
18. *The Hamilton Spectator*, 31 March 1971.
19. *The Hamilton Spectator*, 31 March 1971.
20. *The Hamilton Spectator*, 1 April 1971.
21. *The Hamilton Spectator*, 2 April 1971.
22. *The Hamilton Spectator*, 3 March 1971.
23. Submission to McCombs Inquiry, 25 June 1971.
24. *The Hamilton Spectator*, 19 May 1972.
25. Inquiry Report of Judge McCombs, p. 411.
26. Ibid., p. 406-407.
27. Ibid., p. 409.
28. *The Hamilton Spectator*, 24 July 1972.
29. *The Hamilton Spectator*, 26 July 1972.

Downtown redevelopment: The Civic Square project

Bill Freeman

In their heyday, the 1950s and 1960s, urban renewal programs in Canada were presented to the public as measures of progressive urban reform, designed to rejuvenate deteriorating working-class residential neighbourhoods. In many cases, the reality was very different. Hamilton's Civic Square project shows that, despite all the rhetoric, the real purpose of the project was to clear valuable downtown land occupied by low-income residents and businesses and replace them with high prestige buildings. It was hoped that this would attract more people into the downtown area and ultimately generate higher profits for businesses across the entire business district. The plan is a classic example of how a city government intervenes with taxpayer's money to stimulate the business sector. Unfortunately for everyone, however, the greed of the developers and the politicians compromised the project and resulted in the collapse of the most important redevelopment plan in Hamilton's history.

It is now more than a decade since the federal government cancelled its urban renewal program but Hamilton still suffers from the perverse schemes of planners, politicians and businessmen.

When Civic Square, Hamilton's downtown urban renewal project, was first announced, *The Spectator* stated it was "undoubtedly the most ambitious attempt to resurrect a city ever undertaken in Canada."[1] Almost forty-four acres of the central downtown core of the city were to be cleared and rebuilt with a shiny new cultural and commercial centre which would transform the "steel city" into a "modern metropolis." A decade later, anyone brave enough to venture downtown found a barren landscape and parking lots by the acre. The Civic Square project had become so colossal a failure that it was surprising the central core had been able to survive at all.

In the 1950s and 1960s, urban renewal was promoted as the perfect solution to the problems of the deteriorating inner cities. Under an urban renewal scheme, the federal, provincial and municipal governments would join in covering the costs of acquiring, clearing and servicing land in the deteriorating areas of the city. The land then would be either held by the municipality for public use or turned over to private interests for redevelopment. The municipality would reap the benefits either in improved facilities or higher tax revenues and, in theory, from the rejuvenation of older neighbourhoods.

The Canadian urban renewal program began modestly. In 1954, the National Housing Act was amended to allow federal money to be used for urban renewal. In typical Canadian fashion the structure of the program followed earlier American legislation almost to the letter.

Large cities everywhere in Canada began a

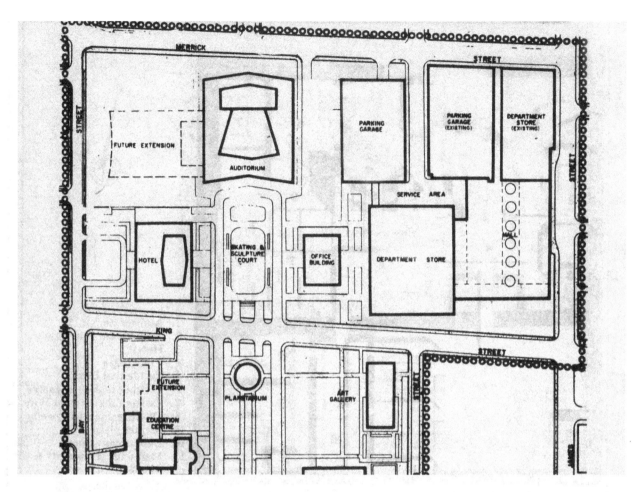

The urban renewal plan for the downtown area submitted by Murray Jones and Associates, June 1965.

scramble for the money, but few municipalities, in the long run, were as successful in getting programs accepted as Hamilton. As early as 1958 the city obtained urban renewal funding for a small project on Van Wagner's Beach, where a number of deteriorated homes were acquired and demolished to make way for a park. The project was hailed a success but, as usual, no one considered what happened to the former residents. It was simply assumed that they were better off living elsewhere.

A few years later another, more ambitious urban renewal project resulted in the demolition of a number of houses and factories in the city's North End to be replaced by a federally financed highrise, approximately 100 public housing units, new schools and a park. In 1973, long after the project was completed, Frank Henry and Peter Pineo, two sociologists at McMaster University, published a study of the community residents dislocated by the North End project. Their study showed that these people suffered considerable emotional upset and financial hardship in terms of moving costs and higher rents. Nevertheless the politicians were enthusiastic, praising the "success" of the scheme.

With Vic Copps' election as Hamilton's mayor in 1962, urban renewal got under way with a vengeance. Ironically, Copps had opposed the implementation of much of the North End project when he was city controller, arguing that the project would result in great hardship for the residents. Once he became mayor, however, his point of view changed.

PRESSURES FOR DOWNTOWN RENEWAL

There were a number of very powerful groups in Hamilton that favoured a massive effort to rehabilitate the downtown heart of the city. The most active group was the downtown businessmen who were deeply concerned that much of their business was being gradually eroded by suburban plazas and shopping centres. They believed that an extensive redevelopment program, creating a new core of civic and commercial buildings, would act as a

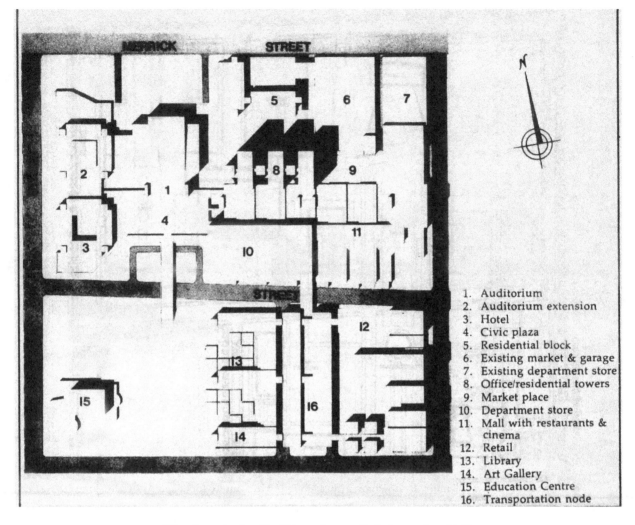

The plan submitted by Triton Centres Ltd., September 1967.

magnet to attract more shoppers and be to the advantage of all downtown business.

Another influential group of prominent business and professional men, well known as backers of many of the city politicians, and with considerable influence in Ottawa and at Queen's Park, were also promoting downtown redevelopment. This group saw the importance of a revitalized city centre to business interests and were strong believers in liberal reformism which would merge business and government interests. The best known of the group was the late Ken Sobel, the owner of CHML radio and CHCH television stations, who was a former employer of Vic Copps and his chief political promoter. It is unlikely that any major program for downtown renewal could have been implemented without the support of this key group and their active promotion of a downtown project made it politically irresistible.

Yet, these were by no means the only people to favour downtown redevelopment. In those heady days of substantial federal funding, no one was questioning the validity of the bulldozing approach. Urban renewal seemed such a good deal for the city that everyone vied to declare its virtues.

THE URBAN RENEWAL STUDY

It was no surprise that on September 29, 1964, Hamilton City Council unanimously approved a resolution authorizing an urban renewal study for the central core of the city. The Toronto firm of Murray V. Jones and Associates was appointed to carry out the study; a little over six months later a report was submitted to council.

Jones recommended two urban renewal projects in the study area: first, redevelopment of 260 acres in the York Street area in the north-west part of the city core, calling for a new series of roads, public housing and some commercial buildings;

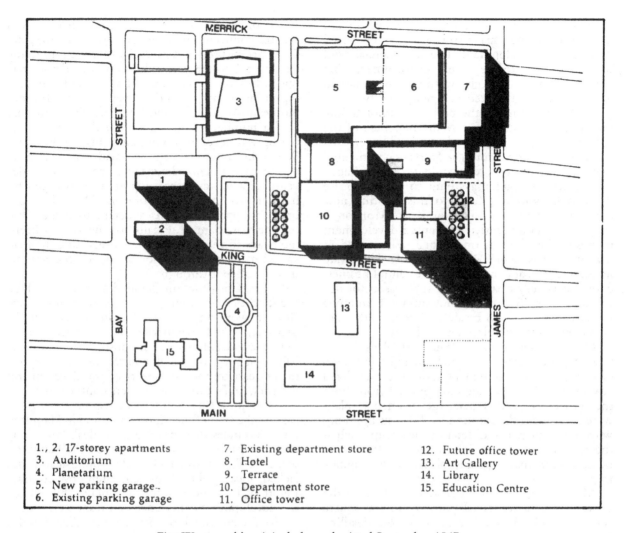

First Wentworth's original plan, submitted September 1967.

and second, the Civic Square project, which would involve the demolition of forty-four acres in the downtown core and redevelopment as a civic and commercial centre. Though Jones gave top priority to the York Street project, arguing that there was extreme deterioration in this area, council ignored this area and turned its attention to the downtown proposal. Unanimous approval was immediately given to second reading of the bylaw designating the urban renewal project area for the Civic Square.

In retrospect, the city might be criticized for proceeding so hastily with Civic Square and ignoring York Street but the criticism would not have been acceptable in 1965. Everyone operating in the political sphere in the city saw redevelopment of the downtown core as the first priority. The York Street area was just a grubby deteriorated slum which the city might eventually get around to fixing up. The possibility of massive redevelopment downtown, transforming the city core into monoliths of steel and glass, sparked the imagination.

The urban renewal plan for the downtown area, as submitted by Murray Jones, called for acquisition and total clearance of almost forty-four acres of land in the central core of the city, adjacent to the new city hall, Gore Park and the main business and commercial districts — a choice piece of property having ready access by public and private transportation as well as a high concentration of pedestrian traffic generated by nearby high-rise apartments, offices and shopping areas. Jones' economic study of this area claimed that it had become obsolete and inefficient. Eighty-two per cent of the buildings were built before 1900, and tax revenue from the area was very low. Altogether there were some 260 businesses, housed in three- and four-storey buildings with 500 people living in apartments over the stores. Some of the businesses, like Eatons, were large and prosperous, but the vast majority were small merchants and manufacturing firms that merely eked out a marginal existence.

Jones' plan included a number of civic buildings (theatre-auditorium, planetarium, education centre, library, farmers' market, art gallery and trade and convention centre) as part of the redevelopment scheme. A segment of the square, 10.4 acres, was to be turned over to commercial development and large areas of open space were to be interspersed through the development. The commercial land would be leased to the developer for ninety-nine years and in return the city would receive rent and increased taxes on the redeveloped property.

The enthusiasm for the project was not simply for the development itself. Many members of the public saw it as a way of attracting additional investment downtown and *The Spectator* commented that the downtown area would soon be ringed with apartment buildings "built to accommodate the people who will flock to this exciting new concept of living."[2] Controller Brian Morison, a lawyer who consistently represented development interests when he was on council, was quoted in *The Spectator* as saying "This will attract the private investment so badly needed in our central business core."[3] It is very clear that the real reason for developing Civic Square was not simply to improve the city centre, but to create a climate in the city favourable to the development industry.

Over the next two and a half years, plans for the Civic Square project were finalized and there was a growing sense of excitement about the revitalized city centre. The city received approval from both the provincial and federal governments, plans were refined for the location of different buildings within the square and different civic groups such as the theatre-auditorium committee and the Board of Education made specific plans for their buildings.

Meanwhile, the call for tenders to develop the 10.4 acres of commercial property in the square was issued. On September 11, 1967, the deadline for submissions, bids from two firms had been received.

The first firm to bid was Triton Centres Limited, a subsidiary of Trizec Corporation (a major Canadian development company then controlled by British interests) which has major investments in Place Ville Marie in Montreal and Yorkdale Shopping Centre in Toronto, as well as other holdings in Hamilton and Vancouver. At the time of the submission of bids to the Hamilton City Council, Triton had few connections with the city's political and business circles.

The other bid on the Civic Square project was made by First Wentworth Development Company, a wholly-owned subsidiary of the Hamilton-based Pigott Construction Company. This company, presently owned and controlled by the third generation of the Pigott family, was originally founded in the 1880s, but it was not until Joseph Pigott Sr., the second generation of Pigotts, took over management in the 1920s that the family fortunes began to climb dramatically. By the end of his tenure as president, the firm was the largest construction company in Canada doing a wide variety of general contracting work and holding a number of investments.

Joseph Pigott Sr. had three sons, all of whom are still connected with the construction company. The current president is William Pigott, reportedly an astute businessman, who runs the day-to-day operations of the company. The second son, Jack Pigott, is a lawyer and a well known Toronto businessman. Joseph Pigott Jr., the third son, has held a number of positions with the family firm, but he was never as prominent as his two brothers. When the announcement was made that Hamilton was to have a major downtown urban renewal development it was Joseph Pigott Jr. who urged his brothers to make a submission. The two older brothers apparently were reluctant to make a bid but Joe was adamant. Finally, for the sake of keeping peace in the family, it was agreed that the firm would make a proposal. Joe was given the responsibility to see it through.

Pigott Construction founded a firm called First Wentworth Development Company to undertake all of its work on the Civic Square project. Unlike Triton, they had no experience in the development industry, and, although their construction company had been very successful, construction itself is one of the least important aspects of the development industry, (in fact most developers contract out their construction). But the new development company carried the aura of the Pigott name and in Hamilton political circles that meant a great deal. For a long time the family had been a force on the Hamilton scene. If Triton was technically sophisticated but lacked local political punch, then, by contrast, Pigott had all the political advantages but lacked the development experience and resources.

To review the bids city council established a joint Review Committee of forty people made up of several professional consultant along with civil servants and citizens. The two plans were quite different. The Triton scheme stressed shopping malls, and improved transportation through the area. They argued that because of the nature of Hamilton's industry and its proximity to Toronto, it was unlikely that a great need would be generated for office space, but space for four office or apartment towers was designed into the plan in case the demand materialized. The First Wentworth plan, on the other hand, stressed office space rather than shopping malls. The Steel Company of Canada had made a commitment to Pigott that they would move the majority of their office staff into the project, and they had a commitment from the Toronto Dominion Bank to locate in the square.

After two months of study the review committee brought in its report on December 18, 1967. They had compared the plans on ten different points. Of the ten points Triton was found to be superior on eight and First Wentworth on only two. In spite of this, the committee concluded that First Wentworth should be awarded the contract.

Why this recommendation was made is still unclear. According to one committee source, the forty-

Buildings coming down at MacNab and York Streets, 1970 (*The Spectator*).

member group was broken into subcommittees which made recommendations on certain aspects of the two plans. After they had finished, a small group of politically sensitive individuals sat down and made the final recommendation to city council. There was dissension by some of the other forty members but it was never resolved. The committee was simply dissolved on the pretext that it had completed its task.

If this is true, it is a classic case of subverted democratic decision making. The committee was not allowed to enter into any meaningful discussion of the overall merits of the two plans. In reality it was not a committee decision at all, but a recommendation, passed off by a small group who were politically trustworthy, as the recommendation of the whole committee.

There may have been some dissension in the committee, but there certainly was none at the Board of Control meeting when the recommendation was considered. All five members voted unanimously in favour of First Wentworth. The following day, however, Triton's president, David Philpot, blasted the Board of Control and the review committee. Replying to them through a newspaper article in *The Spectator*, Philpot pointed out that in spite of the recommendation Triton was found superior in eight out of ten points. He said,

"If the remaining two are so important why not negotiate with us on two rather than Pigott on eight." The only major issue on which First Wentworth was judged superior was on the issue of tax revenue to the city and on this point Philpot hotly contested the findings of the committee. He went on to say: "I feel extremely foolish in submitting the proposal at all. If the decision was to be made on pure economics they could have saved me the trouble with just a telephone call ... Our plan was totally superior. The professionals in this industry are going to have a long hard look at urban renewal projects before jumping in again." He concluded: "It will be interesting to see how many aldermen you have with guts enough to stand up against this decision."[4]

In the next few days the issue generated considerable controversy. Philpot sent letters to every member of council refuting the review committee and showing figures that on the tax issue the committee had misinterpreted the intent of their submission. On December 21, he attended the council meeting and made his presentation, arguing again that the Triton proposal was clearly superior, but all to no avail. After a lengthy debate, Vic Copps summed up the discussion, saying in effect that, although the Triton proposal had great merit, the review committee had not recommended it. He then went on to say that the Pigott family had done a great deal for the city of Hamilton and that the city owed them something. He concluded by recommending First Wentworth. With a vote of fifteen to four, council awarded the contract to the hometown firm.

SQUEEZING OUT THE SMALL MERCHANTS

For some time after the awarding of the contract the political issue of Civic Square dropped out of sight as the negotiations withdrew behind closed doors, but one major issue persistently hounded the politicians over the next two years — the acquisition of the original properties on the Civic Square site. Although there were subsequently innumerable delays in the project the city did not let these interfere with the schedule for expropriation.

The merchants in the area, anticipating problems, formed a group called the Civic Square Tenants and Property Owners' Association. From the beginning they seemed confused about their role. On the one hand they sensed that many of them were going to face hardships due to the dislocation of their businesses. On the other hand, the prevailing belief that the project was going to benefit everyone made it difficult to oppose. Over and over again spokesmen for the group reiterated that they were not opposed to the development but were concerned with protecting their interests.

The majority of the local merchants stood to lose a considerable amount through expropriation, for the simple reason that the commercial section of the Civic Square development was intended to be a prestige project while the vast majority of the businesses located in the area were hardly that. In the first block to be expropriated, for example, there were three butchers, a number of small clothing stores, variety stores and small restaurants. The margin of profit of these stores was certainly not enough to pay the high rents of Civic Square, and even if they had wanted to relocate there, it is unlikely the developer would have accepted them as tenants.

The city had agreed, back in the days when the project was just an idea, that one of their first priorities was to protect the merchants within the boundaries of the square. They offered the merchants what they called the "right of first refusal" on sites within the new shopping mall. The implication of all of the discussions in the early stages was that the new mall would accommodate as many of the merchants as wanted to go into it. But as the day of expropriation came closer it became clear that it would be the developer who would make that decision. Thus, the promise of the "right of first refusal" was not a "right" at all but merely a political slogan to mollify the merchants.

As early as September 1967, before the contract had even been awarded to First Wentworth, the merchants approached city hall for information about demolition schedules, leases in the new development and who would get the first selection in the new mall. The city, of course, could do nothing but delay since many, if not all of these decisions would be made by the developer. By June of 1968, still before the demolition of even the first block had begun, many of the merchants began to panic — and with good reason. First Wentworth had not yet set prices for rental space within the development, but the rumour was that they were going to be very high. Because of the scramble for space in the downtown area the price of good store sites had shot up overnight and even if they could afford it, merchants found few sites available.

John Farnan, speaking for the merchants in his role as President of the Civic Square Tenants and Property Owners Association, pointed out that it takes at least nine months to make the arrangements to move a business, but the merchants were given only seven months to make their plans. It was now only three months before the first of the expropriations were to begin and many of them had not yet made up their minds on what they were going to do.[5]

The city, sensitive to the criticism, decided to make a temporary shopping mall to accommodate the merchants who would be displaced from Civic Square and who wanted to relocate in the new mall, but as it turned out this helped very few of the businessmen. Out of the 260 merchants within the old Civic Square area only a handful went into the temporary mall.

It was the small merchants that particularly suffered and gradually they became embittered. There was talk about how city hall would help them but in fact little was done. Finally, from the city's point of view, the issue was resolved only because it went away. The merchants scattered and tried to salvage what they could, giving up on the city as hopelessly compromised. In the end somewhere between one-quarter and one-half of the merchants failed to relocate and were forced out of business.

However, not everyone suffered from the expropriation. A small group of property owners and speculators made a tidy sum because they knew what was happening and were shrewd enough to use every legal tactic available to them. For example, owners would sign long-term leases of five or more years with their tenants so that the city would be forced, by law, to compensate them for loss of rent.

The speculators, led by millionaire William Fraleigh, realtor Percy Walton, and merchant Edward Farrar (a one time president of the Civic Square Tenants and Property Owner Association, and a member of the urban renewal committee), slightly before and immediately after the announcement designating the Civic Square boundaries, began to buy up properties and acquire options on others — some for as little as $25. They then demanded that the city buy them out for $2-million. One of the aldermen realized what they were doing but was reluctant to blow it into a full scale scandal. He threatened to make the issue public and finally, under pressure, the group reduced its demand and settled for $1,186,500.

SETTING THE STAGE

Except for the problems with the merchants, there appeared to be very little political activity for a period after the contract had been awarded to First Wentworth. In fact this was far from the case. The political decisions that were made in the months immediately following the awarding of the contract in December 1967, set the course of the negotiations and continue to profoundly influence the outcome of the project to this day.

For First Wentworth, the chief negotiator throughout was Joseph Pigott Jr. Pigott is a youthful, good looking man, who exudes the confidence and disdain of an aristocrat. Throughout the negotiations his demands were always expressed in a way that gave the impression that this was the final offer, take it or First Wentworth would get out. It was not unusual for him to shout at the city negotiators in the midst of an argument and pound the desk for emphasis. If nothing else, he gave the impression that he knew what he wanted and intended to get it.

On the side of the city the issue of the negotiations was much more complicated. Early in the Copps administration an urban renewal committee was established, made up of many prominent citizens from business, professional and labour circles. The person appointed to chair this committee was Copp's friend and promoter, the late Ken Sobel. An urban renewal department was also set up to handle all the dealings in relation to the development. The first administrator of that department was Graham Emslie, a former employee of Sobel and a co-worker with Copps at CHML, and who has since gone on to become Toronto's development commissioner. The role of the department was to administer all of the urban renewal projects so they were intimately connected with the Civic Square development, but they were never given more than a skeleton staff to do the job. As a result the city had to depend on expensive outside consultants, particularly the planning firm of Murray Jones and Associates.

The implications of these arrangements, which on the surface seemed innocent enough, were considerable. The creation of the urban renewal department meant that all dealings with Civic Square would be kept out of the normal planning process. Hamilton had long had a sophisticated planning department staffed with many competent professionals but they were completely eliminated from the development negotiations. With the appointment of people who were politically trustworthy to positions of power in the urban renewal department and committee, the stage was set to ease and facilitate the redevelopment of the Civic Square.

The one city department that, in the beginning, was to be part of the negotiating team was the legal department, but not for long. Shortly after the negotiations began Pigott refused to work with Ken Rouff, the city solicitor, because he claimed Rouff was obstructionist. It seems that he tried to protect the city's interests by challenging a number of proposals of First Wentworth; Pigott complained to the politicians, and Rouff was removed from the negotiations. A Toronto firm, Fraser and Beatty, was appointed the city's legal consultant for the project and they sent Donald G. Scroggie to Hamilton to aid in the negotiations. The firm ultimately took over $100,000 out of the city in legal fees.

Another major event in this period was the firing of Professor James Murray, the city's architectural consultant, some nine months after being hired. He apparently did not like the plans of First Wentworth and when they refused to take any of his suggestions into account he threatened not to give his approval. Pigott complained and Murray was promptly fired by the city. For over a year the city did not have an architectural consultant on the project in spite of the fact that this directly contravened provincial legislation governing urban renewal.

In the end, Mayor Vic Copps and Controller Jack MacDonald emerged as the city's chief negotiators. This was strange for a number of reasons. First, council at no time designated these two as the negotiators — they simply assumed the role. Second, this is completely outside the normal functions of politicians; normally negotiations are left to the civil servants who have the technical competence to deal with the issues and the politicians oversee this process, dealing with the broad framework and philosophy of the project rather than the details. Finally, out of twenty-one members of council, Copps and MacDonald were the two politicians in the city with the closest links to Pigott.

While Jack MacDonald has been at city hall he has been well known as the businessman's representative. He is a competent politician with considerable influence because of his intimate knowledge of the city, his hard work, and his ability to convince aldermen of his point of view. He had, at this time, a number of significant links with Pigott Construction Company.

Vic Copps also had strong links with the Pigotts. One of the major sources of support for Copps throughout his long political career in Hamilton was the Knights of Columbus, a group with which

Vic Copps (Courtasy of *The Spectator* Collection, Special Collection Hamilton Public Library).

the Pigott family has been heavily involved. Joseph Pigott Sr. was made a Knight of Malta, the highest position a layman can achieve in the Knights of Columbus; the Pigott Construction Company had built the Knights of Columbus Hall, and had given a large donation toward its construction.

Thus, the stage had been set for the most important negotiations in Hamilton's history.

REVISING THE PLAN

One of the recommendations of the Joint Review Committee was that, if the First Wentworth plan was to be accepted, considerable revisions be made to basic design and planning concepts. Murray Jones was appointed to help in the redesign of the plan. This was in spite of the fact that at least one developer, in considering whether to bid, had enquired if it would be possible to make revisions in the plan once it was submitted and was told that this would not be possible because it would give unfair advantage to one developer over another. The plan Triton submitted was taken as a final draft, though the final working drawings remained to be submitted. Yet, First Wentworth was given every opportunity, and was, in fact, encouraged to redesign the project almost without restrictions.

In June 1968, six months after the vote that had given them the contract, First Wentworth gave an indication of the sort of revisions they were entertaining, when Joseph Pigott told *The Spectator* that an extra 100,000 square feet of the project should be turned over to commercial development. This meant that the size of the commercial section of the square would grow from the original 10.4 acres to approximately 18 acres. Pigott argued that his investigations among private realtors had shown a much greater demand for rental space than had been anticipated. This would be a good deal for the city, he claimed, because it would mean "more dollars at work and more tax revenue for the city."[6] The fact that the extra space would be taken from the land set aside for cultural buildings was ignored.

When the new plan was unveiled it showed an enormous commercial development spreading along King Street, with pedestrian malls linking the commercial and cultural buildings. The library had been taken out of the cultural section of the square and relocated in the commercial development. The farmers' market and art gallery had been eliminated altogether — there was no room for them anymore.

This was a major, as it turned out the major, revision of the plan, making a significant shift in the emphasis of the square away from cultural buildings to commercial development. One might assume that this would generate considerable political debate in the city, and in fact there were a few signs of a confrontation but nothing materialized. At the request of Pigott, the Board of Control met behind closed doors to discuss the project, and when council met on July 17, the revisions won easy acceptance. Out of council's twenty-one members only two voted against the proposal.

It is difficult to understand why council so readily agreed to Pigott's demands. What Pigott told council members was that because of the general rise of interest rates at that time, First Wentworth needed more land and more tenants in order to make an economically viable project. But that argument simply did not make sense. If there were financial problems Pigott should have wanted a smaller development so as to diminish the financial risk. The fact that he was looking for higher profits must have been obvious to council members, yet they were apparently willing to go along with him. Of course, some, like Copps and MacDonald, were already hopelessly compromised and others certainly supported it because they were strongly tied into the development industry and would always support projects of this kind. But many of the remaining aldermen were apparently beginning to panic. They had the horrible vision of being left with acres of vacant land in the downtown commercial heart of the city and no prospect of finding another developer. This was such a frightening possibility that many were willing to agree with almost anything Pigott proposed as long as he would carry the project through to completion. Consequently, as time went on, the plans for Civic Square were constantly being changed. On August 13, 1968, Murray Jones submitted changes to the Board of Control, shifting the theatre-auditorium closer to city hall and further changes, shifting a building here or a pedestrian mall there, were made over the next few months; it never seemed to stop.

PUBLIC AWARENESS

The public was kept almost totally uninformed about these negotiations. Periodically, an article on the negotiations would appear in the press, but the real action was going on behind closed doors. One person who had the opportunity to go over the minutes of the meetings described them as being dominated by Pigott. Over and over again he would demand concessions and each time the city would give in. Citizens began to realize that every time there was a new plan released, further concessions had been given to the developers. Murray Jones, the Toronto planning consultant, seemed hopelessly compromised, to the point that Bill Powell, one of the aldermen who consistently opposed First Wentworth, said he wondered who Jones was working for. Scroggie, the legal consultant, often appeared in the same light.

Through the latter part of 1968 and early 1969, people began slowly to see what was happening. In March 1969, Mr. B.B. Schecter, a city lawyer sitting on the theatre-auditorium committee, complained to *The Spectator* that in the new design of the square the committee had been coerced into accepting four acres of land rather than the six that had been promised to them.[7] The chairman of the committee, John Trimble, denied the charges, saying that the city would come out with a very satisfactory theatre, but the issue was not so easily brushed aside. Much of the money for the theatre-auditorium had been raised by public subscription. When the theatre appeared to be threatened by the small allotment of land many community leaders became embittered with the whole project.

Marvin Wasserman, president of the Hamilton Downtown Association, attacked the project in an interview with *The Spectator* and pointed out that people in the city were worried because the original concept of Civic Square, as the meeting place of Hamilton, had been jeopardized by the frequent changes in the plans and by the enlargement of the commercial section of the square. "The plan was presented three and a half years ago but nothing has been finalized — It is time that the game

Jack MacDonald (*The Spectator*).

of hopscotch with the market, library, theatre-auditorium and art gallery came to a stop."[8]

On the same day another article appeared in *The Spectator*, describing the efforts of Mrs. Sheila Zack, wife of a well-known city merchant, to organize a fight against the First Wentworth plan. Nothing had emerged in five years, she claimed, and she intended to rally interest in Civic Square by contacting different service groups and local labour leaders.

The emergence of these critical articles in *The Spectator* was no accident. In March, a group of people had gone to the newspaper to complain about the news coverage of the project. They claimed that Civic Square was not being adequately covered, important information was not being disseminated, and there was virtually no critical analysis of the project. Because of this *The Spectator* assigned a full time reporter by the name of Peter Calamai to cover the story.

Vic Copps manning the wrecking ball in Civic Square (Courtesy of *The Spectator* Collection, Special Collections Hamilton Public Library).

SUPPORT AND OPPOSITION FOR THE PIGOTT PLAN BY THE 1968–70 HAMILTON CITY COUNCIL

Political Party	Total Support	Opposition	Began with Support, Swung to Opposition	Total
Liberal	4	1	3	= 9
PC	3	1	3	= 7
NDP	2	1	2	= 5
Total	10	3	8	= 21

As this table illustrates, there was little difference in the support of the Pigott Plan by the different political parties. It was a core of three aldermen, Bill Powell, Reg Wheeler, and Bill McCulloch, who led the rebellion against the plan. The background of the three men was quite different: each of them came from a different political party. Powell was a retired wage earner and unionist, Wheeler a foreman in one of the steel mills, and McCulloch a small businessman. The one thing they did have in common, however, was their independence from the major political machines that operate in the city.

The role that Peter Calamai, a reporter for *The Spectator*, played was crucial. From March 1969 on, there was a flood of information on the project. He examined in detail the various plans, he interviewed carefully the people involved and he followed the emergence of the protest groups with considerable detail. It even got to the point that Calamai was accused by some of the other reporters at *The Spectator* of losing objectivity.

The group led by Sheila Zack called itself the Save Our Square Committee (S.O.S.). They created the greatest political protest that has ever been seen in Hamilton. They took full page newspaper ads explaining their position, distributed bumper stickers, found teams of lawyers to review the contracts and architects to criticize the plans.

By far the most important work was S.O.S.'s attempt to convince the councillors to vote against acceptance of the First Wentworth plan. For a while S.O.S. generated a flurry of opposition. A group of aldermen met in one of the aldermen's homes to discuss the plan privately, but in the end, on May 16, 1969, council voted 16 to 4 to accept the First Wentworth revised plan.

In spite of their defeat, S.O.S. was not about to give up. The matter had to be referred to the Ontario Municipal Board for final approval and S.O.S. hoped for success at these hearings. Altogether the evidence was heard for five days in May and June, 1969. Herman Turkstra, acting as lawyer for S.O.S., exposed the enormous inadequacies of the analyses prepared by the planning consultants, Murray V. Jones and Associates. After questioning Jones on the details of an overpass at King Street, Turkstra commented, "You haven't calculated the intensity, you haven't calculated the cost, and you haven't calculated where the money is going to come from."[9] Lukin Robinson, an economist for the Jones firm, admitted, when cross-examined by Turkstra, that he had miscalculated by more than $2 million the estimated residual value of the land at King and McNab Street. Much of the work, he admitted, was prepared in haste for the council meetings and needed to be corrected later. Turkstra commented, "You're talking about the attempt by Board of Control to railroad this thing through in a couple of weeks."[10]

In the end, however, the OMB ruled in favour of the city. Their decision as reported in *The Spectator* read in part: "The board realizes that the scheme in many respects is less than ideal, but on the evidence the board will not upset what it believes to be the reasoned judgement of council. Upon the evidence the board cannot come to the conclusion that the council was necessarily acting out of ignorance and was not fully aware of its responsibilities to the electorate."[11]

Civic Square 1979 showing some of the vacant field awaiting development (Tom Moerman).

FIRST WENTWORTH COLLAPSES

The loss of the OMB hearing was a bitter blow to S.O.S. and as a group they never recovered. However, it was not long before events themselves delivered the results S.O.S. had been unable to achieve. On June 24, 1969, the day after the OMB completed its hearings, council agreed to an extension of the signing of the development agreement from July 8 to July 30. This was the fourth extension given to First Wentworth, making the project already ten months behind schedule.

And so it continued. After more closed door meetings, it was finally made public that First Wentworth was having difficulties raising the money. Joseph Pigott tried to act confidently. There was no panic yet, he claimed, but the tight money situation was making it difficult to get financial backing.

A number of the aldermen were furious. Bill McCulloch demanded that the $100,000 bond put up by First Wentworth be confiscated. "First Wentworth has continually called the tune," he said to *The Spectator*, "and the city has given way all the time. Throughout the negotiations there has never been one change to benefit the city, always the developer. Almost every businessman would like this deal. Access to a one hundred million dollar project without risking any financial commitment." Reg Wheeler, another alderman, said he had continually questioned in the past whether First Wentworth had sufficient money to proceed with the project. "I wasn't given a straight answer until last week."[12]

Gradually the facade of the power of First Wentworth and the Pigott family began to crack. By September, it was widely known that the financial problems of First Wentworth were serious. The mood of council quickly turned against the developer. On September 17, it was learned that there was a clause in the original contract with First Wentworth giving them sixty days after the contract had run out to arrange further financing. Again there was an ugly scene in city council. Accusations were made that council had been tricked by Copps and MacDonald and that the councillors had not been kept adequately informed.

Still the city clung to First Wentworth. In December 1969 another extension was given to Pigott because he claimed he still had a possibility of getting financing. In the end it became a total fiasco. Copps, MacDonald and Pigott flew off to Paris to negotiate with a German financial group only to have the deal fall through. The CNR pension fund was supposedly interested but that evaporated. The matter continued to March 2, 1970, when finally the majority of aldermen, led by Bill Powell, Reg Wheeler and Bill McCulloch, rebelled against the negotiating team and terminated the agreement.

YALE PROPERTIES

As the First Wentworth contract was being terminated, the greatest fear of the politicians was that they would never be able to attract another developer. Acres of prime land in the downtown had been sitting vacant for a year and more property was being cleared every day; an election was coming up the following December and citizen groups were after the heads of the administration, when suddenly, Yale Properties came forward, offering to complete the project.

Yale Properties Limited is a Montreal firm owned and operated by Menshi Mashaal, a successful, Iranian, immigrant businessman and his seven sons. In every way the firm seemed to be highly competent. They were a fully integrated development firm owning three large office buildings in Montreal as well as extensive shopping malls in Montreal and Sherbrooke in Quebec. As far as the city was concerned, Yale's major advantage was that it had a working agreement with the Standard Life Assurance Company and the Bank of Montreal which assured it more than half of the mortgage money required for the project.

Yale delivered results with blinding speed. It was not until March 2, 1970, when the city formally terminated its agreement with First Wentworth, that Yale began work in earnest on its proposal, but within a month Yale's architect, Arthur Lau, had finished his preliminary plans. By August, an agreement had been reached with the city and all the major companies involved. By October, 1970, well before the December election, Yale had actually begun construction on Phase I of the six-phase project.

Beneath the rosy exterior, however, things were not quite so simple, Yale was in an excellent position to negotiate a good contract with the city. They kept the 18 acres of land that First Wentworth had negotiated, rather than reverting to the original 10.4 acres and they took advantage of some of the agreements that First Wentworth had made; particularly their agreement with Stelco, who were to be the prime tenants in Phase I of the project.

Yale's proposal was the fourth major revision of Civic Square. Again buildings were shifted around with the result that they were even more cramped than under the 1967 Pigott plan. The art gallery was relocated across the street from city hall, the new public library was placed over a rebuilt farmers' market on Merrick Street and an enormous townhouse and high-rise development of 810 units was proposed for the corner of Bay and Merrick Streets. But in spite of this further commercialization of the square not one member of council questioned the deal.

It was only four years after Yale became involved, that some of the problems came to light. Yale began construction of Phase I on September 1, 1970 and it was to be completed by October 18, 1972. However, they were held up six months by the elevator strike in 1972. Phase II of the project was to begin construction on October 19, 1972, but this was held back because of the strike and then there were further delays.

On September 24, 1973, already eleven months behind their own schedule, Yale was granted a further extension of six months. In making the announcement, Mayor Copps said, "I understand they are still trying to negotiate for the leasing of the department store which is the main part of the phase."[13]

Again the negotiations withdrew behind closed doors, but when they emerged in April 1974 it was evident that fears had been well founded. Yale had been unable to attract a major department store into the development. In the past the department store had always been talked about as a crucial part of the project because it would be a powerful inducement to attract shoppers into the area. Now Yale was suggesting that the store be replaced by a four- to six-storey office building and that the Lloyd D. Jackson shopping mall would be extended into the ground floor of the building. This was a far cry from the department store in terms of attraction.

Another proposal was put forward. The Library Board suggested that the new downtown library should be relocated in Phase II of the project. When Yale and the city turned the suggestion down, F. E. Wigle, a Library Board member, put the case in a letter to the editor of *The Spectator*. "I am amazed that Yale Properties has not seized on the opportunity to fit into Phase II the bright, exciting, new library structure, which would be a tremendous pedestrian traffic generator." He went on to say: "Reg Monaghan, the city's representative, stated that the library proposal was not amenable to Yale Properties. There was no indication as to whether or not Yale's proposal was amenable to the citizens of Hamilton. Yale hopes to build a 'money machine' in Phase II, and from its point of view, why not? . . . However, it may be that the majority of the citizens of Hamilton are not so much interested in seeing a money machine being built on this choice piece of real estate as they are in seeing something built that will give them a higher quality of life in the downtown area."[14]

More surprising than Yale's refusal to enter into negotiations on the library issue, or its inability to attract a department store into the square, was the proposal to build the four- to five-storey office tower. Hamilton already had a surplus of office space at the time. A 1974 survey showed 250,000 square feet of unrented space in Hamilton. This included five full floors of the Stelco tower (that had not been rented since completion in 1972), owned by Yale and located right next door to the proposed new building. All of these objections were raised at another Ontario Municipal Board hearing early in the new year, but Yale was given approval to carry on with its new design anyway.

The second phase of the commercial section of the square was finally completed in 1977 — years behind schedule. Much of the six-storey office building remained vacant. Some of the stores in the mall stood empty for months, and Eames, a locally-owned department store that had relocated in the mall, subsequently went bankrupt.

The other key elements of the redevelopment plan quietly disappeared. In the 1970 Yale plan the company included an enormous town-house and high-rise development of 810 units at the corner of Bay and Merrick Streets. Later, Yale silently dropped this part of the plan. At no time was there ever public discussion of its omission, and in fact there was never any mention of this major revision in *The Spectator*. Again it indicated that the developer and possibly mortgage companies believed that at least some aspects of the commercial development were not financially viable.

Even more serious was the fact that the hotel, an integral part of the Civic Square plan from the time Murray Jones first submitted his plan to the city council in June of 1965, was in jeopardy. The Hilton chain had long been rumoured to have obtained the contract from Yale for a 420-room, twenty- to twenty-five-storey hotel but their plans were held in abeyance. Reg Groome, President of Hilton Canada Ltd., confirmed in an interview with *The Spectator* that forecast costs increased from $15 million in 1975 to $20 million in 1976. This, he claimed, had sent his firm "back to the drawing boards."[15] It was obvious that Hilton was not going to put its capital into such a risky venture.

Despite the seriousness of the crisis, the politicians and public ignored Civic Square. With the marginal success of the second phase, the withdrawal of the residential development, and the delaying of the hotel, the most pessimistic predictions about the development seemed confirmed. Yet from the late 1960s the project went through crisis after crisis with very little coverage by the Hamilton media. The public had virtually no knowledge of what was really going on.

The reaction of the politicians to those problems was to revert to their broader strategy of looking to the public purse to stimulate development in the square. Many people were upset that the planned library-farmers' market development was to be located on Merrick Street, behind Eatons and away from the business district but city officials now refused to consider any other location. If nothing

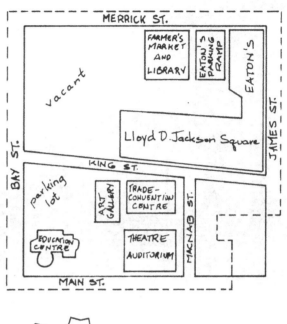

The Yale Plan for the square, March 1970.

else the building would fill an empty piece of land that was obviously unattractive to any other developer.

There was another attempt to fill vacant land in the project area on Bay Street by building an arena on it. Alderman Bill McCulloch made this proposal, but it was rejected by a city-wide referendum in December 1976. Still determined to put the land to some use, Mayor Jack MacDonald, and later Labour Minister John Munro and others joined together to try and get the Pan-American Games in 1983, but the city's proposal was rejected by the games committee. One of the main reasons Hamilton made this proposal was that in this way the city could get federal money to help build an arena and fill in the empty land of Civic Square.

Finally a solution to Hamilton's most pressing problem came from the provincial government. On July 20, 1978 Government Services Minister Lorne Henderson and Premier William Davis came to a city council meeting to announce that the Ontario government would build a $35 million trade and convention centre and provincial office tower in Civic Square. Hamilton politicians were overjoyed.

Civic Square 1979 looking from Bay Street (Tom Moerman).

Again they saw the investment of taxpayer's money as a means of stimulating the whole downtown area. This is how *The Spectator* reported it:

Construction of Hamilton's trade and convention centre is being hailed as the taking-off point for the city's downtown area. City politicians and businessmen are convinced the $35 million centre and provincial office tower will attract new hotels and businesses to downtown Hamilton and give a shot in the arm to other businesses.

Mayor MacDonald went on to talk enthusiastically about how this public investment would stimulate development in the entire city:

"Hotels are the next major target we're aiming for — but close to that is the airport . . ." Mr. MacDonald said he hoped the announcement of the centre would spur a similar announcement by federal transport minister Otto Lang about airport expansion.

Controller Ian Stout was equally enthusiastic:

Once word gets out that the centre is GO, I think you will see them (the hotels) running to us. We can offer them a pretty damn attractive location at Bay and King Streets connected to a new art gallery, theatre-auditorium, shopping, a library-market and a convention centre.

And Alderman Pat Ford, chairman of the Downtown Redevelopment Subcommittee believed that the centre "could be the catalyst to attract two or three hotels to the area."[16]

The uncritical nature of these statements speaks volumes. No one pointed out that the trade and convention centre will probably become an expensive drain on the tax dollar that will have to be maintained by the municipality. The real reason for the politicians' enthusiasm, of course, was that they need a hotel in order to complete the square and they see the trade and convention centre as a way of getting it. Again their strategy is to make a massive investment in public funds to subsidize private interests. But as on other occasions in Hamilton's Civic Square this venture could well end in failure. Contrary to the politicians' predictions, no hotel chain has run to build a new hotel in downtown Hamilton.

URBAN RENEWAL IN RETROSPECT

In Hamilton political circles assessing the Civic Square project as a failure has not been a popular judgement, but by almost every yardstick it has been a disaster.

Of course the project was simply too big for a

city the size of Hamilton to undertake. For years business and political leaders envied the type of aggressive development that was going on in Toronto and other centres. For them Civic Square was an attempt to use the public purse to spark similar development. It was a failure, however, primarily because the demand for new commercial and office space did not exist to sustain a project of this size.

From a planning point of view Civic Square must also be judged a failure. The Murray Jones plan of 1965, with its large courts, open squares and the theatre auditorium on Merrick Street looking south to city hall, is a combination of public and commercial buildings as well as parks. The plan may well have had limitations, but it at least presented a balanced mixture of public and private uses.

Civic Square as it is today reflects of the worst type of planning. The theatre-auditorium, art gallery, trade and convention centre and Board of Education Building are all crammed into the narrow piece of land between Main and King Streets, while it appears that empty and poorly used land will always remain in the large block of property between King and Merrick Streets. The reason for this is that in the negotiations between Pigott and the city virtually no planning was done. When Pigott got the politicians to increase the size of the commercial section of the square, the cultural and public buildings had to be squeezed into what little land was left. The only planning principle used was one based on political power.

The square was also a major commercial failure. One-and-a-half office towers were built, and about half of their floor space was vacant long after completion. The shopping mall of Lloyd D. Jackson Square was a mixed success. Eaton's department store has been extended and they may make another expansion, but virtually all other commercial aspects of the square have collapsed. Because of this failure the number of cultural and government buildings in the area has been increased to further stimulate development, but even this has not been enough to fill the open spaces.

Civic Square did more to disrupt Hamilton than could have been imagined when it all started. Rather than attracting people to the downtown, the redevelopment program drove them to shopping plazas even faster. (In fact since Civic Square began the city has approved two enormous shopping plazas to be built in the suburbs.) What development money was attracted into the area surrounding Civic Square produced blockbusting and spot demolition but very little development.

Clearly blame lies at the door of the city politicians. Pigott and later Yale made it quite clear that they were after a project that would create healthy profits for them and little more. The Hamilton politicians were vulnerable for two reasons: developers, particularly ones like Pigott with a strong power base in the city, have political clout, and the politicians were very susceptible to their influence. More important, once the city became committed to the project, the politicians became dependent on the developer for its completion. The result was that council sold out its original dream, and bought what in retrospect was probably inevitable — years of chaos and a poorly planned and executed development.

1. *The Hamilton Spectator*, 10 April 1965.
2. *The Hamilton Spectator*, 10 April 1965.
3. *The Hamilton Spectator*, 10 April 1965.
4. *The Hamilton Spectator*, 19 December 1967.
5. *The Hamilton Spectator*, 24 June 1968.
6. *The Hamilton Spectator*, 11 June 1969.
7. *The Hamilton Spectator*, 19 March 1969.
8. *The Hamilton Spectator*, 2 April 1969.
9. *The Hamilton Spectator*, 21 June 1969.
10. *The Hamilton Spectator*, 21 June 1969.
11. *The Hamilton Spectator*, 30 June 1969.
12. *The Hamilton Spectator*, 20 June 1969.
13. *The Hamilton Spectator*, 24 September 1973.
14. *The Hamilton Spectator*.
15. *The Hamilton Spectator*, 28 November 1975.
16. *The Hamilton Spectator*, 21 July 1978.

Arenas, libraries and parking garages: Downtown development in the seventies

Marsha Aileen Hewitt

Hamilton was dubbed the "give-away king" in a 1978 Spectator article reporting that it is the only city of its size in Ontario to spend $32,000 annually on gifts to "distinguished" visitors.[1] This amount is twice what Toronto spends on such gifts, and four times as much as what other Ontario municipalities of comparable size spend. The cost of special presentations jumped enormously after Mayor Jack MacDonald took office at the beginning of 1977. In 1977 the city spent $4,883 on special presentations, compared with $273 in 1976. The mayor is fond of giving away statues costing $150 apiece, the work of a local artist. The mayor explained his big-spending style with taxpayer money by saying: "If Hamilton is a great city, which it is, it should act like a great city and not like the bushers of the world."[2]

This is just a small example of the abuse of public funds on the part of the city of Hamilton through giveaways to private individuals and business organizations. Hamilton politicians are particularly inclined to lavish valuable real estate upon developers for relatively little in return. A look at development in Hamilton in the 1970s offers a disturbing picture of just what the people have lost, both in revenues of various kinds and in natural resources, in order for the business groups to grow richer. Three major projects — an arena, a library-farmers' market, and a generous gift to the T. Eaton Company — illustrate how city politicians treat developers.

The argument in favour of granting generous subsidies to private interests is that such "incentives" are essential to the greater economic growth of the city. There have been many times when the eagerness of Hamilton's city fathers to attract investment has depleted the public wealth and enriched the private. The story of the ever-elusive civic arena illustrates how far the city administration is willing to go in order to realize development projects. The driving force behind the original move to bring an arena to Hamilton was former mayor Vic Copps, who was once described as "a nice man afflicted with a monumentality."[3] On the question of an arena, one city politician remarked that "the mayor would almost sell his soul to build an arena in this town."[4]

PHASE I: THE KATZ-TOBIAS ARENA PLAN

The arena-colosseum first became the subject of a definite proposal in June 1973, when Hamilton lawyer Henry Katz and investment counsellor Douglas McKay formed a company known as the

The parking garage that Hamilton city council sold to Eaton's for $1 million (Marsha Hewitt).

"Hamilton Colosseum Group," which was to build a $3-million, 10,000-seat arena in the extreme eastern end of the city. The group's proposal included a request for city financial aid in what was to be a private venture. Copps readily agreed to this proposal, which meant that the city would be put in a dubious position as business partner with a private group. The project also presented grave financial risks for taxpayers, and Copps seemed quite oblivious to them.

The Colosseum Group asked for 18 acres of prime city land at $15,000 per acre. The market value of this land was later estimated at between $70,000 and $100,000 per acre. Moreover, the group asked the city to rent ice time and meeting space in the arena at $35,000 per year over 30 years — all to be paid, of course, out of public funds.

By April 1975 the Katz-McKay proposal had changed in its details, but not in its fundamental content. The city, in order to encourage cautious investors to put up $6 million, would "sweeten the deal" by putting up $2 million, to be paid in $200,000 annual installments over 10 years, as a guarantee for partial repayment of the mortgage.

A number of aspects of this deal show the inherent business bias of the leaders of council. Copps and others blindly accepted Katz's claims that he could find investors for the arena and so pushed the city to give the money to the group. In fact Copps seemed quite unperturbed when Katz refused to divulge the names of those backers who had supposedly put up $4 million in additional financing. He was no more ruffled by Katz's failure to provide any documentation to prove that any such backers existed. Alderman Don Gray, a strong opponent of the project, argued that the city was probably giving away closer to $5 million, since the true value of the land was at least $50,000 per acre, the city had agreed to make a major investment in roads and services for the site, and was providing a direct subsidy of $35,000 for ice time over 30 years.

None of this bothered the mayor and his followers. On April 21, 1975, Board of Control voted to give the Colosseum Group the $2-million guarantee it had requested. However, before this issue could proceed to council for final approval, special provincial legislation was needed to allow the municipality to invest public funds in a private project. The council sent the mayor to Queen's Park and, through the offices of Darcy McKeough, then Minister of Municipal Affairs, the mayor's efforts were supported and the province passed the bill.

Despite these enormous subsidies, Katz and McKay were having trouble raising money for the project. They had reportedly gone as far afield as Europe and the Middle East in a search of the money, but in spite of the arena's "assured" success, nobody came forward to invest. As spring turned into summer it became increasingly obvious that the Colosseum Group could never build the arena.

It was at this point that a Toronto "import-export" businessman named Ted Tobias became involved. Who Tobias was, and how he became involved in the project, was never clear, but in his backroom meetings with Mayor Copps and others he soon arranged for the original agreement between the city and the Katz group, with all of its subsidies, to be transferred to him and his backers.

After muscling the Hamilton Colosseum Group out of the arena project, Tobias issued a string of ridiculous promises, which were accepted by the mayor and many others at city hall, with no questions asked. He promised to bring a World Hockey Association franchise to Hamilton through the combined efforts of himself and John Bassett Jr., President of the WHA Toronto Toros. Naturally the construction of an arena was contingent on getting such a franchise. Later on, amid rumours that the WHA was in financial trouble and in danger of folding, Tobias talked about bringing in an NHL team, despite the territorial rights of the Toronto Maple Leafs. Moreover, to prove his good faith, Tobias promised to "retire from (the import-export) business and devote myself to hockey in Hamilton."[5] At another time the developer proposed bringing in stars like Elvis Presley and other mammoth extravaganzas. He had something for everyone.

From the very outset Tobias played the part of a big-city smooth talker selling a bill of goods to a gullible small town, and the mayor responded enthusiastically. On his own initiative Copps promised Tobias that the city would pay $2,000 for season tickets if general sales were below 10,000 tickets, an offer later rejected by the city hall Arena Committee. Tobias also argued that since he was going to bring Hamilton a "20,000 seat showpiece" complete with box seats and air-conditioning,[6] the city should expand its offer to a 22-acre site instead of the original 18, at the same low price of $15,000. In October 1975, Tobias asked the city to sell or lease him an additional 50 acres of city land for a hotel/recreation complex at the same price. He insisted that his commitment to the arena project would not be compromised if he failed to get this extra land, and added that his new proposal was just an undefined idea. "We've done no research, no planning, no financial investigation . . . we have no idea whether Hamilton needs the hotel."[7] It was as if it had occurred to him as an afterthought that he might like to have this extra land at the bargain basement price.

At this point Tobias began to look like a land speculator hoping to wrest parcels of prime city land from the municipal government at a very low cost in order to re-sell them at market value. This possibility was enhanced when Tobias submitted a new draft agreement with the city in January 1976. This draft dropped an important restrictive covenant from the original agreement with the Katz group that had prohibited the developer from re-selling the arena site. Ken Rouff, the city solicitor, wrote to Board of Control at the time, stating that the new agreement "does not give the city any choice over the sale or assignment of the whole project or on parts of the lands." Moreover, "if the new draft agreement were accepted, the city would have no guarantee of land use control."[8]

On another occasion Tobias told a press conference that he and Copps had discussed further ways in which the city could be of help to his group. One suggestion, apparently, was that the city should sell him a chunk of land in the vicinity of the arena, with a view to allowing Tobias a profit on the land once the arena was built and land values escalated.

For the arena project itself, Tobias demanded city help with drainage, paving and lighting of the parking lot at an estimated cost to the city of $700,000. Copps' response to this and the request for extra land for the hotel was that the city should "seriously consider" these requests because of everything Tobias was going to do for Hamilton. The arena would bring in revenues of "thirty to forty million dollars worth of extra business a year to the city," the mayor said. "He's (Tobias) going to spend $14 million for an arena we can't get anyone else to build. There's going to be between $300,000 and $500,000 in taxes coming in from the arena. And he's going to have a payroll of about $800,000 per year."[9] The mayor at no time produced any documentation for these claims.

By this stage it was obvious that Tobias' request for heavy subsidies was an about-face from his initial pledge not to ask the city for money. When he was asked why he had originally said he had no need of municipal funds for the arena development his reply was: "God only knows."[10]

Although Tobias' proposals for municipal subsidies grew as the months went by, the size of the arena he intended to bestow on the city actually shrank. At first he had boasted about his intention to build an arena much like, but bigger than, the spherical arena in Edmonton. He said he would bring the architects and builders to Hamilton to complete the project. By the end of October 1975, however, the Edmonton model was scrapped and Tobias said he would build the arena if his unnamed contractor could do it for $13 million or less.

In spite of the dubious claims, contradictions and general fuzziness of Tobias' proposals, the city hall Arena Committee recommended that Tobias' group be voted the $2 million "in principle" in return for a one-seventh interest in the project.

When city council received the committee's recommendation, the phrase "in principle" had been deleted.[11] It was no wonder that some council members protested that the Arena Committee was trying to "stampede" the $2-million proposal through council. Alderman Don Gray pointed out the inequities inherent in the recommendation, given that the city stood to gain a 14% share in the venture for its $2 million, whereas Tobias' group would claim an 86% share for its $5 million.

The identity of the backers of the arena project was never revealed, if such backers ever existed. Tobias claimed that his "group" included John Bassett, Jr. and a Toronto businessman named Aldo Lorenzetti. Just what role these men were supposed to play in Tobias' scheme was never clarified. Bassett refused to confirm or elaborate upon his alleged financial involvement with Tobias; all he would confirm was his partnership with Tobias in his "bid" to bring Hamilton an arena. In that case, perhaps the only support that Bassett was lending Tobias was in the form of verbal encouragement.

Tobias also refused to name the "manufacturer of consumer products" he claimed as another backer.[12] On the same occasion, he said that he had a "tentative" arrangement with Canada Permanent Trust Company for a mortgage. Finally he told the local press that it was "nobody's business" what Bassett's specific involvement was in the arena development. The mayor and many others on council saw nothing wrong in his secrecy.

When some aldermen demanded to know whether Tobias had the financial backing that he claimed, Copps became angry and on one occasion managed to suppress the debate by putting the issue off to another council meeting.[13] Tobias' response to council's demands for more information came in the form of a 12-page brochure put together by an advertising agency that contained such details as the size of the arena's parking lot, the exterior construction of the building, the amount of restaurant and lounge space inside and the colour of the upholstered seats. This was as far as Tobias was willing to go; he apparently thought he could dazzle council into dropping their demands for hard financial information.

The whole Tobias proposal was so outrageous that Hamilton investment counsellor Harold Barham, manager of Chisholm Investments, contacted Mayor Copps to tell him that the $2 million sought by Tobias was "sucker bait." The term, he explained, was used in investment circles to mean "if the city goes for it they'll be on the hook for all time." Said Barham: "I told him (Copps) he should let the promoter do his own promoting, not the city. The city is not in the loan business. Let the promoter raise his own capital."[14]

Barham warned that the arena could be a "white elephant" and certainly there is an abundance of historical precedent to show that, often, such multi-purpose colosseums do little more than gobble up millions of tax dollars. The March 1973 edition of *Fortune* magazine explained how such schemes are usually sold to the public:

The taxpayer rarely understands what he is in for when a stadium project is announced. To drum up public support, the advocates of a stadium generally understate the probable cost, which invariably balloons as construction proceeds. They also overstate probable revenues by anticipating multiple use for the structure — rock concerts, races, fireworks displays, and conventions — that in actuality dwindle to a few. The stadium's recurring deficits prove to be much higher than promised, and the taxpayer discovers that civic pride has been compromised by special interests, blind boosterism and inept planning. Tainted with deception, the "can do" spirit becomes vitiated by a lingering bitterness that can undercut a city's ability to finance other and perhaps more important projects.[15]

The real risk that the city of Hamilton could have been taking was enormous. Yet these dangers were not even discussed; all the mayor seemed concerned with was getting Tobias his $2 million. Finally he was able to do it. Council voted 11–10 in December 1975 to give Tobias his subsidies. The method of payment had been amended, however, from issuing the money in a lump sum, as originally recommended by the Arena Committee, to payment in annual installments of $400,000 over five years for 25 years of ice time. There was a further proviso that the first $400,000 would not be paid to Tobias until the arena facility was complete and the owners had paid their first taxes to the city. This stipulation at least ensured that an arena would be built. Even so, these further conditions meant little in terms of protection for the city since council really had no idea of the nature of the venture they had voted to undertake.

At the time the vote was taken, council had no signed proposal from Ted Tobias, nor had it any idea from where the mortgage money was to come. Wrote *Globe and Mail* columnist Dick Beddoes: "The bare majority of Hamilton councillors simply accepted, as an act of good faith, that there is a bountiful Mr. Christmas lurking in the background."[16]

Apparently Tobias was not happy with the installment plan, much preferring the $2 million in one lump sum before beginning construction. Two days after the council meeting, John Bassett, Jr. announced that he was no longer certain the arena would ever materialize since Tobias "didn't get what he asked for."[17]

By this time Mayor Copps seemed to have lost all perspective on the situation. It should have appeared obvious to him that Tobias had no intention of building an arena in Hamilton. Instead the mayor kept up his useless machinations, trying to pave the way for a project that had little reality. In January 1976, when a city alderman demanded that council seek Ontario Municipal Board approval

The footings of the new Library-Farmers' Market being laid in July 1978, already well behind schedule (Marsha Hewitt).

before it signed any agreement with Tobias, the mayor decided to bypass the city legal department in submitting the application.

When council voted to invest $2 million in Tobias' arena project, it was generally believed that the agreement the city was embarking upon would be the same as that struck with the Hamilton Colosseum Group. Apparently, this was not the case. When Tobias' agreement finally came before the Arena Committee in February, there were 10 significant changes from the original agreement, all to the city's disadvantage. Alderman Don Gray, a member of the Arena Committee, was refused a copy of the Tobias agreement by the mayor until the actual committee meeting in which it was to be discussed.

In a letter to Board of Control, Ken Rouff listed and commented on the changes. He wrote:

I have no evidence that "The Tobias Group" is a properly constituted legal entity, nor do I have any information as to what persons comprise "The Tobias Group." If the new draft agreement were accepted, the city would have no guarantee of land use control. The new draft agreement ... omits the right of the city to approve plans and drawings with respect to the type of building to be constructed ... [omits] the requirement that the purchasers furnish the city treasurer with satisfactory evidence of the financing ... does not mention the city's right to use the ice and other facilities for 25 years ... it requires the city to improve three existing highways, to build a new one and install services on it. If the city does not complete the work before the opening of the project, the city could be liable to the purchasers for damages. In effect the new draft agreement, while obligating the city to provide these services, removes the protection which the city had under the previous agreement ... [it] does not give the city any voice over the sale or assignment of the whole project of parts of the lands.[18]

Rouff concluded that the Tobias agreement "emasculates the protection afforded the city's interests and at the same time fortifies and reinforces the interests of the purchasers."

Tobias' demand for so many concessions for himself in return for absolutely nothing of benefit to the city was so blatant that it forced the Arena Committee to recommend to council that it withdraw the offer of $2 million and honour only its gift to Tobias of the 22-acre site at the $15,000-per-acre rate. The committee made this recommendation in an attempt to ward off Alderman Bill McCulloch's notice of motion that council cancel "all agreements or any actions taken by council in connection with the arena project."[19]

Copps feared that McCulloch's motion would pass at the next council meeting because, since the 11–10 vote to award Tobias the money, a pro-arena alderman, Reg Swanborough, had died and been replaced by an anti-arena alderman, Kay Drage. There was every indication that McCulloch's motion would have passed in a reversed 11–10 vote.

Aldermen Don Gray and Dennis Carson, both arena opponents, and both members of the Arena Committee, knew nothing of their committee's new decision until they saw it in a press release. They learned that no committee meeting had in fact taken place to discuss the issue, let alone recommend it. The decision had been taken as a result of a "telephone poll" conducted by the mayor himself of the "majority" of the committee members.

The arena issue involving Tobias came to an end in March 1976, when Mayor Copps suffered a heart attack severe enough to prevent him from returning to public office. The driving force behind bringing an arena to Hamilton was gone, and further dealings between the city and Tobias were half-hearted.

In April 1976, city council's arena committee decided to sever all ties with Ted Tobias and find a new developer to build an arena in Hamilton. Ken Rouff, the city solicitor, informed council at about this time that the Ontario Municipal Board would not allow a municipality to sell industrial land for less than the current market value. Perhaps the most telling comment on the whole situation came from Ted Tobias himself, as part of his farewell to the city: "Hamilton is a fabulous city to be in business in."[20]

PHASE II: THE PAN AMERICAN GAMES

The Hamilton arena controversy did not end with the exit of Ted Tobias. One reason for this was that Mayor Copps was succeeded by another pro-development mayor, Jack MacDonald, in the December 1976 municipal election. The fact that the people of Hamilton rejected the arena project in a city-wide referendum at the same time he took office did not dampen MacDonald's enthusiasm for a huge colosseum. Rather, he decided that the way to get it was to tie the colosseum to a bid to bring the 1983 Pan American Games to Hamilton.

The real reasons why some Hamilton political figures were in favour of the arena are complex. Some believed that the city needed an arena, no matter what the cost to the public. Another factor was that the Pan American Games would provide a stimulus to the tourist and retail industries. The most important reason, however, was that MacDonald and the business community hoped to use the building of sports facilities for the games as a way of further stimulating downtown development. The major facilities for the games were planned to go into the Civic Square project. On this same site, the city had earlier proposed building an arena, but the plan was rejected by the 1976 referendum.

On March 16, 1977, MacDonald called a council meeting and announced that Hamilton would make a bid to host the 1983 Games. He informed an almost incredulous council that he had to have a decision immediately if he were to fly to Mexico in time to meet the deadline for application, which was only four days away. At that point council was handed a 24-page brochure, of which there existed only one copy, complete with colour photos of various parts of Hamilton. The brochure had been prepared by the Pan American Games City Hall Steering Committee, chaired by a former law partner of John Munro, Jack Pelech. Pelech's committee had been active for a year prior to the March 16 meeting and had met frequently. March 16, however, was the first time council had ever heard from the committee or received any information concerning the games.

After the fiasco of the Katz-McKay and Tobias schemes, many aldermen were cautious. They felt that the information regarding Hamilton's submission for the games had been "dumped" on council "at the eleventh hour" and as a result the proposal to seek the games was defeated in a 12–7 vote. Council was angry that it had never received any previous reports from the committee, especially when they had been assured when the committee was formed that it would report back from time to time.

At the March 16 meeting, Mayor MacDonald presented council with a rather sketchy outline of the implications of the city hosting the games. He was particularly vague about the financial arrangements for the estimated $50-million sports facility, but he did assure council that although the province and Ottawa would share the costs, the city alone would receive the revenues. After the meeting, a reporter called Queen's Park to seek confirmation on this and was told that as far as the province was concerned, the revenues were to be shared.

After the meeting in which the proposal for the games was defeated, John Munro himself telephoned several aldermen who had voted against the motion to try to convince them of its great

Architect's model of the new Library–Farmers' Market complex (Bill Freeman).

benefits for Hamilton. One alderman remarked that if he was against the games before, Munro's telephone call merely strengthened his resolve. Several aldermen resented the pressure being put on them to vote for a project the details of which were extremely vague.

Munro's intervention at city hall to promote the games is interesting. Perhaps he was lending his support for the games partly out of loyalty to his friend and former law partner Jack Pelech, chairman of the games committee. Given his role on the committee, Pelech was obviously in favour of having the games come to Hamilton. His committee, in fact, offered to help raise $9 million of the city's share of the costs. Or perhaps, as the federal Minister of Labour, Munro expected that the games would give the construction industry a needed boost which would, in turn, yield him political returns.

The mayor called a special meeting for the next day, hoping that he could persuade council to reverse its decision on the games. A few hours before the meeting, he held a closed session with a small group of aldermen to deliver a pep talk on the value of the games proposal.

The special March 17 meeting was attended not only by John Munro but also by the federal Minister of Sport and Recreation, Iona Campagnolo, who was there to assure council of federal aid. The pressure worked and the council reversed its vote. The politicians imposed certain restrictions, including one that said the city would spend a fixed $7.8 million, with the provincial and federal governments paying $16 million each. It was also announced at this meeting that the province had agreed, apparently sometime between the March 16 and 17 meetings, to let the city take all the revenues. As for the approximately $9 million remaining, the Pan Am Games Committee pledged to raise it privately, but the details of this last fund-raising plan were never clarified.

The pitfalls of this arrangement were immediately obvious to the games' opponents on council. In the first place, the $50-million cost of the facilities was only an estimate and had no detailed documentation behind it to show how that figure was reached. The $16 million agreed to by the provincial and federal governments was a final amount and did not allow for inflation or escalating construction costs. There was also little reason to believe that the city hall games committee could in fact raise the extra $9 million from private and public donations. It was highly unlikely that people would be willing to give money to this type of project, which has so universally proven to be a money-loser.

The dangers were of no apparent concern to Mayor Jack MacDonald. He assured council that Hamilton would avoid the pitfalls of the Montreal Olympic experience because of the "business-like approach" of the Pan Am Games Committee. In its brochure, the committee wrote that the "1983 games will truly be a celebration shared by the people of Hamilton" and that the "vital need for a new colosseum has long been recognized throughout this sports-minded community."

Further indications of the "business-like approach" of MacDonald himself could be seen in the way he presented Hamilton's application for the games to the committee in Mexico that would decide who would host the games. Council had stipulated that a city-wide plebiscite be held within 90 days, if the games were awarded to Hamilton. This MacDonald neglected to tell the committee in Mexico, and when asked why, he replied that he did not want to "prejudice" the committee's decision toward Hamilton.

There was certainly a possibility that the games could be rejected in a plebiscite, if a sampling of published letters to the editor of *The Spectator* was any guide. Many were negative, and cynical about the politicians' motives. The local radio and television media responded with a campaign against opponents of the colosseum and the games.

Alderman Don Gray pointed out that the city was already committed to expenditures of approximately $200 million for the new Art Gallery and Library-Farmers' Market Complex, as well as the Trade and Convention Centre, which had yet to be built. Gray complained that "there is no priority system in Hamilton — everyone is pushing to get his own project approved."[21] Like many other politicians at city hall, Gray was concerned that the city was piling up too great a financial debt, and placing too much of a burden on taxpayers.

While there was plenty of evidence to show that Hamilton could in fact be harmed by having a colosseum, there was little hard documentation to demonstrate the contrary. The problem soon became academic, however, because the games were finally awarded to Venezuela.

THE LIBRARY-FARMERS' MARKET: THE DEVELOPERS HAVE THEIR WAY

While the question of an arena for Hamilton was laid to rest, at least temporarily, Hamilton city politicians were busy with other downtown development projects. One of these was the library-farmers' market project included in the Civic Square project.

The library-farmers' market project was beset with problems from the time city council decided that, rather than co-ordinate the construction of the building with a general contractor, they would use a method known as the Project Management System. The claimed advantage of this system is that work can begin on a project before the plans and drawings are completed, because the work is done in stages under separate contracts. However, the client, in this case the city of Hamilton, is responsible for tendering all the various phases of the project, and in the case of the library-market there were some 41 contracts involved. If the advantage of this system is that it is faster and cheaper, Hamilton has yet to experience its good fortune. By the summer of 1979, the library-market project was already running in excess of $1 million over budget, with only the foundations excavated.

The city decided to use the management system primarily on the advice of its engineer, Bill Phillips, and the architect retained to design the project, Anthony Butler. Once city hall had agreed, Pigott Structures Limited, a wholly-owned subsidiary of the Pigott Construction Company that built the city hall and began the Civic Square, was hired to oversee construction of the project. The management committee appointed by the city was made up of Phillips, the engineer; Butler, the architect; and J. Neilson, vice-president of Pigott Structures.

The first major problem that the project encountered was a dispute over the contract forms to be used. The original set of forms was drawn up by professional associations representing architects and contractors, and was recommended to the city by Anthony Butler. These forms were unacceptable to the city solicitor, Ken Rouff, because of the strong protection afforded the contractors and lack of protection for the city. Among other things, the contract forms contained no clauses holding the builders responsible for any latent defects that might be discovered in the construction of the building after the two-year warranty ran out, and for seeing that the workmanship required by the specifications of the design was in keeping with the building code. Hamilton knew from its city hall experience about the importance of such provisions. Council readily accepted Rouff's recommendation that these two clauses be inserted into the contract.

The contractors who planned to bid on the project protested loudly. At a council meeting in February 1978, W. P. Cooper of Cooper Construction Company spoke on behalf of 10 representatives of the local construction industry, arguing against the clauses added by Rouff. Cooper bluntly threatened that there would be no bids on the library-market project if the amendments remained.

Mayor MacDonald was in full agreement with the industry's point of view and he made several interruptions when Rouff tried to explain his position. The mayor told council that he too had been told that bidding might not take place on the project if the forms as changed by Rouff were adopted by council. He took up the cause of the contractors so zealously that Alderman Bill McColloch wondered aloud if MacDonald was also acting as a spokesman for the contractors.

In spite of such obvious intimidation by the contractors and the mayor, council held firm on the contract forms. Rouff sent the amended contract to Butler, the architect, in early March with several changes in it to protect the city's interests. Butler returned the contract forms three weeks later, late on a Thursday afternoon, with instructions to Rouff that it be approved by the following Monday. All Rouff's amendments had been deleted and the solicitor had one working day to respond to this and suggest other changes.

Pressure on council to drop the protective clauses intensified; Board of Control received a letter dated March 6, 1978, from the management committee warning that if the amendments or "General Conditions" approved by city council remained, prices would be driven up or bids might in fact fail to appear. Phillips, Butler and Neilson, wrote:

We must record our extreme concern of (sic) the effect that the changes made by city council, to the recommended wording of the General Conditions, will have on the tendering process for all of the remaining bid packages, the established schedule and the final cost of the project. We are concerned that the revisions to the general conditions could lead to severely reduced competition, inflated prices and/or qualified tenders.

They closed their letter by saying that, if the contract changes remained, "we cannot be responsible for any delays attributed thereto nor can we be responsible to keep this project within the approved estimate." Given such threats from its own management committee, it is easy to see the impossible situation in which city council was placed. The business group was characterizing city council as a group alienating all the local construction firms to the point where they would probably not bid at all, or if they did, would bid so high that the project would be pushed well over budget, thus increasing the burden on taxpayers. If council were actively to seek outside firms to do the job, as several aldermen suggested, then local industry would suffer. Finally, council was accused of endangering the whole project before the foundations were even laid. Certainly Hamilton was in sore need of a new library; the main library had been built prior to World War I and was no longer adequate. In the face of all these pressures, council held out against the contractors, for the moment, that is.

The local construction firms were as good as their word; a few days later no bids were received for the $200,000 second stage. In a clear show of power, the large local contracting firms such as Cooper, Frid and James Kemp Construction took out bid packages on the work but held back from actually bidding. At a March 13 council meeting, James Barclay, president of the Hamilton Construction Association, told council on behalf of the other city contractors that delays would only raise prices on the project. He also warned that the project might have to be abandoned altogether as long as the amendments to the contract remained. Said Barclay: "I would like to guarantee if this were done (the forms changed) the city would get seven to eight legitimate bids for the project." He went on to refer to any suggestions that the contractors were in collusion with each other in their failure to bid as "absolute balderdash."[22] Controller Pat Valeriano and Aldermen Henry Merling, Kay Drage and Bill McCulloch called the companies' action a "gang-up" against the city.

In a dispute of this sort, one of the problems of the Project Management System quickly emerges: since the work is done in stages and individually bid upon, the absence of bids at one stage of the work can hold up the entire operation, and costs rise. When suggestions came from council to abandon the system in favour of retaining a general contractor, Board of Control received another letter from the management committee, dated March 15, recommending that the present system be kept. The letter pointed out that if council decided to scrap the management system, there would be escalating costs due to a 33-week delay (an estimated time period) not to mention possible court action by Pigott Structures, the construction manager, for cancellation of its contract. The management committee, however, offered no hard documentation to support its claims.

The Hamilton confrontation with the local contractors followed a similar altercation between Toronto City Council, and the Canadian Construction Association and the Ontario Association of General Contractors in 1961 over the $30-million new city hall. In the Toronto dispute, the city was faced with the same contract forms as were being foisted on Hamilton. Contractors took out bid packages but made no bids; the Hamilton firm of Pigott Construction Company was, in fact, one of the contractors involved. Only one company from outside Toronto agreed to take the contract using the city's forms and that company got the job. According to one Toronto city spokesman interviewed by *The Spectator*, the city still uses its own forms and 1961 was the "last time the issue was raised."[23]

While Hamilton City Council was fighting the contractors and the recommendation of its own management committee, Board of Control (with the exception of Pat Valeriano) voted for a resolution that the city adopt the contractor's forms. Finally a compromise was reached that gave the city virtually the protection it had been seeking from the very beginning. After weeks of battle, the new contract forms pushed by the contractors and the architect were abandoned, and both the city and the business groups accepted the standard contract forms that had always been used by the city.

Although the forms accepted by the contractors do not specifically contain the "latent defects" clause, they do allow the city to claim damages under common law that might show up after the warranty. This "compromise" was a clear victory for the city in that the contractors would now have to deal with the city on its terms, rather than their own. The firms were not happy about the outcome of their battle with council, but said they could "live with" the forms. Anthony Butler, the architect, was the most bitter: "This demonstrates why everything municipalities end up doing is second class. It's always a compromise."[24]

The victory won by council was not only short-lived, it was almost completely reversed. By mid-July, bids began to appear on the library-market that were, in Controller Valeriano's words, "11% to 65% higher" than the estimated cost. Valeriano was particularly struck by the bidding pattern of one company, Saltfleet Construction Ltd., whose bids on two of the early stages of the project were under the estimate in one case and very slightly over in the other. When Saltfleet bid on the ninth package, however, its bid was the highest of four companies, at $3,480,332 on an estimate of $2,092,000, or $1.3 million over the projected figure. In Valeriano's view, there was something "not normal" in this sort of shift.

Valeriano recommended that the city wait 30 days and re-tender, in the hope that the companies would bring their bids down. Mayor Jack MacDonald replied, in a lengthy speech to council fully supporting the bids offered, that such an action would undermine the "integrity" of council as an agent with which to do business. Moreover, re-tendering the bids would undermine the entire tendering process: "I implore you [council] not to mess with the tendering system." He felt that if council adopted this course of action, competition would be threatened because the companies would know the city's estimates.

When it was suggested that the city should advertise more widely, and perhaps seek a contractor from elsewhere in Canada, the mayor declared that "every company competent to do the work from Winnipeg to Halifax" knew of the library-market project in Hamilton and were probably not offering bids because of the contract form being used. He produced no letters or documentation from other companies to support his speculations. It is notable that many of his arguments suggested that this was a moral issue, since there is nothing illegal or unusual about re-tendering a contract when the bids received are so high above estimates.

MacDonald's final argument was the one which probably convinced the majority of council members that they should vote to accept the bids instead of re-tendering. Said the mayor: "There's a big hole over there and tons of reinforcing steel . . . we are already committed to go with it." Controller Ian Stout maintained that he had been opposed from the start to "a palace for the printed word" but that council had two choices — go ahead with the bids received or scrap the whole project. Given his views on literacy, he might well have been just as happy to take the latter course. With the exception of Controller Valeriano and Alderman Bill McCulloch, the only two who voted against accepting the bids, the tenor of the comments that night was in agreement with MacDonald and Stout.

As soon as the vote was taken and before the end of the meeting, city engineer Bill Phillips and architect Anthony Butler rushed out of the chamber to shake hands with and congratulate the businessmen who had attended the meeting. This burst of enthusiasm and self-satisfaction took place in full view of the entire council chamber; Alderman McCulloch later commented on the blatant manner in which the city employees and the businessmen responded to their victory.

Most of the council members who voted to accept the high bid explained their decision on the basis of fear of what the contractors might do if council tried to face them down in this conflict over high prices. Barclay had already made threats that the project would never materialize if the city insisted on exposing the contractors. Still, when the construction industry was in a slump, it is hard to believe that contractors could have continued to resist an $11-million job for very long. Re-tendering by a city council unwilling to go higher than the prices estimated by their consultants might have brought in bids closer to the city's expectations. Instead, the politicians buckled under pressure from the construction industry and its friends at city hall.

EATON'S TAKES THE PARKING GARAGE

While all the wrangling over the library-farmers' market was going on, another deal was quietly being made by city hall with one of its good corporate friends, the T. Eaton Company. Their department store on James Street is also a part of Civic Square, and when Eaton's intimated possible plans for expansion, the city was delighted. At one time the city had tried to attract a second department store into the square but failed. Instead, an office building was put in the location designated for a new department store despite the fact that, at that time, literally floors upon floors of office space stood empty in the huge "Century 21" tower in the heart of the city. Expansion of the Eaton's store was what the city had to settle for as a second-best alternative to a new department store in the Civic Square project.

In the spring of 1978, the city negotiated with Eaton's to sell the company 800,000 square feet of prime downtown land adjacent to the store at the very low price of $1 million. That works out to about $55,000 an acre for an 18-acre site. City officials valued the land at $2.5 million but given its location inside the square its market value was more likely double that amount.

The land was divided into four parcels which surrounded the store. In its agreement with the city, Eaton's was committed to rebuild and expand its present store — maybe. For the city officials, this was the reason for the sale, but Eaton's refused to allow a clause in the agreement enabling the city to reclaim the land if the company failed to expand. In the signed agreement, the only penalty

Interior view of the Edmonton Coliseum, which at one point in Tobias' plan was to be the model for a Hamilton Coliseum.

Eaton's was required to pay if it did not honour its commitments was a once-only $300,000 penalty. Alderman Bill McCulloch commented that "for $300,000, they can completely lock the land up for eternity. They don't even have to build on it."[25]

The cheap real estate was not all that Eaton's got from the city: behind the store there is a parking garage whose full capacity is 531 spaces. This parking facility was part of the land deal between the city and Eaton's. Eaton's purchased the garage plus all the revenues from it. According to two city Parking Authority officials, the revenues from the garage were a "major contributor" to its general income. In 1977 the net income from the parking facility was $124,729.

The 1977 net revenues do not represent the full operating capacity of the facility since 112 spaces are closed three days a week to accommodate a farmers' market; on market days, only 247 spaces are in use. An additional 172 spaces had been permanently closed because of deterioration of the structure and were declared unsafe by the city when it was the owner. As soon as Eaton's took possession of the garage, its consultants said the unsafe portions were fine for public use and they were opened to the public. No renovations were done. One Parking Authority official said that when the city closed those 172 spaces, they were in "urgent need of repair" and that there was a definite question of "the public's safety involved." The same official also stated that with all parking spaces in use, the net revenue of the parking garage would be $215,000 per year.

In 1979 the farmers' market was scheduled to be relocated so that Eaton's would have full use of the garage each day of the week. Until the farmers' market was relocated, the city of Hamilton agreed to operate it and give the profits from the market, which in 1977 amounted to $30,000, to Eaton's. Not only has Eaton's purchased a piece of land with no real restrictions on it at a low price, it has also received a large money-making operation — the parking garage — from the city.

The manner in which the most recent sale of land to Eaton's was negotiated is worth noting. According to Alderman McCulloch, his Planning and Development Committee had no knowledge that a deal with Eaton's was taking place until the terms and conditions of the tentative agreement were presented to council as a fait accompli. Alderman Pat Ford, of the Downtown Redevelopment Subcommittee of the Planning and Development committee, was on the negotiating team with Eaton's but never told McCulloch or anyone else on council about the negotiations.

McCulloch was angry that his committee was kept in ignorance and charged that the way in which the negotiations with Eaton's were handled precluded council and public input. The negotiating team for the city included Bill Phillips, the city engineer; Jack Jones, the Board of Control secretary; Dan Weiss, city real estate director; Alderman Pat Ford, who according to Weiss "only came once or twice" to the sessions;

and, of course, Mayor Jack MacDonald.

Only three members of city council voted against the sale to Eaton's; one of those opposed, Bill McCulloch, felt there was "no advantage to the city but a heck of a lot to Eaton's... We are saying whatever you want, you can have it."[26] The mayor disagreed because "we got $1 million in cash with which we can provide parking elsewhere."[27] According to some members of city council, all the politicians saw when they voted to give the land to Eaton's was the million dollars. The loss of the revenues from the parking ramp seemed to make no impression on their view of the deal. Perhaps the situation was best described by Alderman Fred Lombardo, who felt that the sale to Eaton's was the biggest give-away since "the Indians sold Manhattan for $24, and they still got a better deal than we did."[28]

A year later it was learned that Eaton's had leased the parking garage to a private developer for more money than the department store paid the city. Moreover, Eaton's leased land adjacent to the garage to Enfield Properties of Waterdown. This company has plans to build a bus terminal. These transactions between Eaton's and the developers happened immediately after Eaton's purchased land from the city. It appears that Eaton's had no intention of using the land in order to extend its department store.

This is the usual approach to development in Hamilton. And responsibility for this state of affairs must be placed squarely with city hall and municipal politicians who are strongly compromised by the developers. Those few politicians who at times oppose the predominating bias are in the minority on council and are too poorly organized ever to seriously challenge the rest of council and the mayor. Opposition members on council never caucus together on how to fight some of the destructive policies pushed by the mayor. The opposition, when it exists, operates on an individual basis and these individuals are not themselves consistent in their attitudes, but tend to deal with issues as they arise. As long as this situation continues at city hall, and business-minded politicians continue to be elected, the developers in Hamilton will always have their way. Taxpayers will continue to pay for the business community's privileged position in return for badly conceived projects of little value to the public.

1. *The Hamilton Spectator*, 28 June 1978.

2. *The Hamilton Spectator*, 27 June 1978.

3. *The Hamilton Spectator*, 11 December 1975.

4. *The Hamilton Spectator*, 27 October 1975.

5. *The Hamilton Spectator*, 12 June 1975.

6. *The Hamilton Spectator*, 11 October 1975.

7. *The Hamilton Spectator*, 11 October 1975.

8. Letter to Hamilton Board of Control, written by Ken Rouff, 30 January 1976.

9. *The Hamilton Spectator*, 11 October 1975.

10. *The Hamilton Spectator*, 27 October 1975.

11. *The Hamilton Spectator*, 28 October 1975.

12. *The Hamilton Spectator*, 6 November 1975.

13. *The Hamilton Spectator*, 11 November 1975.

14. *The Hamilton Spectator*, 22 November 1975.

15. Charles G. Burke, "It's Promoters Versus Taxpayers in the Super Stadium's Game," *Fortune*, March 1973.

16. *The Globe and Mail*, 10 December 1975.

17. *The Hamilton Spectator*, 11 December 1975.

18. Rouff letter, 30 January 1976.

19. *The Hamilton Spectator*, 13 March 1976.

20. *The Hamilton Spectator*, 24 April 1976.

21. Interview with the author, July 1977.

22. *The Hamilton Spectator*, 14 March 1978.

23. *The Hamilton Spectator*, 20 March 1978.

24. *The Hamilton Spectator*, 21 March 1978.

25. *The Hamilton Spectator*, 4 May 1978.

26. *The Hamilton Spectator*, 4 May 1978.

27. *The Hamilton Spectator*, 6 May 1978.

28. *The Hamilton Spectator*, 10 May 1978.

Hamilton Harbour: Politics, patronage and cover-up

Marsha Aileen Hewitt

After 14 months and $7 million of taxpayer money, Canada's longest and costliest trial finally ended in mid-1979. After more than 40 years of bid-rigging — inflated contracts and elaborate kickback schemes — the entire Canadian dredging industry and some of its top executives were tried and convicted for conspiracy to defraud the Canadian public. (Many of those convicted immediately launched appeals.)

The sequence of events that led to the revelation of one of the worst corporate scandals in Canadian history took place in Hamilton. The discovery of a fraudulent contract for dredging work in Hamilton Harbour — standard practice in Canada's dredging industry, it appears — provided a startling demonstration of the way some large enterprises regularly did business with the public. If it had not been for events in Hamilton in the early 1970s, and the dogged persistence of a few individuals in uncovering the truth (or at least part of it), the corruption of the dredging industry and some of its more prestigious executives might never have been known. Even now the whole story has probably not come to light.

Hamilton Harbour used to be called "Lake Geneva" by the 18th-century settlers who lived in the area. The beautiful land-locked harbour, ringed by the Niagara Escarpment, lies at the western end of Lake Ontario and provides excellent shelter for boats and ships. The Bay was a favourite recreational area of Hamiltonians until well into the 20th century. Lansdowne Park lay at the foot of Wentworth Street, bathing beaches dotted the shoreline, and farther east were Sherman's Inlet and Huckleberry Point. All were popular for fishing, swimming, and picnicking.

Many Hamiltonians still remember the steamers that left from the foot of James Street for day and night cruises around the Bay and into Lake Ontario. Boathouses along the shoreline offered rowboats and canoes that could be rented for the day. In winter, the frozen waters of the Bay were covered with skaters and ice fishermen. Ice boating and curling were also familiar winter sports.

Hamilton Harbour is also one of the finest inland harbours in the world, and by the mid-19th century it was becoming an increasingly important commercial centre. This aspect of the harbour has resulted in Hamiltonians being robbed of one of their finest natural resources through the gradual destruction and isolation of the harbour. The primary responsibility for this state of affairs lies with the Hamilton Harbour Commission, which tends to act as a real-estate broker for private enterprise. As a result of the Commission's selling off waterlots and miles of shoreline at astonishingly low rates to big industry and private developers, the face of Hamilton Harbour has drastically changed. The 10 square miles of water surface is now reduced to seven square miles— 30 per cent less than what it used to be.

A pleasure steamboat at the Beach Strip Canal, in pre-World War I days (Public Archives Canada).

Since 1929, a total of almost 2,000 acres of water has been filled in, almost exclusively for the benefit of industry, particularly Stelco and Dofasco. The total price at which these waterlots were sold was little more than $2 million. None of the sales was ever tendered, nor was there public notice that the lots were even available; these deals were privately arranged between the Commission and the industries. Firms like Stelco simply asked the Commission to buy lots, and the sale was finalized upon completion of the price negotiations.

One unanswered question is how prices of waterlots are determined. Stelco rarely paid more than $1,500 per acre, a remarkable fact when one considers the site upon which the company rests is prime industrial land. A few years ago, one harbour-based steel company sold several acres of waterlots it had acquired at $1,500 per acre to another company for $23,000 per acre.

All that is now left untouched by industrial development of the Bay is its western end, but even this is endangered, not by industry but by a private development scheme that has already resulted in the filling in of over 50 acres of water.

The central issue to be resolved is the question of who has ultimate power over the fate of the harbour: the city or the Commission? The city has always maintained that the role of the Commission is to act as trustees on its behalf. As City Solicitor Ken Rouff wrote in 1972:

The Hamilton Harbour Commissioners are a corporation called into being primarily to act on behalf of the City of Hamilton as trustee of the city's interests. With the possible exception of the power conferred upon the commissioners to act as delegates for the federal government with respect to the federal navigation and shipping power, it is nowhere contemplated or intended that that corporation is to become a power unto itself, free to act without reference to the wishes of the city council.[1]

Yet since the inception of the Hamilton Harbour Commissioners' Act in 1912, the Commission has acted as a "power unto itself," allowing the city no say as to the development of the harbour. How this came about is a complex issue, best determined by an analysis of the structure of the Commission and its political context.

THE HAMILTON HARBOUR COMMISSION: A POWER UNTO ITSELF

The Hamilton Harbour Commission oversees the development of the harbour almost exclusively. It is a three-member body composed of two federal appointees and one appointed by the city. The federal posts are filled through political patronage. The real purpose of this patronage, besides rewarding the party faithful, is to ensure that business interests, the traditional support of the local politicians, are protected. When the Conservatives were in power under Diefenbaker, two Hamilton Tories, Argue Martin and J. Edmund McLean, were the federal commissioners. The most powerful Liberal political patron in Hamilton since 1962 has been John Munro. In May 1964, Munro appointed E. Delbert Hickey, a Hamilton lawyer who is also a member of the prestigious Hamilton Club, and Joseph Lanza, a Hamilton tailor, to the Hamilton Harbour Commission. Lanza, a one-time city alderman, was convicted in the 1940s on bookmaking and gambling charges.

The Liberal party connections of Hickey, former chairman of the Commission, and Lanza are extensive. Both ran unsuccessfully for the federal Liberals; Hickey was an officer of the Wentworth Liberal Association for 23 years prior to his appointment to the Commission, and Lanza was twice Munro's campaign manager. Munro tried but failed to get Lanza a citizenship court judge position in 1969. According to lawyer Joe Kostyk, a loyal Munro supporter who collected over $40,000 for Munro's 1974 campaign: "John wanted him to get it, that's for sure." The National Parole Board's refusal to issue Lanza a pardon for his criminal record has been reported by the Hamilton media.

Since the Commission was incorporated under its own act and is not under the jurisdiction of the National Harbours Board, no one seems to know to whom the Commission is responsible. In February 1972, then Minister of Transport Don Jamieson stated publicly that he could not and would not interfere with any filling in of the harbour because the Hamilton Harbour Commission is an "autonomous" body and therefore out of his jurisdiction. A few days later, Chairman Del Hickey contradicted Jamieson, saying: "Despite his statement, I feel we are responsible to Mr. Jamieson."[2]

The ambiguity regarding the accountability of the Commission gave the chairman and his fellow commissioners virtual license to do whatever they pleased with the harbour. In fact, the arrogant behaviour of the Commission in relation to the city or any group that tried to challenge its indiscriminate filling in of the Bay caused Tom Beckett, a Liberal and former chairman of the Hamilton Region Conservation Authority, to say that he had "nothing but condemnation" for Hickey's Commission, adding that "this body appears to be responsible to no one on Earth."[3]

The virtually unchecked power of the Commission and the resultant lack of public participation in the harbour's development has created the present situation in which the harbour is treated, for all practical purposes, as real estate to be sold off to industry when required, at bargain-basement prices.

LANDFILLING: INSTANT REAL ESTATE

The most destructive policies of the Hamilton Harbour Commission have involved the landfilling of waterlots. Hamilton's steel companies, Dofasco and Stelco, have benefitted enormously from landfilling, which has allowed them to expand their operations considerably. Both east-end harbour-based steel industries have also improved their docking facilities with landfilling so that they are more easily able to land the iron ore that comes up the St. Lawrence Seaway by ship.

The harbour also provides the steel companies with a convenient way to dispose of slag, the major waste product in steel production: slag is the basic landfill material used by the companies.

Since 1912, the steel companies have been able to fill in as much of the Bay adjacent to their properties as they wished. There seems to be no limit to the amount of water Stelco and Dofasco can fill in, although the size of the harbour has been greatly reduced.

THE LAND SWAP

In 1971, the Hamilton Harbour Commission was quietly negotiating a deal with Stelco and Dofasco that would allow the companies to fill in the harbour by yet another 328 acres. This deal involved an exchange of land and waterlots between the Commission and the steel companies whereby the Commission would acquire 313 acres of waterlots along the Beach Strip.

The completion of this deal was announced publicly November 11, 1971, to the surprise of many people on city council as well as the Hamilton Region Conservation Authority. City Controller Herman Turkstra was angered that the city had not been first consulted, and that there was no accounting as to why the deal was necessary in the first place. He described the situation as "three men, responsible to no one, agreeing with . . . men

The Royal Hamilton Yacht Club at the Beach Strip. The building was destroyed by fire in 1915 (Public Archives Canada).

responsible to two bodies of shareholders, to take an asset that belongs to the citizens of Hamilton and convert it to the use of the companies, without the public's being aware of it."[4]

When the Commission first announced its deal with the companies, it said that the total acreage to be given them was 103, which was later found to be untrue. The Commission also said that it would give the city 176 acres of its newly acquired Beach Strip holdings for a public park. According to Turkstra, a park at that location was unfeasible for two reasons: first, if the province was to carry out its plans to extend the Queen Elizabeth Highway over the Skyway Bridge, it would need that site, and second, a park of that size would require 1.75-million cubic yards of fill, an amount almost impossible to acquire. Hickey certainly would have been aware of these obstacles; therefore, he must have mentioned the park in order to soften the impact of the land swap. Hickey's Commission had been plagued that entire summer by protesting environmental groups concerned about additional landfilling in the harbour, and pressure was rising to stop further filling.

The Hamilton Region Conservation Authority was upset because it had already agreed with the Commission to begin a joint waterfront study of the Bay. Tom Beckett was outraged at the Commission's duplicity in keeping the deal a secret from the Authority when the former knew full well that a freeze on all further landfilling was necessary until the study was finished.

John Prentice, a member of the Conservation Authority at the time, was concerned about the swap because the area to be filled by the steel companies was the deepest part of the Bay. Thus the fill would displace the largest amounts of water in the Bay, dangerously depleting the oxygen content that is already non-existent at water depths greater than 30 feet.[5] Once all the oxygen was gone from the Bay, it would become septic and no longer able to dilute pollutants. The deputy director of the Municipal Laboratories, A. V. Forde, supported this warning, adding that increased landfilling was endangering the quality of Hamilton's drinking water.

The other danger of filling in this area was that the channel connecting the Bay with Lake Ontario would become too narrow for the Bay to flush itself out into the lake, this being the only way the Bay rejuvenates itself. If this flushing-out process stopped, the Bay would become a cesspool.

In spite of the warnings, the deal went ahead. Those on council who protested to the Commission met with an abrupt response from Hickey: "As far as we're concerned, the deal has been finalized."[6] City Solicitor Ken Rouff challenged the legality of the swap on the grounds that harbour lands held in trust for the city could not be disposed of without the approval and consent of council. In response, Hickey merely scoffed and allowed the companies to fill.

Hamilton City Council was far from unanimous in its opposition to the land swap, however. When some city aldermen argued against it, they were almost jeered at by Mayor Vic Copps. When confronted with the serious environmental dangers to the Bay as a result of this filling, Copps retorted: "Our greatest problem in this city isn't ecology. It is unemployment. This deal will help ease that problem."[7] The land swap did not create more jobs for Hamiltonians. Copps was strongly supported by Controller James Campbell, who did not seem to mind that the Bay was being filled for various projects. He said: "If filling is taking place for that development then it's my position that the Bay should be filled . . . go ahead and fill it."[8]

The ensuing political controversy about the Bay over the next few months reveals a great deal about the political power of the steel industry in Hamilton.

Ice fishing in Hamilton Harbour came to an end in the 1920s with increasing pollution of the bay (Public Archives Canada).

The then provincial Environment Minister, James Auld, became involved in the issue and he granted power over landfilling in the harbour to the Hamilton Region Conservation Authority, which stopped the steel companies from reclaiming the land.

The executives of Stelco and Dofasco used all the considerable political pressure at their command to ensure that they could continue filling, and soon gained the support of Mayor Vic Copps and a number of other business-backed council members. Meanwhile the companies continued to fill the waterlots granted them by the Commission as if they were above the law. They had strong backing for this from Del Hickey, chairman of the Commission. Hickey said flatly that he had no intention of following the new legislation and would never recognize the authority of the Conservation Authority over landfilling. He maintained that "the dumping regulations are not well thought-out or even reasonable."[9]

Auld remained firm on the issue of exemptions until mid-June, when he startlingly and inexplicably reversed his position: he asked the Conservation Authority to allow Stelco and Dofasco to fill in their waterlots even though they had not even applied to the Authority for permits. Auld directly undermined his own legislation, and from then on rapidly backtracked. He said he regretted his previous stand and that he had misunderstood what the steel companies had wanted to do with the reclaimed land. According to his public statements, Auld had the notion that all the companies wanted was to fill in 100 acres for the sole purpose of adding more pollution-control equipment.

But on August 4, it was learned that both steel companies had a quite different notion about the amounts of filling in to be done, and its purpose: Dofasco was to get 120 acres of waterlots to fill in and Stelco 208, for a total of 328 acres. Of the total acreage involved, 16.2 acres were to be used for the installation of pollution-control devices.

Meanwhile the Hamilton Region Conservation Authority was determined to exercise its newly-won powers; however, the group was willing to compromise. It offered to let Dofasco have 96 acres to fill in and Stelco 86; the companies refused to budge. In early July 1972, the Conservation Authority gave Stelco and Dofasco an ultimatum: apply for permits within 10 days or face prosecution. The companies applied for permits on the last day, but had never ceased their filling operations. On August 23, the Conservation Authority met to vote on their applications. It voted twice, each vote resulting in a tie, and in each case broken by Chairman William Powell against the companies. On September 14, the Ontario Cabinet overturned the Conservation Authority's decision and allowed Stelco and Dofasco to fill. The reason the province gave for its action was that the Conservation Authority was so evenly split on the issue that the government felt it had to step in and "assume leadership." This move was fully supported by Auld and the Minister of Natural Resources, Leo Bernier, who had been as firmly against the exemptions as Auld.

When Bernier announced the reversal of the Conservation Authority's decision, he contacted the news media before informing the Authority. William Powell angrily lashed out at the Conservative government, suggesting that Stelco and Dofasco used "high pressure tactics" in their appeal against the Authority's decision. Said Powell: "I'll bet the lobbyists from the two steel companies were just about camping down there [at Queen's Park] . . . I can smell the whole situation from here."[10]

THE LAX LANDFILL PROJECT

An issue of equal importance to environmentalists in Hamilton was a plan to fill in the western end of the harbour, the only area left that is at all suitable for recreation.

In the spring of 1957, a Philadelphia-based organization, Luria Brothers Co. Inc., approached the Commission to buy land on the harbour bed in front of waterfront property that they already owned in the northwest end of Hamilton. This deal was for 40 acres of waterlots and shore-front. The site is located in the only remaining portion of the harbour which might have been suitable for recreation. Lauria's plan was to erect a scrap metal processing plant on the reclaimed land. The deal was completed in November 1958 at the low price of $1,500 per acre, or $60,000 in all.

For some reason, Luria's Canadian agents, Samuel and Sheridan Lax, were given this parcel of land and waterlots on April 3, 1959. Not long afterwards, the city began planning an urban renewal program in the North End, adjacent to the Lax site, and when Hickey, Lanza, and city appointee Kenneth Ronald Elliott came to the Commission a little later, they expressed a wish to co-operate with and assist in the urban renewal project by making available to the Lax brothers 51 more acres of shorefront and waterlots.

By this time, the scrap metal plant idea had been abandoned in favour of a new idea for development of the Lax property: a multi-million-dollar residential complex of high-rise apartment blocks with marina facilities and parkland. Some 15,000 people would occupy the development, to be known as "Bayshore Village," and Lax began filling in 1968.

Conveniently for Lax, the city was involved at that time with tearing down a fair portion of the escarpment for the Claremont access roadway project, and what better place to dispose of the escarpment but in the Bay? The Lax brothers bid for and won the fill from the roadway project (they were the only bidders) for one cent per cubic yard. In 1973, the filling stopped due to mounting opposition from environmental and citizens' groups, and

E. Delbert Hickey.

the city zoned the land already filled as a "holding zone." This zoning classification means that no development can take place on the Lax site without city approval.

When Lax stopped filling, over 50 acres of harbour had been filled, and this reclaimed land lies vacant and ugly, slicing across the west end of the Bay. The city now wants a public park with marina facilities on the Lax site, but there is the problem of price, and who will pay for it — the city, the province, or the federal government? A *Spectator* article of May 17, 1974, said that the Lax' price for their land was $6.76 million. It was bought for $212,000. William Powell, chairman of the Hamilton Region Conservation Authority, commented that the Lax waterlots "should never have been sold in the first place . . . The thing was . . . a steal . . . a mistake by the harbour commissioners."[11]

But how was Luria/Lax allowed to obtain the waterlots in the first place? In a CTV documentary done for W5, entitled The Seaway: Paydirt and Patronage, aired in the summer of 1975, Argue Martin, chairman of the Commission when the original transaction with the Luria Brothers took place, explained that the sale occurred because the Commission needed money. No other considerations entered the picture — no considerations of port planning or development.

When Hickey, Lanza and Elliott took over the Commission, they supported the "Bayshore Village" plan, offering Lax even more harbour property as an added encouragement to his investment. The Lax scheme was unusual because it was the only

Kenneth R. Elliott.

instance of a plan for private residential development at the harbour and, as such, was unrelated to the development of the port of Hamilton.

The business interests of Commission members complicate the story of the Lax development. Ken Elliott became a vice-president and director of a cable television company, Northgate Cable, in December 1969. This company's territory is the north and west area of Hamilton, including the Lax property. Completion of "Bayshore Village" would have added about 4,000 families to Northgate Cable's portion of Hamilton.

Del Hickey, while chairman of the Commission, was an executive officer of Ronark Developments, a wholly owned subsidiary of Ronyx Corporation Ltd. Sam Lax was then a director of Ronyx; Del Hickey is today vice-president of Ronyx. While Hickey was on the Commission, the mailing address of Ronyx Corporation Ltd. was his law firm of McBride, Hickey, Green, McCallum and Mann at 20 Hughson St. South.

ELLIOTT AND THE COMMISSION

It was in 1969 that Ken Elliott's integrity as city representative on the Commission was first questioned. The issue came up when Elliott's interest in Northgate Cable came to light.

The facts came out in public when Elliott applied to the CRTC for permission to buy half of the company's twenty thousand shares for less than $500; his application was turned down. Up to that time, Elliott had been popular at city hall because he kept the politicians well informed about harbour matters.

Elliott clashed with his fellow commissioners in January 1966, when he publicly revealed that the Commission had awarded a five-year contract to the higher of two bidders. The favoured one was Hamilton Terminal Operators Ltd. (HTO), a cargo-handling firm that had worked for the Commission at its overseas terminals since 1960. Because of its "proven competence," the Commission decided to waive a $100,000 performance bond. On January 31, 1968, only two of the five years of the contract having been completed, HTO went out of business and the Harbour Commission, at the urging of John Munro,[12] took over the work, buying the necessary equipment from the defunct company. The cost to the Commission for this fiasco was approximately $500,000.

Elliott's popularity with city council began to wane in 1971, the year Hamilton lawyer Herman Turkstra began his term as controller. Turkstra has a solid reputation in Hamilton as a brilliant courtroom lawyer as well as a man of high moral principles. The story of his fight to remove Elliott from the Commission and to probe the harbour is fascinating because it very quickly became a fight with his fellow city councilmen as well. Turkstra was a key figure in uncovering corruption at the harbour through the activities of Elliott.

It was over the issue of the land swap between Dofasco, Stelco and the Commission that Turkstra first tried to have Elliott removed as the city appointee to the Harbour Commission. At that time, Elliott was in the employ of United Smelting and Refining Co., a company that sells scrap metal to Stelco, and Turkstra felt that Elliott's support for the landswap constituted a conflict of interest. On November 30, 1972, Turkstra tried to persuade council to remove Elliott as its appointee to the Commission; Turkstra's motion was overwhelmingly defeated 19–2. This move, however, was only the beginning.

THE BARFNECHT AGREEMENT

The end of the Hickey-Lanza-Elliott administration began with allegations made by a Bolton, Ontario, scrap dealer named Kenneth Barfnecht, who contacted Turkstra in the summer of 1972 with allegations of corruption at the harbour. On July 21, 1972, Barfnecht made a formal statement to Turkstra, then chairman of the Harbour Subcommittee, which revealed that he and Elliott

Signs like these appear all along the shoreline of the harbour, reminding the people of Hamilton that the harbour is off-limits to them (Marsha Hewitt).

had agreed to enter a business partnership in breaking ships at the harbour.

A formal business agreement had been drawn up on May 31, 1972, by Brian Morison, Q.C., himself a former city controller and lawyer for the Harbour Commission. Within the terms of the agreement, Elliott and Barfnecht were to be partners in the new company; Elliott's role would be to procure ships for breaking, acquire sites at the harbour as well as obtain the permission needed from the Commission for the operation of the business. Clearly Elliot, as a commissioner, was in conflict of interest; he had entered into a business venture which depended in part on Harbour Commission approval.

A third party, Robert A. Henderson of Aldershot Contractors' Equipment Rentals Ltd., was to be brought into the agreement. He wanted to receive one-third of the company profits paid to him in trust under a different name. The agreement was never signed because Barfnecht saw his company's profits shrinking as a result of various personal extravagances being demanded by Elliott. If it were not for this, the deal would have gone ahead.

While these negotiations were going on between himself and Elliott, Barfnecht had already brought three ships into the harbour and had begun dismantling them for scrap. On June 8, one week after his proposed partnership with Elliott had fallen through, Barfnecht received a letter from the harbour commissioners forbidding him to cut ships at the dock where he was located. He removed his ships to another harbour site and they were impounded in the dead of night for non-payment of a $3,000 rental fee. Barfnecht was being charged far in excess of the usual one cent per foot for docking his ships — that is, $12.00 a foot. He later received a $2,500 refund from the Commission as the result of a court action. It was never revealed how the Commission happened to overcharge Barfnecht.

When the ships were impounded, they were located on the property of Aldershot Stevedoring. Barfnecht claimed that the manager, Frank Paten, had given him permission to dock there but the company later denied this. The president of Aldershot Stevedoring is Robert A. Henderson, the same person originally involved in the aborted business agreement with Barfnecht and Elliott.

It is hardly surprising that Barfnecht became convinced Elliott was using his influence with the Harbour Commission to ruin Barfnecht's business because the latter had refused to go into partnership with Elliott. He then decided to take all the damning information he had about Elliott and other harbour activities to the RCMP. His allegations included extortion, drug trafficking, smuggling and conflict of interest.

The RCMP sent Barfnecht to the OPP and the

The piece of land slicing through the water in the centre of the photograph is the Lax landfill site. Even though most of the property was filled in 1971 it remains the subject of controversy (Marsha Hewitt).

Hamilton police, on the grounds that all the charges (except drug trafficking) were out of their jurisdiction. He went to Dr. Pierre Camu, administrator of the marine transportation branch of the federal Department of Transport who directed him to a St. Catharines authority who told Barfnecht: "If you don't like what's going on in Hamilton harbour, why the hell don't you get out?" He then went to the deputy minister of Transport, who in turn contacted the solicitor for the marine branch of the Department of Transport, John Gray. A meeting was ultimately arranged with the RCMP and it was decided that a preliminary RCMP investigation into the harbour would be launched. As it happened, the RCMP investigation did not begin until a full year later.

Barfnecht, in the course of his search for an authority who would begin an investigation into his charges, saw two local Hamilton politicians, NDP MPP Norm Davidson (Hamilton Centre) and Tory MP Lincoln Alexander (Hamilton West). Although both politicians' ridings border the harbour, neither would offer him any help. According to Barfnecht, Alexander's reaction was based purely on political opportunism: "Linc said it was a biggie and could go either way. If it went one way, it could destroy the Liberal Party and if it went the other, well, he wouldn't want to be on my coattails."[13] Alexander, the most important federal Conservative in this area, has never spoken out strongly on the harbour.

THE HISTORY OF THE RCMP's HARBOUR INVESTIGATION

August 1972: Barfnecht contacts the RCMP.

September 12, 1972: Controller Campbell tells council that the Solicitor-General of Canada has begun an investigation into harbour. No such investigation was going on.

September 1972–February 1973: No investigation. Solicitor-General Warren Allmand claims the RCMP could not investigate due to a "jurisdictional dispute" with Hamilton city police. RCMP asked city police to investigate Barfnecht charges on November 7th and agreement was made. In December RCMP checks back and finds out no investigation going on. Hamilton police later claim no such agreement made and that according to their records no meeting about the issue ever occurred.

February 23, 1973: Allmand makes formal request to RCMP to begin investigation.

May 1974: RCMP issues statements saying "investigation was commenced in September 1973 by criminal investigation section."

May 3, 1975: Dr. Morton Shulman charged investigation delayed due to political interference.

The RCMP never explained the year delay in their investigation, merely insisting it began in September, 1973.

Aerial photo of the Stelco property, about 1976 (Hamilton Public Library).

While this was going on, Turkstra began preparing evidence against Elliott. The issue he wanted to explore was Elliott's conflict-of-interest dealings. Turkstra, unlike some of his fellow council members, saw that the involvement of Elliott in a ship-breaking operation at the harbour could easily be aided by his position on the Commission. City Solicitor Ken Rouff agreed with this, saying:

If this agreement places ... the harbour commissioner, our appointee, in the position where he is operating a business, and it turns out later that for the successful operation of that business he must apply to the Harbour Commission, then he's wearing another hat. That sort of thing is a conflict of interest.[14]

The 1912 Harbour Commissioners' Act forbids commissioners from having "any transactions of any pecuniary nature, either in buying or selling, with any members thereof, directly or indirectly." Yet in a strictly legal (not moral) sense, it appears that this stipulation can be interpreted fairly broadly, as it was by Toronto lawyer J. J. Robinette when consulted by the former Commission on the question of Earl Perkins, port director of Hamilton Harbour.

It was revealed in a Spectator article on December 10, 1971, that Earl Perkins was, and had been for some 11 years, part owner of a cargo-handling firm at the harbour called Direct Seaport Services. This company handles about one-fifth of all the rubber imported into Canada. It employs longshoremen to unload, weigh and inspect the rubber; Perkins' job as port director is to oversee relations between the longshoremen and the Harbour Commission, ensuring that these relations are "harmonious." He makes recommendations to the Commission as to rental rates for storage facilities on harbour property and many things that would directly involve his company. In fact, according to Del Hickey, Perkins "supervises everything" at the harbour.[15]

When confronted with the fact that Perkins' involvement with Direct Seaport might be seen as a conflict of interest, Hickey replied that: "There is no conflict that I can see — Mr. Perkins devotes more than 50 hours a week to his job as port director."[16] The Commission then asked J. J. Robinette for his opinion and on January 20, 1972, he stated that Perkins was not in conflict of interest due to his partnership in the company. When then Minister of Transport Don Jamieson was asked his opinion of the whole affair, he refused to get involved in an issue that was, in his view, "strictly the business of the Hamilton Harbour Commission."[17]

The Perkins story is significant because it casts light on the way in which the Harbour Commission works, and provides a context in which to judge Elliott's involvement in conflict-of-interest situations. Elliott was not the only one using his position in the harbour administration for his own benefit, but whereas Perkins was protected by legal opinions, Elliott was ultimately fired on the grounds of an intent to go into business at the harbour. The reason Elliott was fired was because there was some accountability in his case, given that he was the city appointee and thus responsible to city council, which ultimately removed him. The rest of the harbour administration in Hamilton is virtually responsible to no one but itself.

Turkstra tried to probe the extent of Elliott's business connections at the harbour when he invited Marvin Frank to a Harbour Subcommittee meeting at city hall on August 4, 1972.[18] Frank is president of several companies, including A. J. Frank & Son, a scrap metal company located at Hamilton harbour. Turkstra had reason to believe that Elliott might have been financially involved with Frank's company, using his position on the Commission to promote Frank's business interests.

In response to Turkstra's probings, Marvin Frank vehemently denied that Elliott had ever received financial reimbursement for any work done for Frank's company. Barfnecht, who was present at this meeting, contradicted him, saying that Elliott used to help Frank obtain ships for breaking. Barfnecht was referring to two American ships for which he claimed Frank had sent Elliott and then Hamilton Alderman Aldo Poloniato to Europe to find markets for selling them.

Barfnecht made his statements contradicting Frank in the recorded August 4 meeting of the Harbour Subcommittee.[19] He further claimed, contrary to Frank's statements, that he and Elliott brought the American ships through the Welland Canal for Frank. When the job was done, Barfnecht signed a timecard of A. J. Frank & Son; Elliott paid him $200 on behalf of the company for his help bringing in the ships.

As the meeting continued it became fairly apparent that Elliott acted as an agent for Frank while he was a commissioner. Turkstra wanted to know if Elliott was receiving any money for his work. He confronted Frank with information he had that Elliott seemed "to be operating as your employee," bidding in Frank's name for the ships and making the arrangements for their sale and transfer to Hamilton. Said Turkstra: "The question is a pretty simple one: what's Ken doing running all over the place ... putting himself forward as your agent?" All that Frank would ever admit was that "Elliott is a friend of mine." He finally walked out of the meeting, saying: "I'm not staying any longer, gentlemen. I've got high blood pressure, I've got diabetes, I'm getting over a heart attack, I'm leaving now," and then he disappeared.

ELLIOTT FIRED AS HARBOUR COMMISSIONER

On August 28, 1972, Hamilton City Council convened to decide what to do about the revelations made at the August 4 meeting, where Barfnecht's agreement with Elliott was made known. For the second time in eight months, Herman Turkstra confronted city council on the issue of Elliott using his position as harbour commissioner for his personal interests. Unlike the previous occasion, Turkstra had the support of more than one alderman because the evidence against Elliott was too blatant to shrug off this time. This meeting was a bitter confrontation between pro- and anti-Elliott factions within council and turned out to be the first in a series of nasty clashes among council members.

Turkstra had the support of Ken Rouff, the city solicitor, who agreed that Elliott's agreement with Barfnecht constituted a conflict of interest. The opposition to this claim voiced by some aldermen rested upon the fact that the agreement was not actually signed, and it was felt a demonstrated intention to go into business with Barfnecht was insufficient grounds to remove Elliott from office. This was the centre of the controversy that night, and a motion was put forward to ask Elliott for his resignation. One of Elliott's supporters on council was Aldo Poloniato (the alderman who accompanied Elliott to Europe on behalf of A.J. Frank & Son) who suggested that "what we should be doing right now is rapping his knuckles and saying to Ken Elliott 'Don't get yourself involved in anything like that ... we don't like it'"[20]

This was the general tenor of the arguments against the motion to remove Elliott. Those sharing Poloniato's opinion had a difficult time wading through the basically ethical question of a public representative using his position for personal benefit. Turkstra rose in council to try to outline as clearly as possible just what was involved and why council ought to be concerned at what Elliott was willing to do. He described the commission as "three men who have an absolute monopoly and who are not elected but who are appointed," reasoning that "the obligation on those three men to administer the harbour in a scrupulously fair fashion becomes very important."

After much debate on the issue, it was decided to accept the motion that Elliott be requested to resign from the Harbour Commission.[21]

The matter did not end there, however: Elliott refused to resign. On September 5, he launched a libel suit against Controller Turkstra, Aldermen James Custeau, James Kern, Vince Agro, Bob Morrow, Pat Valeriano and businessman Ken Barfnecht. On September 12, city council met again to decide what to do about the recalcitrant Elliott, and it proved a lively meeting.

It was moved by Dave Lawrence that Elliott be fired outright. This motion provoked vicious opposition from Controllers James Bethune and, in particular, James Campbell. Bethune saw the issue as one of "character assassination," declaring the move by council to dismiss Elliott a "smear," an action "most unfair and corrupt."

Alderman Bill Scandlan decided it was "a vendetta by some members of council;" all this impassioned indignation moved Controller Campbell again to jump to his feet to apologize to Elliott, on behalf of council and the city of Hamilton, for what council was attempting to do. Campbell's defence of Elliott was particularly enlightening when he offered himself and his business partner, Bethune, as a shining illustration of political integrity to prove unequivocally that Elliott in no way compromised himself in his intended agreement with Barfnecht:

. . . it wasn't long ago that I discussed with Controller Bethune maybe we should build some apartments . . . and I suppose very shortly we are coming up with a situation and I think we still are that we might sign an agreement pretty soon to become partners in some construction work and I suppose that we are going to have to go to the planning board to get some zoning changes . . . and do you know under the terms of reference set down now if we stick to a single standard that Bethune and I now, that the word is out are liable to be asked for our resignation at any moment because that's exactly. . .

At this point Campbell was drowned out by resounding booing and cheering from the spectators' gallery, where about 90 citizens frequently interrupted the evening's debate in this way. Mayor Copps was forced to demand order, threatening that he'd allow no "demonstrations" in his council chamber.

The next day, September 13, Elliott issued a writ against the City of Hamilton for unlawful dismissal. His claim was that, first, the city had no authority to remove him from his post as its own representative to the Harbour Commission, and second, that he was not guilty of a conflict of interest. He appealed to the fact that Commission Chairman Del Hickey knew about his plans with Barfnecht and saw no impropriety in it. His agreement was "never signed nor put into effect and . . . the chairman of the Harbour Commission had full knowledge [of it] and . . . I made a complete disclosure [of it] and . . . there had been no action by the Harbour Commission" against his plans.[22]

TRYING FOR AN INQUIRY

Coincident with the struggle in council to fire Elliott was another struggle to convince the federal government to initiate a public inquiry into the operations of Hamilton Harbour. Some council members felt that the revelations concerning Elliott alone justified an inquiry since there were several other points council wanted cleared up about the harbour. Predictably, there were those on council who were opposed to an inquiry and they tended to be, with a few exceptions, those same people who had all along supported Elliott.

Besides the motion to fire Elliott before council the night of September 12, there was another motion stating that "the Federal Government be petitioned to conduct a full-scale public inquiry into the activities of the Hamilton Harbour Commission." The motion was tabled, however, because of a curious and sudden revelation made by Controller James Campbell, who stated that he had already gone to Ottawa August 31, 1972, and had placed the document containing Barfnecht's allegations against Elliott in the hands of then Solicitor-General Jean-Pierre Goyer. He said further that he had been assured that an investigation would be immediately forthcoming. Herman Turkstra proposed "on the strength of this assurance" tabling the motion for one month in order to "await a reply from Ottawa."[23]

As it turned out, Campbell had not gone to Ottawa on the 31st and he had never met the solicitor-general. Amid later angry denials from Goyer that he had ever seen Campbell, it was learned that the latter had (according to *his* explanation) sent a registered letter to Goyer containing the findings of the Harbour Subcommittee. On the 11th, Campbell was in Ottawa, but the man he saw was the executive assistant to Goyer, John Cameron. There was a federal election going on at the time, and Cameron did not tell Goyer anything about the visit from Campbell, instead sending a letter to Allan Baker, his counterpart in the Ministry of Transport, who in turn passed the letter on to the deputy minister of the department for relay to its legal advisor, John Gray.

It is not surprising that while the Barfnecht document was making its tortuous way through the

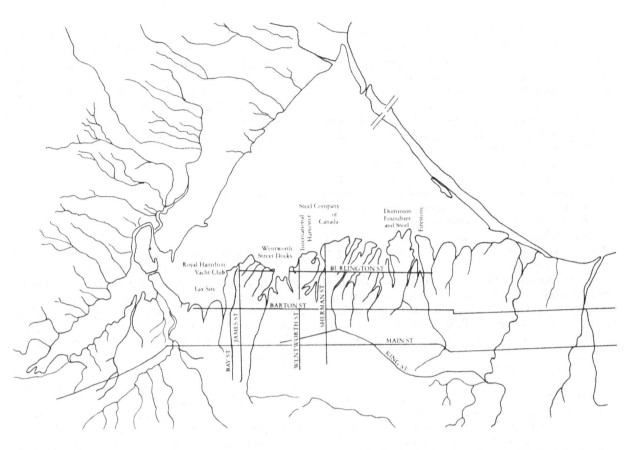

These maps show the original harbour and what the headlands look like today. Approximately one-third of the bay has been filled in, and almost all of that has been used for industrial purposes.

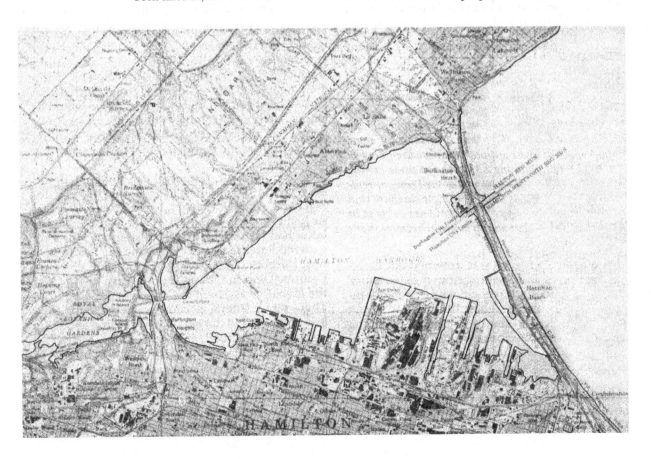

labyrinthine recesses of the federal civil service, the ministers themselves heard nothing about it. Baker later said he "thought" he told Jamieson about the document, but wasn't sure. One thing is sure: Campbell's story was not accurate. That Goyer and Jamieson were busy campaigning for the election probably explains the fact that the Barfnecht document was so long kept at the level of the civil service. At any rate, this was the explanation given by the ministers and their assistants at the time.

As it happened, some Hamilton politicians were not unhappy that the inquiry was not proceeding. Alderman James MacDonald was against an inquiry because of the expense it might incur. At the September 12 meeting, Controller Anne Jones objected that: "We can't have a public inquiry every time someone raises something in the paper . . . the reporters have such an exciting way of putting things."[24] On October 10, 1972, when the tabled resolution calling for the public inquiry from the September meeting was raised, it was defeated 11–7.[25]

The next day, Board of Control met to consider a request from Turkstra's Harbour Subcommittee to hire an independent firm of auditors to study the Harbour Commission's books in order to ascertain the amount of surplus profits owed the city by the Commission.[26] Turkstra had an idea that between 1962 and 1972, the Commission had accrued $2.5 million in surplus profits, but auditors were required to ensure that this sum was indeed surplus profit and not something else. Mayor Copps and Controller Bethune objected to doing this, saying that the matter could easily be resolved by inviting Chairman Hickey to a Board of Control meeting to explain his interpretation of surplus profits. Hickey had on several occasions said publicly that Hamilton would never get any share of harbour profits at any time, even though the 1912 Act states specifically that all surplus profits rightfully belong to the city.[27]

One can imagine the frustration of the members of the Harbour Subcommittee in the face of this opposition to doing something about the harbour. The final exasperation was expressed by an angry Herman Turkstra toward the end of October, when he accused Mayor Copps, Controller Bethune and Alderman Aldo Poloniato of being part of "a concerted campaign to prevent at all costs a proper examination of the role of the Hamilton Harbour Commission in the life of this city."[28]

He accused them of harassing him in his efforts as chairman of the Harbour Subcommittee to probe harbour activities. Turkstra circulated a letter he wrote the mayor in response to the latter's not informing him of a meeting of the three levels of government, to which all interested parties were invited, to discuss environmental issues relating to the harbour. Turkstra felt that as head of the harbour committee at city hall, he should have been given the opportunity to attend this meeting by simply being told of it.

Turkstra felt a conspiracy existed within council to cover up all matters relating to a probe of the harbour. He wrote: "I have reached the point, Mr. Mayor, where I am sick to the pit of my stomach with this kind of undercover scurrying around." He further challenged Copps and the others to ask for his resignation on the basis of non-confidence in himself and his committee, and then move for the dissolution of the committee. In response, Mayor Copps said that he believed the function of the Harbour Subcommittee "is best served if it keeps council informed on environmental matters." Controller Bethune said he'd be happy if the committee disbanded altogether.[29]

On October 31, 1972, the day of the federal election, council finally passed a motion calling for a public inquiry into Hamilton Harbour. On December 15, Justice R.E. Holland dismissed Elliott's case against the City of Hamilton, providing at last the legal ratification of Elliott's firing. On March 30, 1973, Controller James Campbell ran for the vacant position on the Harbour Commission. Although his business partner and fellow councilman James Bethune cut short a Florida trip in order to return home to vote for him, Campbell lost the vote to B.M. Alway, the then city appointee to the Commission.

THE DREDGING SCANDAL

On May 30, 1974, Kenneth R. Elliott was arrested by the RCMP, charged on 11 counts including fraud, bribery, forgery, conspiracy, and breach of trust. Charges were also laid against Reginald Leigh Fisher, a Hamilton business consultant, for conspiracy to defraud the Hamilton Harbour Commission of $365,000 as well as bribery, forgery, and conspiracy. Robert A. Henderson of Aldershot Contractors' Equipment Rentals Ltd., the same man who was to be part of the Elliott-Barfnecht business agreement, was also charged on a lesser offence. Two others were also charged with lesser offences: Robert P. Henderson (no relation to the other Henderson), a marine engineer and retired employee of the federal department of Public Works; and Harry Atkins, a former OPP officer. They were convicted and received fines ranging from $10,000 to $40,000, and were put on a two-year probation. Ken Elliott and Reginald Fisher were convicted and sentenced July 10, 1975, receiving prison terms of six and three years respectively.

Among several others named but not charged by the RCMP were Marvin Frank, Joseph Lanza, E. Delbert Hickey, and Ontario Minister of the Environment George Kerr. As part of the evidence it was shown that Elliott alleged his colleagues on the

Harbour Commission accepted kickbacks on the Stratherne Street dredging project. The allegations were never proven.

Three dredging companies bid on the job, two allegedly conspiring to bid high so that the J. P. Porter Co. could receive the job. The other two companies were McNamara Corp. Ltd. and Canadian Dredge & Dock Co. Ltd.; the vice-presidents of all three companies, Horace Grant Rindress (Porter), Albin Louis Quinlan (McNamara) and Robert J. Schneider (Canadian Dredge) were named in the indictments but not charged.

Rindress told the court that Ken Elliott told him he had to pay an additional $10,000 beyond the kickbacks to the other commissioners for George Kerr, who allegedly demanded the money as a contribution to his 1971 election campaign fund as a form of compensation for his having to endure heavy pressure from environmental groups over the harbour. Kerr resigned his post temporarily in February 1975 to clear his name in court; the charges were never proven and Premier William Davis reinstated him into the Ontario Cabinet.

The significance of the Hamilton Harbour scandal cannot be properly understood unless it is perceived in its larger context of the Canadian dredging industry.

In 1970 the oil barge *Irving Whale* went down off the coast of P.E.I. It contained one million gallons of bunker oil in its hold. At one point, the federal government thought it might try to salvage the sunken barge, and in October 1971, tenders were called and the contract was awarded to a consortium of three companies. Donald A. Kerr, a partner in Atlantic Salvage and Dredging Co. Ltd., as it was then called, put in a lower bid than the consortium, but was refused the contract because, according to federal officials, Ottawa on the advice of a consultant felt that the consortium could better handle the job.

Prior to the closing of the tenders, Kerr was offered a $50,000 bribe to bid high on the contract by a high-ranking executive of the Foundation Co. of Canada, one of the members of the consortium. Kerr informed the federal Department of Transport, and the contract was cancelled. Soon after this, Inspector Rod Stamler of the RCMP was called in to investigate. His official report of June 1973 recommended that a vice-president of Foundation and a vice-president of a Toronto consulting firm be charged with conspiracy. The office of the Attorney-General in Nova Scotia decided not to press charges.

The *Irving Whale* incident precipitated RCMP investigations into the workings of the Canadian dredging industry as a whole, and the Hamilton scandal was discovered during that larger investigation. What emerged from the RCMP investigation and the subsequent trial was, in the words of the prosecutor, Clayton Powell: "A long-standing conspiracy among a group of Canadian companies and executives to rig tenders, maintain artificially high prices for dredging services and share the spoils illegally."

Rindress told the court in the Hamilton case that price-fixing has been going on in the dredging industry for at least 30 to 40 years. He said that the companies maintain "score cards" to keep track of whose turn it is to bid high on a given contract, and how much the company awarded the contract must pay as compensation to the others who bid high. No wonder *The Toronto Star* described the Canadian dredging scandal as "one of the worst corporate scandals in Canadian history."[30] In March 1975, charges were laid against 14 executives and 13 dredging firms for conspiracy to defraud the federal and Ontario governments of $4 million through price-fixing. Predictably, there was an uproar in Ottawa from both opposition parties for public inquiries into the entire affair and demands for tighter government controls in the dredging industry. Hamilton City Hall had been asking for an inquiry since 1972. Federal Minister of Public Works Bud Drury's reply to an NDP suggestion that the industry be nationalized to prevent further public rip-offs was: "The assumption . . . that the government can do it better . . . is not an assumption I'm prepared to accept."[31] Drury admitted in the House that his department continued to award contracts to companies charged before the courts with price-fixing. In fact, in March 1975, it was learned that Trade Minister Alistair Gillespie had given contracts totalling over $104 million to Marine Industries, even though at the time it was under investigation for bid-rigging and was subsequently charged and later convicted. Meanwhile, Drury assured the House that government controls were being implemented to prevent future defrauding of public funds; from now on, dredging companies must provide "written proof" that no "collusion" (bid-rigging) has occurred on the submission of bids for government contracts. Said Conservative James McGrath: "That's like the FBI asking Bonnie and Clyde for assurances to keep the peace."[32]

McGrath also challenged Drury on the grounds that when he was president of the Treasury Board, he ignored reports from then Auditor General Maxwell Henderson that alleged "irregularities" existed in the dredging industry. Henderson told W5 reporters in the 1975 documentary on the Seaway that millions of dollars have been wasted on dredging operations; he even once refused to approve the books of the National Harbours Board. Drury did admit in the House that no real bidding competition for dredging contracts has existed for years, especially where large operations are concerned like Vancouver Harbour or the Fraser, Mackenzie, and St. Lawrence Rivers.

On May 5, 1979, some dredging firms and prominent Canadians were convicted of fraud. Harold McNamara of Toronto, former president of McNamara Corporation, was found guilty on seven counts of fraud conspiracy. Also convicted was Jean Simard, of the Quebec-based Simard family, who are powerful Liberals and involved in a number of businesses. Simard was found guilty on three counts of fraud, as were his companies J.P. Porter and Marine Industries.

Former Liberal party fund-raiser Hugh Martin was acquitted of the single charge against him, but his Toronto-based company, Canadian Dredge and Dock, was found guilty on five counts.

The Hamilton scandal proved to contain implications that reverberated as far as Ottawa. It also provided a microcosmic view of how price-fixing works in the dredging industry, suggested the possible involvement of provincial and federal politicians in a cover-up, and gave the opposition critics a focus whereby they could formulate questions in the hopes of constructing a total picture. Unfortunately that whole picture is as yet incomplete, in spite of the convictions.

JOHN MUNRO AND THE ELLIOTT TAPES

During the trial of Elliott, the court heard a taped conversation between Elliott and Rindress which contained a mysterious reference to Cabinet Minister John Munro:

R: "Have you got any political clout, anything to help?"
E: "Nothing."
R: "After all you did for those guys."
E: "The way I busted my ass for all them politicians, the money I've got them over the years. Now they all go run and hide, including Munro. That's one thing that irks my ass more than anything — Munro."
R: "Well, he started this whole thing, didn't he?"
E: "You bet your ass he did."[33]

The mention of John Munro in relation to the many-faceted controversy around Hamilton Harbour was not new at this point. Prior to this, Munro had consistently opposed a public inquiry into Hamilton Harbour, saying the city hadn't evidence of wrongdoings from which an inquiry could justifiably proceed. It was known that Munro was responsible for the appointments of Hickey and Lanza to the Harbour Commission, and both men were prominent Liberals. Hickey and Lanza were not, however, reappointed to their posts because, according to Jean Marchand, they were "suspect in their ethical standards."[34]

With the removal of the old federal appointees, Munro backed the appointment of two Hamilton Liberal Party supporters to the Commission, lawyer Edward Tharen and businessman Peter Flaherty.

Tharen, the chairman of the Harbour Commission, is a past president of the Hamilton and District Liberal Association and contributed $1,000 to Munro's 1973 campaign. Flaherty is also a member of the same Liberal Association and was a campaign manager for Munro. Flaherty's appointment is particularly significant: he is part-owner of a company called Flaherty Manufacturing, which in 1972 received a $40,000 contract for lapel buttons from the federal department of Health and Welfare, Munro's former cabinet post. No tenders were ever called on the contract and no one knows if there was competitive bidding on it — officials in the department tend to think there wasn't. It was later discovered that a requisition for the pins went directly to Flaherty in place of the traditional tendering procedure "by mistake."

The same week that Elliott was arrested, John Munro's Hamilton East constituency offices were raided by the RCMP. The police were interested in Munro's campaign contributors. They had a tape of a conversation between Munro and Seafarers' International Union President Roman Gralewicz in which Munro either asked for or was offered $500 for his campaign. Receiving money from the SIU put Munro in an odd position; as Minister of Labour, he had direct jurisdiction over any disputes between the SIU and the shipping companies of the Great Lakes. Munro returned the money the following September, having had second thoughts concerning the propriety of his accepting the money and the way in which it might be construed. A police source in Ottawa told a Toronto newspaper that Munro had called Gralewicz soliciting the money, but this has never been proven. Solicitor-General Warren Allmand has refused to make available the Munro-Gralewicz tape or any transcript of it, saying he was satisfied that no soliciting for donations occurred on Munro's part.

Since the demands for a public inquiry into Hamilton Harbour began coming from the City of Hamilton in 1972, Munro has consistently said he could not support any such inquiry. In June 1974, while the federal election was on, then NDP leader David Lewis came to Hamilton while campaigning and remarked that Munro was deliberately preventing an investigation into the harbour controversy. David Lewis's statements came one week after Elliott was arrested and charged in the harbour case.

Lewis's remarks provoked an angry response from Munro, who denied the allegations and challenged Lewis to a public debate. Meanwhile, in the wake of Elliott's arrest, there was much furor about the harbour, including many repeated demands for an inquiry. The harbour affair and Munro's connection with it (whatever that may be) was shaping up to be a major election issue and Munro was finding himself attacked on many sides. Munro had always maintained that an RCMP investigation had begun into Hamilton Harbour in the fall of 1972; the RCMP has always insisted that their investigation began one year later, in September 1973. This discrepancy has never been explained.

None of the above incidents were reported in *The Hamilton Spectator*, the city's only newspaper. On June 6, 1974, a *Globe and Mail* reporter wrote:

The Hamilton Spectator, *circulation 113,000 and the only newspaper in the city, has on the advice of its lawyers decided not to print any stories about land use around Hamilton Harbour or the policies of the harbour commission.*

The *Globe* published all Lewis's charges that Munro was impeding an investigation into the harbour, the calls for a public inquiry, and the Munro television interview. No legal action was brought against the Toronto paper for doing this. Furthermore, none of the statements about the harbour from Munro's political opponents contesting his riding were ever published by *The Spectator*.

In early December 1974, the NDP and Conservative opposition parties in Ottawa began an intensive interrogation of Munro and the Liberal government about the Hamilton Harbour issue that lasted until the end of February 1975. As the opposition pressed for a full accounting of Munro's possible connection to both the harbour and the SIU issues, the Liberal government stonewalled, always giving the same reply against an inquiry: lack of sufficient evidence of wrongdoings. At the end of February Munro — having tearfully offered his resignation to Prime Minister Trudeau, who refused it — went into hospital suffering from "nervous exhaustion." He was distressed by the "innuendo" implicit in the questions asked of him in the House.

THE COVER-UP

On July 24, 1975, John Munro, in response to mounting pressure from Hamilton City Council for an inquiry into the harbour, placed the blame for the entire scandal (as it affected Hamilton) on the city for appointing Elliott as its representative in the first place. Alderman Don Gray, present chairman of the now-called Harbour Advisory Committee, described Munro's statement as a "panic reaction." Alderman Bill McCulloch said he suspected Munro had something to hide because of his steadfast opposition to an inquiry.[35]

On August 6, 1975, the city sent letters to Prime Minister Pierre Trudeau and Transport Minister Jean Marchand requesting an inquiry; the reply was merely that the letters had been received. Munro then said there would be no inquiry unless the city could show evidence of corruption at the harbour; when the city drew up a list of charges of possible wrongdoings, many of which were mentioned at Elliott's trial, Munro dismissed them as "unsubstantial."[36]

There are still many suspicions and questions to be resolved from the dredging scandal. The most pressing is whether Elliott was the sole culprit in the piece. Certainly it was never proven in court that Hickey or Lanza accepted kickbacks for the dredging operation on which Elliott was charged. Elliott was one man on a three-member commission: it has not yet been explained how he could pursue his illegal activities at the harbour without someone in the harbour administration knowing about it.

The Hamilton Harbour scandal was a large-scale affair, leading to the discoveries of corruption in the entire dredging industry and raising suspicions about Hamilton Harbour in general, yet out of the Hamilton case only five men were convicted, two went to jail and Elliott received the heaviest sentence — six years in prison.

There is also the question generated by Jean Marchand's statement that Hickey and Lanza were not reappointed due to suspicions concerning their ethical standards; he never explained that statement.

Nor has the delay in the RCMP investigation ever been explained: on May 3, 1975, then MPP Dr. Morton Shulman suggested the delay was caused by political interference. The conflicting stories between the RCMP and the Hamilton police force have been left up in the air. The RCMP insists it got an agreement from the late Chief of Police Len Lawrence on November 7, 1972, that his force would begin an investigation. When the RCMP checked back in mid-December, they discovered no such investigation was even started. The Hamilton police department says today the meeting is not recorded in their files. Conservative MP James McGrath felt "that this delay was a deliberate attempt to contain the investigation to Hamilton."[37]

The other thing to be explained is the references to Munro on the Elliott tape, as well as his statement about all the money he got for "politicians over the years." Elliott's words could be pure bravado, a trait to which he was certainly inclined, but Munro is closely linked to Hamilton Harbour. His supporters were appointed to be the federal representatives on the Harbour Commission and yet he is the very person who has consistently said he is opposed to an inquiry.

There are also questions concerning the surplus profit the city has never seen from the Harbour Commission — there is an estimated $15 million involved. The city also wants to know how the Commission determines the sale of waterlots and harbour lands, and who are its insurance agents and lawyers. But the Commission to this day refuses to release this information.

In November 1975, city council made its fourth attempt in three years to persuade the federal government to hold an inquiry, but Minister of Transport Otto Lang turned the request down.

On October 28 of that year, Munro said that "answers to questions raised by council can be answered by the Harbour Commission itself."[38] Like the government which appointed him, former commission chairman Ed Tharen refused to give the city any information about harbour operations.

THE STORY CONTINUES

On July 23, 1976, the City of Hamilton filed a writ in the Supreme Court of Ontario against the Hamilton Harbour Commissioners and former commissioner Kenneth Ronald Elliott for an extensive accounting of Harbour Commission activities since April 1, 1948. Among the items the city sought information on were:

- all contracts entered into by the Commission for dredging, construction, reconstruction and development of the harbour;

- all transactions of purchase and sale, lease or other dispositions of lands and how land values were arrived at; and

- a financial statement covering a 10-year period ending December 31, 1971, showing the whereabouts of the surplus profits.

This legal action was the city's last recourse for a public inquiry into its own harbour. Events uncovered well after Elliott's conviction underscored the urgent need for an inquiry. In February 1977, Morris Lax, a Hamilton scrap metal dealer, was convicted on three counts of making false entries in a company account. Lax made the entries on behalf of Marvin Frank, who owns a scrap metal business located at the harbour. Lax helped Frank transact a phoney sale of pipes so that Frank could really give the money to Elliott in partial payment for a dredging contract. At his trial it was learned that Lax was running a huge money-laundering operation, involving some $2 million, along with some 15 Hamilton businesses. Morris Lax's scrapyard on Railway Street is located right across from the Monarch Vending Machine Company, which is associated with Hamilton organized crime figure John Papalia.

The federal government has proposed new legislation that would kill any possibility for a public inquiry. The Canada Ports Act, Bill C-6, would bring all Canadian ports and harbours under the centralized authority of the Minister of Transport. If passed, this legislation not only would threaten any inquiry, but also would seriously undermine or wipe out altogether many rights the city now has in relation to the harbour. The most crucial blow would come under Section 20 of the bill, which deals with land use control. It states: "A Commission has jurisdiction to regulate and control the use and development of all land and other properties within the limits of the port for which the Commission is established." Under Section 14 the Governor-in-Council will "define the limits of the port for which the Commission is established."

These two sections alone would rescind the city's right to jurisdiction over harbour lands not related to navigation and shipping. The city's rights in harbour land use control were upheld in the Ontario Supreme Court in November 1976. The ruling stated that the city has control over land use unrelated to navigation and shipping, which is crucial if the Lax site is to be developed for public recreational use, rather than for industry. Bill C-6 would seriously undermine the city's control in this area.

Hamilton presently has the right to appoint one member to the three-member Harbour Commission. Under Bill C-6, the city would have only the power to nominate members to the local port commission for appointment by the Minister of Transport.

The city of Hamilton would also lose its right to inspect the financial records of the Commission since under the new bill, the Minister of Transport would appoint an auditor who would report to him. All surplus profits, which under the 1912 Act belong to the city, would go to the Receiver General. Hamilton Harbour would be lost to the city and the federal government could develop it in any fashion it pleased, completely free of public input.

In 1963, John Munro opposed a similar bill put forward by the federal government and he argued hard against it. At the time, Mayor Vic Copps went to the Senate to appeal the bill, then called "S-38" and he told the Senate that the city had "a stake in the harbour that represents an asset which it would be . . . accurate to say is worth $100 million." The current value of that investment is estimated to be considerably higher. This investment includes cash grants, land and waterlots given by the city to the Harbour Commission, plus surplus profits that the city at that time had not claimed. Copps further argued that if the bill became law, it would mean for Hamilton "nothing more nor less than expropriation without compensation."[39] Presumably such action by the government today would amount to the same thing.

Munro gave his hearty support to Copps' position at the time: "I am giving my argument in complete endorsement of the case put forward (by Vic Copps)." Munro has not explained the change of mind that led him to support the current bill, C-6. Given his somewhat awkward position in the Hamilton Harbour scandal and the references to him on the Elliott tapes, perhaps it is not so unusual that he could support the new bill. If Bill C-6 should ever become law, an inquiry into the operations of Hamilton Harbour will never take place.

The present Hamilton Harbour Commission chairman is John Agro, Q.C. A long-time Hamilton Tory, Agro shows no indication of bringing a change to the image of the Commission. Upon taking office, Agro pledged to run a more open administration, because of his concern that in the public mind, Hamilton harbour is perceived as "a bedrock of fraud, payoffs, manipulations, easy bucks. This is why the people must get first hand information."[40]

Agro is, however, no more open about the internal workings of the Commission, nor any more inclined to open up the harbour for recreational use, than his Liberal predecessors Del Hickey and Ed Tharen. In his first public report (Hamilton Harbour Commission 1977 Annual Report) he stated that the harbour is a "marine enterprise operating for the benefit of industry and commerce." In the Hamilton Harbour Port Master Plan (June 1978), the "General Policy" statement reads: "The Hamilton Harbour Commissioners shall actively encourage increased recreational activities in the harbour *to the extent that it does not conflict with shipping, navigation and their related activities*." (Author's italics.) Seen in an historical context, this means that the policies of "industry first — the public last, if ever," are expected to continue at the Harbour Commission.

1. Brief of Ken Rouff to Hamilton City Council, 11 January 1972.

2. *The Hamilton Spectator*, 17 February 1972.

3. *The Hamilton Spectator*, 3 December 1971.

4. *The Globe and Mail*, 12 November 1971.

5. *The Hamilton Spectator*, 3 December 1971.

6. *The Hamilton Spectator*, 22 December 1971.

7. *The Hamilton Spectator*, 1 December 1971.

8. *The Hamilton Spectator*, 15 February 1972.

9. *The Hamilton Spectator*, 3 April 1972.

10. *The Hamilton Spectator*, 19 June 1972.

11. *The Hamilton Spectator*, 17 May 1974.

12. In 1962, newly elected MP John Munro wanted an inquiry into the operations of Hamilton Terminal Operators Ltd., but it never took place.

13. *The Hamilton Spectator*, 12 March 1975.

14. August 28, 1972, Ontario Supreme Court, Ex. No. 10.

15. *The Hamilton Spectator*, 10 December 1971.

16. *The Hamilton Spectator*, 10 December 1971.

17. *The Hamilton Spectator*, 31 December 1971.

18. Ontario Supreme Court, Ex. No. 15.

19. Ontario Supreme Court, Ex. No. 5.

20. Minutes of September 12, 1972, meeting of city council, Ontario Supreme Court, Ex. No. 11.

21. Those for the motion: Controllers Turkstra, Jones, Aldermen Morrow, Agro, Valeriano, Lawrence, Custeau, Wheeler, Ford, Stowe, Kern. Opposed: Mayor Copps, Controllers Campbell, Bethune, Aldermen Cline, Poloniato, Lombardo, MacDonald, Edge.

22. *The Hamilton Spectator*, 14 September 1972.

23. *The Hamilton Spectator*, 13 September 1972.

24. *The Hamilton Spectator*, 13 September 1972.

25. Those opposed to an inquiry: Mayor Copps, Controllers Bethune and Campbell, Aldermen Ford, Edge, MacDonald, Scandlan, Stowe, Lombardo, Cline, Poloniato, and Custeau.

26. Between 1911 and 1966, the city of Toronto collected approximately $78,974,566 in surplus profits from its Harbour Commission. (*The Hamilton Spectator*, 26 January 1966.)

27. In 1966, then Alderman Bill Powell said that when he asked the Hamilton Harbour Commission where the surplus profits had gone, he was told "it's none of your business what happened to the money." (*The Hamilton Spectator*, 26 January 1966.)

28. *The Hamilton Spectator*, 21 October 1972.

29. *The Hamilton Spectator*, 23 October 1972.

30. *The Toronto Star*, 1 March 1975.

31. Hansard, 2 May 1975.

32. Ibid.

33. *The Globe and Mail*, 31 May 1975.

34. *The Toronto Star*, 1 March 1975.

35. *The Hamilton Spectator*, 25 July 1975.

36. *The Hamilton Spectator*, 19 August 1975.

37. *The Hamilton Spectator*, 10 March 1975.

38. *The Hamilton Spectator*, 29 October 1975.

39. Proceedings of the Standing Committee on Transport and Communications, 30 October 1963.

40. *The Hamilton Spectator*, 21 December 1976.

Index

Pages numbers in italics refer to illustrations.

Abella, Irving, 53
Agro, John, 99, 166
Agueci, Alberto, 80, 81–82
air pollution, 98
Aldershot Contractors' Equipment Rentals Ltd., 155, 161
Aldershot Stevedoring, 155
Alexander, Lincoln, 156
Alinski, Saul, 100, 101, 102, 103, 104
All Souls Church, 108
Allmand, Warren, 156, 163
Alway, B. M., 161
Amalgamated Association of Iron, Steel and Tin Workers, 40, 48
Amalgamated Society of Engineers, 40
American Federation of Labor (AFL), 39, 46, 47, 55
Anderson, Helen, 54
arena, 26, 133, 136
    city legal department, 140
    Copps, Victor, 136–141
    Hamilton Colosseum Group, 137, 138
    Arena Committee, 138–39, 140, 141
    hotel/recreation complex, 138
    Katz-Tobias Plan, 136–41
art gallery. *See under* Civic Square
Atkins, Harry, 161
Atlantic Salvage and Dredging Co. Ltd., 162
Auld, James, 152

Baker, Allan, 159, 161
Ball, John, 38, 58
Baptist Creek train disaster, 18
Barclay, James, 144, 145
Barfnecht, Kenneth. *See under* Hamilton Harbour
Barham, Harold, 139
Barton, Warren
    Carter, Mo, 95
    editorial policy, 92, 95, 98
    Globe and Mail, The, 95, 97
    Hamilton Harbour, 92
    Muir, John, 95
Bayshore Village, 153–54
Beach Strip, *149*, 150, *151*
Beasley, Thomas, 18
Beckett, Tom, 150, 151

Beddoes, Dick, 139
Bernier, Leo, 152–53
Berton, Pierre, 81
Bethune, James, 159, 161, 166
blockbusting, 106, 110, 135
Bluestein, Max. *See under* organized crime
Board of Control system, 24, 30, 32, 33–34, 35
Board of Education, 28, 31, 41, 97, 124
Board of Health, 106
Board of Trade, 15. *See also* Chamber of Commerce
Bolshevik Party. *See under* Communist Party of Canada
bounties, 10
Boytovich, Joseph, 76
Branigan, Doug, 107, 108
British Labour Party, 39, 43, 46
Brooks, Stewart, 93, 97
Buchanan, Isaac, 19
Buffalo, NY, 77, 79, 80, 81, 82
Bullock, Gordon, 96, 97
Burman, Frank, 114
business, ideology of, 10–11, 14, 27, 35, 37, 38, 136. *See also* political power
Butler, Anthony, 143–45
Buttrum, John, 105
Butty, Julius, 62, 72
Buzza, Pat, 109

C. C. Parker, 114
Calamai, Peter, 92, 98, 129, 130
Cameron, John, 159
Campagnolo, Iona, 142
Campbell, James, 30, 119, 151, 156, 159, 161, 166
Camu, Pierre, 156
Canada Permanent Trust Company, 139
Canada Ports Act (Bill C-6), 165–6
Canadian Congress of Labour, 54. *See also* Canadian Labour Congress
Canadian Construction Association, 144
Canadian Dredge and Dock Co. Ltd., 162–3
Canadian Labour Congress, 57
Caplan, Gerald, 54
Carr, Leeming, 70
Carson, Dennis, 141
Carter, Mo. *See under* Barton, Warren
Central Mortgage and Housing Corporation (CMHC), 65, 66, 86–8, 110
Central Ornamental Ironworks Ltd., 117
Century 21, 24–5, 145
Chamber of Commerce, 15, 32, 43, 84
CHCH-TV, 32, *71*, 122
Cheeseman, W.J., 65
Chisholm Investments, 139
CHML (radio), 32, 122, 127

167

Christ the King Church, 104, 108
Ciarillo, Dominic, 82
Citizens' Guide to City Politics, A, 26
city council, structure of, 28
City Hall, *117*
    Building Committee, 114–16, 119
    Dukeshire, Victor, 115–16, 118
    Eaton's, 112, *116*, *118*
    German, Alex, 113, 114–15, 116, 118
    judicial inquiry, 113–14, 117–19
    MacDonald, Jack, 112, 114, 119
    marble (falling), 92, 113–16, 118, 119
    Old City Hall, 112, *113*, *115*, *116*, *118*
    Pigott Construction Co. Ltd., 112–19
    roofs (leaking), 113, 115, 118
    Rouff, Kenneth, 114, 115, 117, 119
Civic Square
    art gallery, 123, 128, 129, 132, 134, 143
    Copps, Victor, 121, 122, 125–26, 127–28, 131–32
    department store, 132–33, 135
    downtown redevelopment, 24, 35, 56, 120–35
    farmers' market, 123, 128, 132, 133, 136, *140*
    First Wentworth Development Company, 35, 92, 124–32
    high-rise development, 132, 133
    hotel, 133–34
    library, 123, 128, 129, 132–33
    Lloyd D. Jackson Square, 98, 132, 135
    MacDonald, Jack, 127, 128, 131–32, 133–34
    merchants (small), 123, 126–27
    opposing groups, 56
    Pigott, Jr., Joseph, 124, 127, 131
    planetarium, 123
    Review Committee, 124–25, 128
    Save our Square (S.O.S.), 35, 92, 130–31
    Spectator, The, 120, 124, 130
    Steel Company of Canada (Stelco), 124, 132–33
    supporting groups, 121–22
    Tenants and Property Owners Association, 126–27
    theatre-auditorium, 123, 124, 129, 135
    townhouse development, 132, 133
    trade and convention centre, 123, 134, 135, 143
    Triton Centres Ltd., *122*, 124–25, 128
    urban renewal project, 24, 35, 92, 120–21, 122–25
    Yale Properties, 132–35
Claremont access roadway, 153
Clark, Donald, 29, 49
classless society, 29
Cline, Mac, 115, 116, 118
Cold War, 54
Coleman, Tom, 92, 94, 97, 98
Communist Party of Canada, 44, 46, 47, 48, 49, 53, 54, 57, 58
    Bolshevik Party, 40, 43
    Labour Progressive Party, 54, 70
Conservative Party, 29, *35*, 48, 67, 96
Cooke, Stew, 56
Cooper, W.P., 143
Cooper Construction Company, 143, 144
Co-operative Commonwealth Federation (CCF), 35, 45, 48–49, 52, 53–56, 70
    ILF merges with, 48
Coppley, George C., 43–44, *44*
Copps, Victor, 29, 30, 128, 130
    arena, 136–39, 141
    on business subsidy, 11
    Civic Square, 121, 122, 125–26, 127–28, 131–32
    downtown redevelopment, 23–26
    era, 33–34
    harbour, 11, 151, 152, 159, 161, 165
    Munro, John, 69, 99
    on municipal parties, 57
    political support for, 30, 33
    role as mayor, 30
Corktown. *See* neighbourhoods
Costa Nostra. *See* organized crime: Mafia
Cotroni, Vic, 81, 83, *84*, 85
Cranfield, Earl, 117
crime. *See* organized crime
Crocker, Joseph, 52,
Crockett, Will, 40
Cross, Edgar, 114, 116
Cross, Stiles and Brown, 116
Custeau, James, 159

Davidson, Norm, 156
Davidson, Tom, 58
Davis, William, 134, 162
Deering Agricultural Implement Company. *See* International Harvester
demolition, 23, 101, 110, 121, 123, 126, 135
Department of Health and Welfare, 66, 108, 163
department store. *See under* Civic Square
Department of Transport, 156
depression (economic)
    of 1861, 19
    of 1913, 65
    of 1920–23, 43
    of 1930–40, 22–23, 46, 47–48
Desjardins Canal, 10, 15
    train disaster, *18*–19
Desroches, Ben, 38, 58
Diamond Jim's, 83
Diefenbaker, John, 150
Direct Seaport Services, 157
Discharged Soldiers and Sailors Federation, 43
Dominion Foundries and Steel Co. (Dofasco), 40,

49, 67, 149, 150, 152–54
Doneff, Paul, 77
Donnelly, Jack, 82
Doonesbury (comic strip), 95
Downtown Businessmen's Association, 32
Downtown Redevelopment Subcommittee, 134, 146
downtown redevelopment, 23–26. *See also under* Civic Square
Drage, Kay, 141, 144
dredging scandal. *See under* Hamilton Harbour
DREE Grants, 10, 27
Drew, George, 54
Drury, E. C., 42, 45, 162
Dudzic, Stanley, 87–88
Duke, Clinton: judicial inquiry, 82, 83, 93–94, 99
Dukeshire, Victor. *See under* City Hall
Dundas (town), 15, 75, 117
Dundurn Castle, *16*, 17
Dunn, Alexander, 19–20
Durand Community Group, 35
Durand. *See* neighbourhoods
Durso, John, 77

Eames Department Store, 133
Eaton's (T. Eaton Co.)
    Jackson Square, 135
    old city hall, 112
    parking garage, *137*, 145–47
    See also under City Hall
Edmonton, 138, *146*
elevator strike, 132
elites, theory of. *See under* political power
Elliott, Kenneth, 98, 153–55. *See also under* Hamilton Harbour
Emslie, Graham, 127
Evans, Ramsay, 114–15, 117
extortion. *See under* organized crime

Fairclough, Ellen, 63
Family Service Agency, 88
Farmer, Tom, 91
farmers' market, 136, 140, 142, 143, 145, 146. *See also under* Civic Square
Farnan, John, 126
Farrar, Edward, 126–27
Ferguson, G. Howard, 45
Fergusson, J. R. Company Ltd., 117
Firestone, union at, 53
First Wentworth (Development Company), 35, 92. *See also under* Civic Square
Fisher, Reginald Leigh, 161
Flaherty Manufacturing, 66, 163
Flaherty, Peter, 66, 163
Flatman, Fred, 39, 40, 43, 44, 47
Flett, John, 46
Foley, Bill, 33, 56

Ford, Pat, 134, 147
Forde, A. V., 151
Fortune, 139
Foundation Co. of Canada, 162
Fraleigh, William, 126–27
Frank, A. J. & Son, 158
Frank, Marvin, 158, 161, 165
Fraser and Beatty, 127
Frid Construction, 144
Frisina, Alf, 24–26

Galente Organization. *See under* organized crime
Galt–Guelph Railway. *See* Railways
gambling. *See under* organized crime
Gardiner, Reg, 54
Gasbarrini, Danny, 80, 82, 94, 99
Genesse, Fred, 76
Geneva, Lake, 148
German, Alex. *See under* City Hall
Gilkson, J. T., 17
Gillespie, Alistair, 162
Gisborn, Reg, 55, 56
Globe and Mail, 64–66, 72, 74, 95, 97, 98, 139, 164
Gompers, Samuel, 39, 43, 44, 46
Gordon, L. M., 70
Gore Park, 123
Goyer, Jean-Pierre, 159, 161
Gralewicz, Roman, 163
Grand Trunk Railway. *See under* railways
Grant, Campbell, 94
Gray, Don, 137, 139, 140, 141, 143, 164
Gray, John, 156, 159
Gray, Malcolm, 97
Great Western Railway. *See under* railways
Groome, Reg, 133

Halcrow, George, 40, 41, 42, 43, 45, 70
Halford, H. J., 41
Hamilton Apartment Association, 33
Hamilton Blast Furnace Company. *See under* Steel Company of Canada
Hamilton Colosseum Group. *See under* arena
Hamilton Construction Association, 144
Hamilton and District Labour Council. *See under* labour
Hamilton Downtown Association, 129
Hamilton Labour Council. *See under* labour
Hamilton Harbour
    Barfnecht, Kenneth, 154-58, 159, 161
    Canada Ports Act, 165–66
    Commission, 10, 64, 66, 86, 99
    composition and structure, 150
    Dofasco, 149, 150, 152
    dredging scandal, 148, 161–65
    Elliott conflict of interest, 158–9
    Elliott dismissal, 158–9

Elliott lawsuit, 159
filling of, 149, 150–4
Hickey, E. Delbert, 150–54, 157–59, 161–64, 166
Lax Landfill project, 153–4, 165
RCMP, 161, 162, 164
recreation, 8, 148
Stelco, 149, 150, 152, 154
Subcommittee, 155, 158, 159, 161
Turkstra, Herman, 150, 151, 154–161
Hamilton–Port Dover Railway. *See under* railways
Hamilton Regional Conservation Authority, 7, 150–53
Hamilton Steel and Iron Company. *See under* Steel Company of Canada
Hamilton Terminal Operators Ltd. (HTO), 154
Hamilton Welfare Rights Organization, 26–7
    Alinski, Saul, 102, 103
    Board of Control, 103
    clothing exchange, 103
    co-op store, 103
    founding, 102
    Munro, John, 102, 103, 104
    Poor People's Conference, 103
    sit-in at Welfare Office, 103
    termination of grant, 103–4
    Welfare Advocacy Service, 103
Harbour Commissioners' Act, 149, 157
harbour. *See* Hamilton Harbour
Harris, Ray, 102
Haslem, Edgar, 43
Henderson, Lome, 134
Henderson, Nora Frances, 50, 51, 52
Henderson, Robert A., 155, 161
Henderson, Robert P., 161
Henry, Frank, 121
Hepburn, Mitchell, 48, 54, 70
Hickey, E. Delbert (Del), 92, 150, 151, 152, 153, 154, 157, 158, 159, 161, 162, 163, 164, 166
Hilton Canada Ltd., 133
Hilton, Hugh, 50, 52
Hincks, Francis, 16
Hinsberger, Ed, 104
Hohler, Kate, 105, 106
Holland, R. E., 161
Home Juice Company, 83
hotel. *See under* arena *and* Civic Square
House of Industry, 19
Howe, Bill, 56
Huckleberry Point, 19, 148
Hume, Gordon, 100
Hunter, Harry, 49, 54

Imperial Tobacco, 86, 87
incumbents' re-election, 34
Independent Labour Party (ILP), 35, 38–47, 49, 78
    merger with CCF, 48
Independent Steelworkers Association, 49
International Harvester, *20*, 53
International Wing of the Unemployed, 44
Irving Whale, 162

Jackson, C. S., 53
Jackson, Lloyd D., 24, *29*, 52
Jackson Square, 98, 132, 135
James Kemp Construction, 144
Jamieson, Don, 150, 158, 161
Jonah, Ephraim, 66, 88
Jones, Anne, 113, 161
Jones, Jack, 146
J. P. Porter Co., 162, 163
just society, 102

Katz-Tobias Arena Plan. *See* arena
Kaufman, Benjamin, 82
Kennedy, Robert, 82
Kern, James, 159
Kerr, Donald A., 162
Kerr, George, 96–97, 161–62
Kidd, Paul, 98
King, William Lyon Mackenzie, 50
Kiwanis Club, 33
Knights of Columbus, 32, 33, 112, 127–28
Knights of Labour, 39
Kostyk, Joe, 150

LaBarre Roofing Co., 115
labour, 20, 35
    American Federation of Labor (AFL), 39, 46, 47
    as an opposition group, 35, 38
    CCF, 45, 48, 49, 53, 54
    coalition with farmers, 41, 42
    Cold War, 54
    Communist Party of Canada, 44, 46, 47, 48, 49, 52, 53, 57, 58
    depression of 1920–23, 43
    election (1933) in *The Spectator*, 48
    election (1943) in *The Spectator*, 49
    Hamilton and District Labour Council, 38, 54, 57, 58
    Hamilton Trades and Labour Council, 44
    ILP merges with CCF, 48
    ILP, defeat of, 45
    Independent Labour Party (ILP), 38–45, 49
    Labour News, 39
    Lawrence, Sam, *29*, 45–53, 55
    Mitchell, Humphrey, 47, 48, 50
    NDP and municipal politics, 56–7
    Rollo, Walter, 39–43
    Steelworkers, 48–54, 56, 58, 73
    Stelco strike (1946), *47*, 49–53, *55*

United Electrical Workers (UE), 53, 54, 57, 58
Labour Progressive Party. *See under* Community
   Party of Canada
Labour Representative Political Association, 47
Lake Erie Boy's Town, 97
Lang, Otto, 134, 164
Langs, John G., 65
Lansdowne Park, 148
Lansky, Meyer, 82
Lanza, Joseph, 86, 150, 153, 154, 161, 163, 164
Lau, Arthur, 132
Lawrence, David, 55, 56, 114, 159
Lawrence, Len, 74, 164
Lawrence, Sam
   CCF, 45–52, 70
   early career, 45–46
   ILP, 44, 46–47
   municipal policies, 47
   political career, 29, 35, 45–53
   Stelco strike (1946), 49–53
Lax development, 35, 92. *See also under* Hamilton
   Harbour
Lax, Morris, 165
Lax, Samuel, 153, 154
Lax, Sheridan, 153
LeBarrie, Donald "Red", 80, 82, 94
Legislative Assembly Standing Committee on
   Railways. *See under* railways
Leitersdorf, Joseph, 117   Lewis, David, 98, 163–64
Lewis, John L., 48
Liberal Party, 29, 32, 41, 42, 46, 48, 150, 156, 163
Library Board, 31, 132–33
library-farmers' market, 133–34, 143–45
Lions' Club, 33
LIP grants, 105, 110
Lloyd D. Jackson Square. *See* Jackson Square
loan sharking. *See under* organized crime
Lobo train disaster, 18
Lombardo, Fred, 147, 166
London and Gore Railway Company. *See under*
   railways
longshoremen, 10, 81, 157
Lorenzetti, Aldo, 139
Lorimer, James, 26
Luria Brothers Co. Inc., 153
Lypka, Michael, 65

MacDonald, Jack, *129*
   arena, 136, 141–43
   city hall inquiry, 93, 112–19
   Civic Square, 92, 127, 128, 131–32, 134
   Eaton's, 148
   election, *35*
   library-farmers' market, 143–45
   political policies, 30
MacDonald, James, 161

Macdonald, John A., 19
MacDonald, Mickey, 76
Mackenzie Rebellion, 15
Maclean's, 93
MacNab, Allan, *15*, 16–19, 41
MacNab, Mary, 41–43
Mafia. *See under* organized crime
Magaddino Family. *See under* organized crime
Magaddino, Stefano, 79, 81–82
Main Place, 87
Manthorpe, Jonathan, 64
marble falling. *See under* City Hall
Marchand, Jean, 163, 164
Marck, Albert, 62
Marine Industries, 162, 163
Martin, Argue, 150, 153
Martin, Frank, 86–87
Martin, Hugh, 163
Martini, Quinto, 63
Mashaal, Menshi, 132
Masons, 33, 45
Mauro, Vincent, 81
McAuliffe, Gerald, *96*
   Clinton Duke Affair, 93–94
   Globe and Mail, 97
   Kerr, George, 96–97
   Lake Erie Boy's Town, 97
   Oakville-Trafalgar Hospital, 96
   Preston, Peter, 97
   St. Joseph's Hospital, 91–92
McBride, Hickey, Green, McCallum and Mann,
   154
McBride, Malcolm, 42
McClure, Tom, 54
McCombs, Theo, 112, 113, 117–18
McCulloch, Bill
   arena, 141
   Civic Square, 56, 130, 131, 132, 133
   Eaton's, 146–47
   harbour, 164
   library-farmers' market, 144, 145
McGrath, James, 162, 164
McKay, Douglas, 136
McKenzie, Bob, 56, 58
McKeough, Darcy, 137
McLaren, Joseph, 114
McLean, J. Edmund, 150
McMaster, Ross, 14, 27
McMenemy, John, 46, 52
McMurrich, J. Cameron, 93
McMurtry, Roy, 74
McNamara Corporation Ltd., 162
McNamara, Harold, 163
Medical Research Council, 65
Merling, Henry, 144
Millard, Charles, 49, 52, 53, 54

Mills Steel, 117
Mindale, Paul, 92
Ministry of Transport, 159
Mitchell, Humphrey, 47, 48, 50
Moerman, Tom, 108
Monaghan, Reg, 133
Monarch Vending Machines, 80, *86*, 165
money laundering. *See under* organized crime
Montreal, Bank of, 132
Moon, Peter, 64, 92, 97
Morgan, John, 58
Morganti, Dominic, 66, 87–88, 105
Morison, Brian, 24, 124, 155
Morrison, Robert, 93
Morrow, Bob, 108
Morrow, George, 108
Mount Hope Airport, 98
Muir, John, *95*
    Barton, Warren, 95–97
    editorial policy, 90, 94–95
    McAuliffe, Gerald, 96–97
    Munro, John, 98, 99
    Warnick, Paul, 95–99
Municipal Laboratories, 151
Munro, John Carr, 63, 64, 65, 68, 69, 70, 71, 102
    arena, 141–2
    Civic Square, 134
    class voting, 70–72
    constituency meetings, 69
    early career, 63
    election organization, 68–70
    Globe and Mail patronage story, 64–66
    Hamilton Harbour, 150, 154, 163–66
    Hamilton Welfare Rights Organization, 102–104
    immigrants and ethnic voting, 67, 68–72
    intervention in judicial process, 62, 72
    lawyers, 66
    machine strategy, 72
    NDP, 67, 70–72
    organized crime, 86–88
    patronage system, 63–68
    political machine, 62–72, 98–99
    recruitment of workers, 66
    Spectator, The, 98–99
    Victoria Park Community Organization, 102, 105, 108, 110
    York Place, 87–88
Murray, James, 127
Murray Jones and Associates, *121*, 122–24, 127, 128, 130, 135

narcotics. *See under* organized crime
National Harbours Board, 150, 162
National Parole Board, 65, 86, 150
National Policy, 19

neighbourhoods
    Corktown, 8
    Durand, 8
    York Street, 8
Neilson, J., 143, 144
New Democracy, The, 40, 41, 42, 44
New Democratic Party (NDP)
    harbour, 162
    municipal politics, 33, 35, 56–57
    Munro, John, 67, 70–72
    Spectator, The, 98
    York Place, 105
New Don. *See under* organized crime
Nichols, Tom, *97*
    Barton, Warren, 92, 95
    McAuliffe, Gerald, 91–92, 93–94
    publishing policy, 91–92
    Special Senate Committee on the Mass Media, 91–92
    Warnick, Paul, 92, 99
Nine Hour Day Movement, 39
non-partisan politics, 28, 29, 35
North End urban renewal, 121, 153
Northgate Cable, 154

Oakville-Trafalgar Hospital. See under *Spectator, The*
occupations of council members, 33
O'Leary, Dennis, 64
One Big Union, 40, 43, 44
Ontario Association of General Contractors, 144
Ontario Municipal Board (OMB)
    arena, 140, 141
    Century 21, 25
    Civic Square, 130–31
    Yale's approval for second office tower, 133
    York Place, 105
Ontario Provincial Police. *See under* police
Opportunities for Youth (OFY), 105, 110
opposition groups, 12, 35–37. *See also under* labour
organized crime
    Acapulco meeting, 82–3, 84
    Bluestein, Max, 80–81
    business infiltration, 74
    Duke inquiry, 82, 83
    extortion, 79, 80
    Galente organization, 79
    gambling, 74, 79, 80, 82, 84, 85, 86, 88
    loan sharking, 74, 79, 80, 82, 85, 88
    Mafia, 74, 79, 81, 83, 85
    Magaddino Family, 79, 81, 82
    money laundering, 74, 82, 83, 165
    Munro, John, 86–88
    narcotics, 74, 76, 77, 79, 81–85, 88
    Papalia, John, 79–83, 88
    Perri, Rocco and gang, 5, 75–79
    prostitution, 74, 79, 84

Three Dons, 79
Toronto Star interview, 76
York Place, 87–8

Pan American Games, 134, 143
    steering committee, 141, 142
Papalia, Angelo, 80
Papalia, Anthony, 79
Papalia, Dominic, 80
Papalia, Joe, 80
Papalia, John, *81*
    Bluestein beating, 80–81
    connections, 94, 165
    early history, 79–80
    heroin smuggling, 81–82
    later career, 83
    See also under organized crime
Papalia, Rocco, 80, 82
Parking Authority, 146
participatory democracy, 102
Paten, Frank, 155
patronage system, 28, 29, 62–68
Pelech, Jack, 66, 86–88, 141, 142
pension fund, 132
Perkins, Earl, 157, 158
Perri, Bessie (née Starkman)
    early history, 75–76
    murder, 76–77
    funeral, 77
Perri, Rocco, *75*
    early history, 75–76
    bootlegging, 75, 76
    Royal Commission, 76
    disappearance, 77
    later career, 77–79
Perrin, Richard, 82
Pettigrew, Jack, 82
Phillips, Bill, 143–45, 146
Philosophy of Railroads, 16
Philpot, David, 125
Pigott Construction, 92, 93, 112, 115, 124, 135. *See also* City Hall; Civic Square
Pigott, Jack, 124
Pigott, Joseph, Jr., 113, 116. *See also* Civic Square
Pigott, Joseph, Sr., 124, 128
Pigott Structures Ltd., 143–45
Pigott, William, 113, 116, 117, 124
Pineo, Peter, 121
Place Ville Marie, 124
planetarium. *See under* Civic Square
Planning Board, 31, 159
Planning and Development Committee, 146
pluralist theory. *See under* political power
police
    Hamilton Police, 156
    Ontario Provincial Police (OPP), 52, 82, 94, 156
    Quebec Police Commission, 74, 86
    RCMP, 52, 74, 77, 98, 155–56, 162, 164
political machines, 28, 62–73
political parties and municipal politics, 29, 33
political power, 9–12
    business, ideology of, 10–11, 14, 27, 35, 37, 38, 59
    elites, theory of, 9–10;
    pluralist theory, 9
Poloniato, Aldo, 158, 161, 166
Porcupine Mines Social Club, 80
poverty, 14, 22–23, 26–27, 100. *See also* welfare
Powell, Bill, 56, 129, 130, 132, 166
Powell, Clayton, 162
pragmatism, 29
Prentice, John, 151
Presbyterians, 100
Preston–Berlin Railroad. *See* railways
Preston, Peter, 97
Price, Jack, 66
Price, Rubin and Partners Inc., 66
Pritchard, Ada, 114
Progressive movement, 28, 29
Prohibition, 42, 75–79, 85, 86
project management system, 143–44
prostitution. *See under* organized crime
public housing, 57, 96
Pugliese, Tony, 80

Quart, Gary. *See under* Victoria Park Community Organization
Queen's Park, 137
Queen Street Residents' Association, 108
Quinlan, Albin Louis, 162

railways
    Galt–Guelph, 17
    Grand Trunk, 16
    Great Western, 15–19
    Hamilton–Port Dover, 17
    Legislative Assembly Standing Committee on Railways, 15
    London and Gore, 15
    Preston–Berlin, 17
Raney, W. E., 42
Rindress, Horace Grant, 162, 163
Robinette, J. J., 157, 158
Robinson, Lukin, 130
Rodger, Foster, 115
Rollo, Walter. *See under* labour
Ronark Developments, 154
Ronyx Corporation, 154
Roscoe, Stanley, 113, 114, 116–18
Rose, Fred, 54
Rotary Club, 32, 84

Rouff, Kenneth
    arena, 138, 140–41
    city hall, 112, 114, 115
    Civic Square, 127
    harbour, 149, 151, 157, 158
    library-farmers' market, 143
Russell, David, 21

Salsberg, J. B., 48
Saltfleet Construction Ltd., 145
Save Our Square (SOS), 35, 92, 130
Scandlan, Bill, 56, 159
Scheckter, B. B., 129
Schneider, Robert J., 162
Scopelletti, Rocco, 82
Scroggie, Donald G., 127, 129
Seafarers' International Union (SIU), 163
Seaport, The, 98
Sefton, Larry, 54
Senate Standing Committee on Transportation and Communications, 11
senior citizens, 107
Sherman's Inlet, 148
Shulman, Morton, 156, 164
Simard, Jean, 162, 163
slum landlords, 106, 110
Smith, Gary, 95
Sobel, Ken, 32, 122, 127
Southam Co. See under *Spectator, The*
Special Senate Committee on the Mass Media, 91, 92
Spectator, The
    advertisers, 90, 95
    Barton, Warren, 92–95
    circulation, 90
    Civic Square, 24, 98, 120, 124, 130
    Duke judicial inquiry, 93–94
    election of 1933, 48
    election of 1943, 49
    harbour, 163–64
    Kerr, George, 96–97
    Lake Erie Boys' Town, 97
    McAuliffe, Gerald, 92–93, 96, 98–100
    McMurrick slaying, 93
    Muir, John, 94–99
    Munro, John, 98–99
    national policy, 19
    Nichols, Tom, 91–94
    Oakville-Trafalgar Hospital, 96
    role of, 90
    Southam Co., 91
    subsidies to industries, 20
    Warnick, Paul, 92–99
Standen, Margaret, 114
Standard Life Assurance Co., 132
Starkman, Bessie. See Perri, Bessie

Star Vending Machine Company, 80
state, role of, 10–11, 35
Steelworkers Organizing Committee (SWOC), 48, 49. See also United Steelworkers of America
Steel Company of Canada (Stelco)
    Civic Square, 124
    founding, 19, 20–21
    Hamilton Blast Furnace Co., 21–22
    Hamilton Steel and Iron Co., 21
    harbour, 149, 150, 152, 154
    ideology, 14
    strike of 1946, 49–53;
    subsidies to, 20–22
Stiles, Douglas, 116–7
St. Joseph's Hospital. See under McAuliffe, Gerald
Stout, Ian, 134, 145
Stowe, Jim, 55, 56
Strathcona Community Project, 100, 108. See also Victoria Park and Northwest Community Organization
Stratherne Street dredging project, 162
Studholme, Allan, 39, 46, 70
Stunden, Violet, 108–109
subsidies, 136
    Barton Township tax concession, 20
    industry, 19–22, 27
    railways, 15–19
    real estate, 23–26
    See also business, ideology of
Swanborough, Reg, 141
Swartz, Sheldon, 85
Sylvestro, Tony, 79, 80

tariffs, 10, 19, 27, 42
Terminal Towers, 24
Temperance Movement, 75
Tharen, Ed, 64, 163, 165, 166
theatre-auditorium. See under Civic Square
Thorold train disaster, 18
Tobias, Ted, 138–141
Toronto Dominion Bank, 124
Toronto Maple Leafs, 138
Toronto Star, 76, 81, 162
Toronto Toros, 138
Town Tavern, 81
trade and convention centre, 143. See also Civic Square
Trades and Labour Congress, 146
Travers, Jim, 7, 86
Trimble, John, 129
Triton Centres Ltd. See under Civic Square
Trizec Corporation, 124
Trudeau, Pierre Elliott, 56, 102, 164
Tuchtie, Walter, 74
Tuckett Tobacco property, 86
Turkstra, Herman

Civic Square, 30
Hamilton Harbour, 150, 151, 154–61

United Church, 100, 101
    funding from, 105, 106, 108, 110
United Electrical Workers (U. E.), 53, 57, 58
    expulsion from CCL, 54
    admission to CLC, 57
United Farmers of Ontario (UFO), 41, 42
United Smelting and Refining Co., 154
United Steelworkers of America, 53, 56, 58
urban renewal, 11, 23–24
    committee for, 127
    department of, 127
    federal program, 120–21
    North End program, 121, 153
    Van Wagner's Beach program, 121
    York Street program, 101, 110, 122, 123

Valeriano, Pat, 144, 145, 159
Van Wagner's Beach. *See under* urban renewal
Venezuela, 143
Veterans' Land Act, 65
Victoria Park Community Homes Inc., 110
Victoria Park Community Organization
    Alinski, Saul, 100–101
    Committee to Reform Victoria Park, 108
    Community Convention, 107–108
    community development, 104–105
    Community Forum, 106
    Community Home Improvement Program (CHIP), 106–107, 108–110
    Hamilton Welfare Rights Organization, 4, 102–104
    Munro, John, *102*, 104, 105, 108
    Quart, Gary, *101*, 101–110
    United Church, 100, 105, 107, 108, 110
    York Place, 105, 107
    York Street urban renewal, 101
Victoria Park Welfare Committee, 102, 108
Violi, Paolo, *78*, 85
voter turnout, 31–32

W5, 153, 162
Walsh, Bill, 54
Walton, Percy, 126–127
Warnick, Paul
    editorial policy, 92
    Muir, John, 95–97
    resignation, 99
Warrender, William, 108–109
Wasserman, Marvin, 129
Watergate scandal, 95
Weatherstone, F. J., 64
welfare
    in 19th century, 14–15
    in 20th century, 22–23
    in 1970s, 26–27
    advocacy, *25*, 105
    Hamilton Welfare Rights Organization, 102–104
    recipients of, 26, 102
    See also poverty; subsidies; business, ideology of
Weiss, Dan, 146–147
Welch, Robert, 25
Welland Canal, 77, 158
Wernick, Louis, 77
Westinghouse, 19, 65
    union at, 53
Whatley (chief of police), 44
Wheeler, Reg, 33, 56, 130, 131, 132
Whisper (boat), 52
Whittaker, Richard, 29
Wigle, F. E., 132–33
Winnipeg General Strike, 39–40
Woodsworth, J. S., 44, 48
Workers' Unity League, 48, 49
World Hockey Association, 26, 138
Wyatt, Rene, 105

Yale Properties Ltd., 25. *See also under* Civic Square
Yorkdale Shopping Centre, 124
York Place, 66, 87–88, 105, 106, 107, 110
York Street, *104*
    merchants, 101
    urban renewal, 101, 122–23
    widening, 101–102, 110
    See also under neighbourhoods

Zack, Sheila, 129, 130
Zion United Church, 100, 108